DOLTON PUBLIC LIBRARY DISTRICT

3 1146 00151 8301

849-2385

D1307446

DOLTON PUBLIC LIBRARY DIST
849-2385

Cosmic Connections

Cosmic Connections

By the Editors of Time-Life Books

TIME-LIFE BOOKS, ALEXANDRIA, VIRGINIA

CONTENTS

CHAPTER 1

Seeking Meaning in the Stars

The world learned in the spring of 1988 that President Ronald Reagan's wife, Nancy, had sometimes dictated changes in her husband's official schedule on the basis of an astrologer's predictions. Moreover, it was revealed that prior to a summit meeting Mrs. Reagan's astrologer had drawn up a horoscope of Mikhail Gorbachev, presumably to help the president prepare for negotiations with the Soviet leader. This widely reported news drew cries of consternation and derision from editorial writers and many public figures: In the nuclear age, how could the most powerful man in the world allow himself to be influenced even to a small degree by a pseudoscience that had been discredited and rejected by rational thinkers centuries earlier? Just what were people to make of White House occupants who set store by mystical mumbo jumbo involving planets and stars and signs of the zodiac?

In fact, a great many Americans—and even more people in other parts of the world—found nothing strange at all about the Reagans' interest in astrology. For these people, the study of the relationship between the heavens and the affairs of humankind is not mumbo jumbo or pseudo anything, but a valid, workable framework for viewing life and, at times, for discerning what to expect, in a general way, from the future. There are enough of these believers to make President Reagan's refusal to publicly proclaim disbelief in astrology (on the grounds that he did not know enough about the subject to judge) a politically astute act.

Astrology's popularity is particularly evident in the Orient, where the ancient art never slipped into the general disrepute that was its lot for so long in the West. In many Asian societies, even the most respected, best-educated families will not set a date for a wedding or buy a property without first consulting an astrologer to determine whether the timing is propitious. No less an occasion than the granting of independence to India was re-scheduled—from August 15, 1947, to the stroke of midnight on August 14— because the original day was declared unfavorable. In Bangkok, executives are careful to consult astral authorities before making crucial decisions. When the Coca-Cola company opened its first bottling plant in Thailand, the directors waited until the stars gave a clear go-ahead. "If you refuse to take the astrologer's advice," one official explained, "the Buddhist priests will refuse to bless the bottling machinery at our opening ceremony. Then nobody in Thailand will drink Coca-Cola." In the Himalayan kingdom of Sikkim, where Crown Prince Thondup Namgyal took New York debutante Hope Cooke as his bride, the wedding was delayed a year, until 1963, at the behest of court astrologers.

In the West, the Enlightenment had sent astrology into eclipse in the eighteenth century, along with magic, witchcraft, and other occult pursuits. But to the distress of many scientists and others devoted to rationality, astrology has made a comeback in the twentieth century. More than 10,000 professional astrologers practice their art in the United States alone, and their devotees number some 50 million. The number of adherents may be on the upswing: A 1987 Gallup poll indicated that more than half of Americans age thirteen to eighteen believed in astrology. Ninety-two percent of the country's daily newspapers were publishing horoscope columns by 1988, up from only 78 percent nine years earlier. The columns are usually among the papers' most-read features, even though many serious astrologers condemn them as shallow and worthless.

In the Western world as a whole, it has been estimated, one out of every 10,000 people is involved in astrology as a student or practitioner—the same proportion as those who are practicing or studying psychology. And in Western languages, there are in print some 1,000 books that deal with serious astrology—roughly the same number as books on the subject of astronomy.

Such figures only highlight the fact that astrology in recent years has become a powerful factor in the lives of many Americans and Europeans, extending far beyond newspaper horoscopes avidly examined for the promise of love, money, or prestige. Unlike Eastern astrologers, who devote themselves almost entirely to predicting the future, most practitioners in the West emphasize psychological counseling based on what the stars and planets tell about the client's character and personality. But fate is not ignored. Every reader of popular magazines knows that many wealthy film stars consult their astrologers on matters of business as well as romance. Less well publicized are the high-rolling financial speculators who telephone their astrological advisers as frequently as they call market analysts. "Millionaires don't use astrologers," tycoon J. P. Morgan is alleged to have said, "but billionaires do." The stock market predictions of leading financial astrologers such as Arch Crawford command Wall Street's attention and may earn the prognosticators six-figure annual incomes.

Astrological consultants thrive even in such narrow fields as residential real estate. "If you sell when Mercury is in retrograde," one Los Angeles adviser warned a client early in 1986, "there will be a slip-up in the contract, or the sale won't go through." So house owner Susan Wallerstein waited a month for the planet to return to its forward course before sticking her For Sale sign in the ground. The house found a buyer by sunset of its first day on the market, for $5,000 more than the seller had hoped to get for it.

Thus is astrology—which has been variously described from different viewpoints as an art, a science, a language, a system, a philosophy, and a fraud—employed as a tool in such purely modern enterprises as stock trading, psychological counseling, presidential scheduling, and figuring out the Los Angeles property market. Yet it is an ancient creation, an exceedingly old device whose influence was felt in

the conduct of human affairs thousands of years ago. The degree of its antiquity was not revealed to the modern world until in the middle of the nineteenth century, through the work of a young, Oxford-educated, Iraqi archaeologist named Hormuzd Rassam—who, as far as anyone knows, had no particular interest in astrology.

In 1853 Rassam began shoveling into a mound of ancient debris near his home on the Tigris River. He and his men worked by starlight, as quietly as they could; a rival French team already held claim to the spot. Rassam risked the ire of his fellow archaeologists because he felt sure that here lay his best chance of unearthing the secrets of the great Assyrian empire that once dominated the region. He was seized by excitement, therefore, when in late December his men uncovered the remains of a building.

Clearing away the accumulated dust of the ages, he broke into a large gallery, its walls carved with magnificent bas-reliefs of a royal lion hunt. And stacked in the middle of the room, under heaps of rubble and drifted sand, lay thousands of small clay tablets inscribed with cuneiform script.

Rassam had found the palace library at Nineveh, the ancient Assyrian capital. It had been erected sometime between 668 and 627 BC by King Ashurbanipal, mightiest of Assyria's rulers, and it contained the richest concentration of ancient Middle Eastern wisdom ever assembled. As scholars pored over the tablets—there were more than 25,000 of them—and as they puzzled out the meanings of the texts, written in the Akkadian language of ancient Babylonia and Assyria, the full import of Rassam's discovery became clear. There were state histories, religious documents, royal decrees and correspondence, literary works, medical texts, dictionaries, and grammars, some dating back to more than a thousand years before Ashurbanipal's time. And among the earliest and most intriguing items was a set of astronomical tables with various prophecies attached.

"On the fifteenth day of Shebat," one read, "Venus disappeared in the west for three days. Then on the eighteenth day Venus became visible in the east. Springs will flow. Adad will bring his rain and Ea his floods. King will

BC, it was dedicated to the moon god Sin; from the top of the eighty-foot watchtower Chaldean astronomer-priests traced, with astonishing accuracy, the movements of celestial bodies.

send messages of reconciliation to king." The ancient Mesopotamians, of course, did not refer to the planet by its current name, Venus; their word for it was Ishtar. But by using context information, the interpreters of the tablets were able to translate the names of heavenly bodies in dozens of inscriptions: "When Jupiter stands in front of Mars . . . a great army will be slain"; "When the Moon rides in a chariot, the yoke of the King of Akkad will prosper"; "When Leo is dark, the heart of the land will not be happy"; "When Venus stands high, there will be pleasure of copulation."

And so on for some seventy tablets, which were christened the Enuma Anu Enlil, from the opening line of the first tablet: "When the gods Anu and Enlil. . . ." Here was evidence of one of humankind's early attempts to read its destiny in the heavens, a practice later known as astrology, from the Greek words for "star speech."

The desire to know the future is as old, no doubt, as consciousness itself. Tribal sages since time immemorial have studied nature's many quirks and attempted to relate them to worldly prospects. The flights of birds, the behavior of serpents, the colors of sunsets, and even the steaming entrails of slaughtered animals have been searched for indications of events to come.

But nowhere do the possibilities of correspondences seem so vivid or likely as in the steady, predictable march of the heavens. The sun rises on schedule; the constellations circle as though by divine edict, ushering in the seasons and providing a tally of days past and to come. As a matter of fact, one of the oldest artifacts in the world is a slab of bone carved 34,000 years ago by an observant Cro-Magnon forebear, with notches apparently marking the phases of the moon—a timetable, perhaps, for the migrations of animals that early man regularly hunted for food. As hunting gave way to agriculture, primitive farmers became aware of planetary motions and of the sun's annual progress from south to north and back again. They planted their seeds accordingly, because they had learned that those heavenly movements presaged seasonal changes in weather and the ad-

This boundary stone from the second millennium BC is representative of those issued to Babylonian landowners as property markers. The stone, called a kudurru, is inscribed with the owner's name and planetary glyphs, or picture words, representing gods. The crescent moon (top) symbolized the lunar god, Sin; the eight-pointed star, Ishtar, or Venus; and the four-rayed wheel, the sun god, Shamash. The scorpion (center), often used as a sign of war, later symbolized the zodiacal sign ruled by the fiery planet Mars.

vent of the annual floods that brought water as well as nourishing new soil to their fields. The relationship between what happened in the sky and what occurred on earth appeared to be one of cause and effect. Who knew what else the heavens might portend and into what other areas of human activity their influence might possibly reach?

The visible manifestations of the cosmic forces have been on display since the world began. On a clear night, with an open horizon, some 2,000 stars appear to the naked eye, shining out from the celestial canopy in patterns that plead for imaginative speculation. To the people of ancient Egypt the brighter glints were the souls of departed pharaohs, who had sailed in spirit boats up the Milky Way to their final resting place. The ancient Greeks embodied an entire mythology—replete with dramatic tales of the squabbles among the families of the gods and the feats of ancestral heroes—in the various constellations. The first Chinese emperors were sired by meteors that fell from the sky and impregnated woman, or so the legend told. And what is considered the first Chinese dynasty, the Hsia, is said to have collapsed in the public turmoil that followed an eclipse of the sun.

On the other side of the world, in ancient America, the Maya of Mexico and Guatemala were obsessed with the planet Venus, which they equated with their serpent deity, Kulkulcan. They devised a calendar for the movements of the planet over a 384-year period.

But no ancient people studied the sky more intently, or took its portents more to heart, than the inhabitants of Mesopotamia— the fertile land between the Tigris and Euphrates rivers. Long before Assyrian scribes copied out the tablets in Ashurbanipal's library, their forebears in the region were recording the motions of the stars and planets. So began astronomy, the science of observing the sky, and from it grew astrology, the practice of reading fate or religious meanings into the movements of the heavenly bodies.

Systematic astral observations began with the Sumerians, who migrated to Mesopotamia around 5000 BC to farm and stayed to build the world's first civilization. Their mud-brick settlements along the rivers grew into cities, with glittering palaces, temples, and other public structures. Commerce developed, and with it came the need to keep records. The Sumerians learned to multiply, divide, take square roots and cube roots, and use recipro-

The Shifting Zodiac

Ancient astronomers believed in a universe with the Earth at its center and a vast globe revolving around it. On the inner surface of this sphere lay the stars, which moved around the Earth but never changed in relation to each other. Roaming among them were the seven known "planets" of the ancients: the Sun and Moon, Mercury, Venus, Mars, Jupiter, and Saturn.

In this scheme of things *(below)*, the Sun followed a line, called the ecliptic, in its seeming annual orbit around the Earth. The ecliptic, in turn, formed the center of a band within which the other planets traveled. Inscribed on this band were twelve constellations. The Greeks called this glittering belt the zodiac. Its constellations gave their names to the twelve astrological signs.

The zodiac was divided into twelve thirty-degree arcs, each named for the constellation it contained. As the Sun rose each day, it traveled against the backdrop of a constellation that moved with it. But the Sun moved slightly faster than the constellation. So, after about thirty days, the Sun would be projected against the next constellation; during a year, it went through all twelve signs.

Over the centuries, the signs became firmly fixed to segments of the calendar. The zodiacal year began with the first day of spring—on which the Sun began rising in Aries.

The clockwork cosmos imagined by the ancients was elegant—but wrong. Among other things, it envisioned the Earth as stationary, not as a globe spinning on its axis. Furthermore, Earth wobbles as it spins. Scientists call the wobble precession. It is slow; one wobble takes 26,000 years to complete. Nevertheless, its course alters Earth's orientation to the stars. Reference points change: 2,000 years ago, the Sun did indeed rise in the constellation Aries on the vernal equinox. Now, however, the wobble has gone far enough for the vernal equinox to occur with the Sun just leaving Pisces. The celestial slippage that occurs over the eons is called the precession of the equinoxes.

This phenomenon, illustrated on the following two pages, has split modern astrology into two schools. The sidereal faction, found mostly in India, acknowledges the precession and adjusts the signs of the zodiac accordingly. In India, someone born on April 1 is a Pisces. In the West, however, astrologers of the so-called tropical school consider that person an Aries, even though the Sun was actually traveling in the constellation Pisces at the time of birth.

Tropical astrology's geocentric scheme shows the zodiac revolving around the Earth like a cosmic wagon wheel. The white line running along the rim is the ecliptic, defined by the annual path of the Sun—the white light at the sphere's right. Spokes of the wheel mark off the zodiac's signs (pages 79-91), consisting of twelve segments of thirty degrees each; the zodiacal year begins with Aries, which is shown in red. The wheel's entire expanse is referred to as the ecliptic plane. In relation to the plane, Earth tilts on its axis.

ARIES

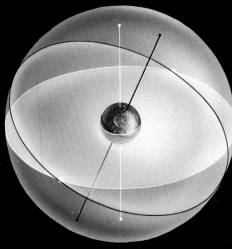

Although modern astronomy envisions a cosmos quite different from that of the ancients, it still maps the heavens in much the same way. The diagram at left shows how astronomers calculate the equinoxes. The horizontal ellipse is the plane of the ecliptic. The paler, tilted ellipse is the celestial equator, an imaginary plane created by projecting Earth's equator onto the celestial sphere. The points where the ellipses intersect form the vernal and autumnal equinoxes. The Sun first crosses the celestial equator in its apparent yearly orbit about March 21 to mark the vernal equinox—and, tropical astrologers say, the start of the zodiacal year.

Like a spinning top that is slowly losing momentum, the Earth wobbles on its axis, describing a great circle in space once every 26,000 years (right). The wobble continually changes the points at which the celestial equator and the plane of the ecliptic intersect to create the equinoxes. The vernal equinox shifts backward along the ecliptic through one full constellation every 2,166 years (the time-span indicated between points A and B)—one-twelfth of the time it takes the Earth to complete its wobble.

THE MOVING ZODIAC

At the vernal equinox some 2,000 years ago, the constellations and the zodiacal signs were one and the same (top). Aries, shown in red, was the constellation rising with the Sun on the vernal equinox. The beginning of Aries marked the beginning of the zodiacal year. Because of precession, however, the vernal equinox has moved backward along the ecliptic, carrying the signs of the zodiac with it. The signs and the constellations no longer correspond. The vernal equinox now begins with the Sun just finishing its month-long tour with Pisces (bottom). Sidereal astrology takes note of actual stellar positions, but tropical astrology does not. The latter maintains the calendrical connection between Aries and the equinox, but in fact the sign and the constellation are no longer synchronous. In essence, then, the tropical astrology favored in the West is more metaphorical than real.

The modern notion of astrological ages, such as the much-discussed Age of Aquarius, is based on the precession of the equinoxes. The constellation that rises with the Sun on the vernal equinox stays the same for more than 2,000 years and gives its name to the age. Thus the Age of Aries was ending about 2,000 years ago, and Pisces was beginning. Pisces is now yielding to Aquarius, but there is debate over exactly when the change occurs. This is because the constellations, defying schematics, do not fit neatly into their thirty-degree segments. Depending on where each one begins and ends, the Age of Aquarius may have already begun—or, as some astrologers maintain, it may dawn as late as the twenty-fourth century.

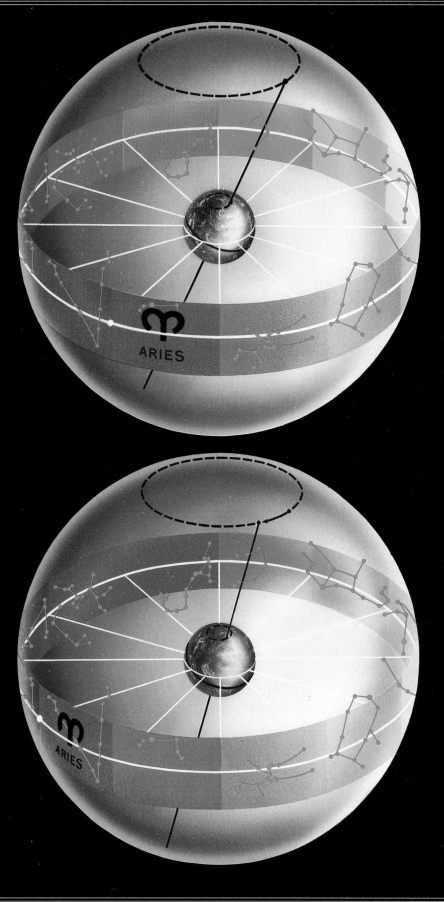

ARIES

ARIES

Ancient astrologers knew as early as 3000 BC that the stars provided a stationary backdrop for the planets' movements across the sky. Gradually, the stars were organized into identifiable patterns that formed the twelve constellations of the zodiac, shown on these pages. The merging of the scientific knowledge of the Chaldean and Greek cultures in the third century BC provided the basis for the constellations' current names.

cal numbers. They also invented the world's first known writing—the cuneiform of the tablets.

The Sumerians were deeply religious, and their gods, as it happened, were none other than the pinpricks of light that so brilliantly illuminated the

PISCES

night sky. As the gods circled about, their behavior could reasonably be perceived as having a profound effect on human affairs. A conjunction between two planets, for example, meant a competition between two deities for the same space in heaven. Surely a similar conflict would soon take place on earth. By the same logic, the Sumerians believed that the gods would communicate their wishes through various celestial omens such as particular cloud formations or shooting stars.

TAURUS

Much effort went into satisfying the gods' desires. Sumerian priests drew up a calendar of religious festivals, based largely on the phases of the moon but keyed to other heavenly signals as well. One sequence celebrated the annual love affair between Ishtar—the planet Venus—and the handsome shepherd Tammuz, who was represented by the constellation later known as Orion. Tammuz shone brightly in the winter sky, but in summer he faded from sight, retreating into the underworld as the sun heated up. Eventually Ishtar went down to fetch him, and the priests would chant prayers and light torches to illuminate her way.

SCORPIO

Any disruption of the normal celestial round brought fear and confusion, for the safety of both gods and humans was thrown into doubt. Eclips-

es were deemed particularly dangerous. During a lunar eclipse it appeared that the moon god, Sin, was being gobbled up by demons and suffering great pain. So when the shadow began to cross, the priests lit their tapers and started their chants, while the people draped cloaks over their heads and shouted for their lives. The method worked, for the noise always seemed to drive the demons away. The shadow passed, and the moon emerged unharmed.

CAPRICORN

The Sumerians thrived for many centuries, until elbowed aside by newer arrivals. These included Semites from Arabia, who around 2350 BC united Mesopotamia with the kingdom of Akkad, the first regional empire; another Semitic people known as Amorites, whose capital at Babylon in the eighteenth century BC was a place of legendary splendor; then Hittites, Kassites, and finally the Assyrians, whose conquests swallowed up

VIRGO

all previous realms. As each new power added its overlay of custom and belief, the region's culture grew increasingly subtle and complex. Astrology was no exception.

The earliest surviving lists of cosmic omens, including the Babylonian tablets found in Ashurbanipal's library, tended to be catchall assortments of astrology, astronomy, religious practice, weather prediction, and just about everything else the scribes could think of. "If the sky is bright when the new moon appears, and it is greeted with shouts of joy, the year will be good," read one forecast. "If it thunders in the month of Shebat there will be a plague

LIBRA

CANCER

of locusts," ran another, based, no doubt, on lengthy experience with locusts and thunderstorms.

Virtually all the early predictions related in some way to the welfare of the state; the idea of an individual horoscope, based on a person's birth date, was still centuries in the future. A forecaster's only client was the king himself, and the astrologer's main task was to discern the will of the gods so that the ruler could fix state policy accordingly. And what monarch could resist feeling content when he heard

AQUARIUS

that "if the sun stands in the place of the moon, the king of the country will be secure on his throne"? Or that "if Jupiter seems to enter into the moon, prices will be low"?

With their nations' futures on their shoulders, royal soothsayers in Babylonia and Assyria used every possible means to read ahead. Besides studying the stars, they analyzed the flight patterns of birds, interpreted royal dreams, deciphered the figures made by a drop of oil as it splattered into a beaker of water. Bizarre childbirths called for immediate explanation: "If a woman gives birth to a pig, a woman will seize the throne; if a woman gives birth to an elephant, the land will be laid waste." It is hard to imagine the occasions that led to such maxims. The art of read-

GEMINI

ing animal entrails gained special importance, for it was thought that the priest's knife, entering the sacrificial lamb or goat, froze a moment in cosmic time that reflected the condition of the entire universe. The liver, being the largest organ, received particular attention. Some seers devoted themselves entirely to hepatoscopy, the art of its analysis.

But the most powerful and direct connection between

the Mesopotamians and their gods remained the lights in the sky. As part of their efforts to please and observe their deities, the lords of Babylon and Nineveh built temples on the summits of lofty stepped pyramids, called ziggurats— the Tower of Babel in the Old Testament is perhaps the

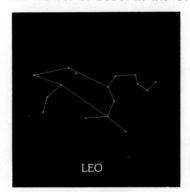

LEO

most famous. At the beginning of each year, according to Babylonian myth, the gods would assemble atop the ziggurats to decide the fates of the people. The rest of the time the priests would use the towers as stellar observatories. And the more the priests discovered, the more complicated their jobs of tracking and interpreting the movements of the heavenly bodies proved to be.

The complex geometry of the heavens has always been a source of wonder and frustration. To a seer on a ziggurat, most

ARIES

stars seemed to circle above in an unvarying sequence, rising in the east and setting in the west like familiar travelers in the sky. The astrologer would discern patterns, with one cluster shaped like a tuft of hair, another like a scorpion, still another like a strutting lion. The sequence's timing would shift from season to season, but this too was predict-

able. Each spring, during the Babylonian period, the constellation we call Taurus would appear on the dawn horizon; a month later the dawn constellation would be Gemini.

But a number of prominent orbs refused to fit into this regular format.

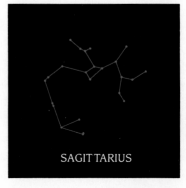

SAGITTARIUS

Ishtar, the Babylonian goddess of love, fertility, and war depicted in this alabaster figure from the third century BC, was thought to be the daughter of either the sky god or moon god. Since Venus is the first object to appear in both the morning and the evening skies, forming a symbolic link between the sun and the moon, Ishtar was identified with that planet.

The most obvious exception was the sun. Even a casual observer knew that in summer the sun rose earlier, stayed up longer, and took a higher path than it did in winter. The point each morning where it broke above the horizon moved progressively northward. Then, at midsummer, it reversed itself, marching south again and following a lower course in the sky. It was apparent that although the sun's movements were somehow related to the great arc that other heavenly bodies described across the celestial canopy, they were also independent of it. The sky watchers also had the key to a nearly infallible prediction. By counting the days after the sun started moving north, they could estimate when the Mesopotamian rivers would rise with the spring flood, and when it would be time for farmers to plant their crops.

Another gleaming exception to overall celestial conformity was the moon. Not only did it rise and set at odd times of the day and night, but it was constantly changing shape as well. Gloriously bright at the full, it dwindled to the smallest crescent, then to nothing—only to reawaken in newborn splendor. The cycle took about twenty-nine and a half days, and it provided the seer with a handy way to mark time. Each cycle became a month, and twelve months added up to roughly a year. There was one major problem, however: The moon cycles did not match up with the annual rhythms of the sun. As a result, the seasons would lag behind the calendar, and every few years the seers would have to add an extra month to make them come out right.

Certain days of the month were set aside for ritual observance, and on some days all activity was strictly to be avoided. The last days before the new moon, when the old moon "crossed the river of death," were seen as particularly unlucky. On the twenty-ninth of Tebit the king did not leave his palace, lest he "meet with witchcraft in the wind of the street." Any man who ventured out-of-doors on the twenty-ninth of Nisan would surely die—or so the seers maintained. Indeed, from the time of King Hammurabi's reign in the eighteenth century BC, all activity was taboo on the first day of each of the moon's seven-day-long quarter phases. The observance of this day of rest passed on to other cultures: thus the origin of the Jewish Sabbath and, later, of the Christian Sunday.

Both sun and moon were important deities in the pantheon of Mesopotamian sky gods, and so were other bodies whose movements seemed even more erratic. These were the planets, and the seer on his ziggurat could pick out five in all. The most brilliant was Venus—Ishtar, to the Babylonian seers—star of both morning and evening, who sometimes shone forth even when the sun was up. Since her brightness fluctuated in an enticing manner, she was seen as the goddess of youth, beauty, and amorous love. But Ishtar was also known as the Lady of Battles and was depicted riding on a lion with a weapon in her hand. Jupiter was another intensely bright planet, whose regal and steadfast glow the seer associated with Marduk, king of the gods. Marduk could unleash storms and cataclysms, but he was generally gracious, and he presaged worldly power and renown. Mars, on the other hand, with his red, malevolent light, was known as the war god Nergal, harbinger of death and destruction. The remote, slow-moving Saturn—Ninurta to the seer—reigned as the pale and flickering deity of time, old age, and scholarly pursuit. With a cycle around the heavens of almost thirty years' duration, Ninurta took the long view of things. His opposite in personality and effect was Mercury, or Nebu, as fast as quicksilver, whose darting path earned him a reputation for foxlike trickiness.

Tracking the planets' courses led seers to much befuddled speculation. The planets appeared to roam the sky at will, with no logical relationship to one another or to anything else. Mercury danced back and forth in the vicinity of the sun. Saturn might linger in a single constellation for years on end, as though chained in place. Sometimes a planet would march ahead in good order, then pause or even reverse itself and move backward. The seers referred to these whimsical orbs as *bibbus,* or wild goats—an oddly irreverent term for the gods of human destiny. But their movements were recorded meticulously and with special attention to the days on which they emerged near the horizon just after sunset.

As the wild goats cavorted about the sky, the so-called fixed constellations provided convenient reference points for plotting their movements. The seers divided the heavens into three broad avenues, which carried the stars along as though on conveyer belts. The northernmost circuit appeared to revolve around the North Star when viewed from the Northern Hemisphere of the spinning earth, and its constellations never set below the horizon. According to some authorities, this belt belonged to Anu, the ruling sky deity. Enlil, god of wind and rain, controlled the middle belt, whose stars were seen to rise and set with the daily turning of the earth. The southernmost belt, with stars that might vanish for months on end in the winter, when the Northern Hemisphere was tipped away from them and the sun, was the domain of the water god Ea, who would periodically surface to rescue humankind in times of crisis, then fade back into his native ocean. Envisioned as a wise old man wearing a fish-shaped cloak, Ea gave the world its science, its art, and its writing, as well as its knowledge of magic.

In the seventh century BC, the Middle East, always a cockpit of clashing cultures and armies, entered an especially tumultuous period that transformed the intellectual climate. The Assyrian empire reached the zenith of its power, then suddenly collapsed. New cultural influences poured in from Persia in the east and from the Greek-speaking westerners who lived on the shores of the Aegean Sea. The ancient city of Babylon, fallen into decay under the Assyrians, rose to new brilliance under the energetic Chaldean king Nebuchadnezzar. Through Jewish chroniclers, posterity would receive an ill opinion of Nebuchadnezzar, since he ransacked Jerusalem and brought the Jews into Babylonian exile; the Book of Daniel asserts that he went mad and ate grass. But during his reign, from 605 to 562 BC, he rebuilt Babylon into a place of unrivaled splendor, with Hanging Gardens that ranked among the world's great wonders and a splendid new seven-tiered ziggurat for inquiring into the celestial mysteries.

As though inspired by this royal setting, the Babylonian seers went about compiling their tables of astronomical data with redoubled energy. They refined the calendar, devising a method for adjusting the lunar months to the solar year in a more orderly manner. Observations became more exact, with researchers using mathematics to pinpoint various astral bodies. A scribe might report that "on the eighteenth day of the month, the goddess Ishtar was 2 degrees 55 minutes above the King"—the King being Regulus, the brightest star in Leo. Sundials and water clocks helped in the timing of stellar events. For precision, the researchers split the day and night into standardized periods: twelve hours from one noonday to the next, with each hour divided into sixty minutes, and each minute into sixty seconds. Every standard clock face in the world thus reflects the work of the Babylonian astrologers, although their time units were exactly twice as long as ours.

The principal constellations also came under study. A fair number had been identified in earlier times, to be sure. But the seers of Babylon were mainly concerned with the

Ancient stargazers in the Outer Hebrides observed the skies from the Callanish megaliths, erected about 1800

BC. They used the data they collected to predict such events as tides, eclipses, and propitious planting times.

The Mystery of Eclipses

In 2136 BC, according to Chinese legend, Imperial Emperor Chung K'ang was horrified one day to see darkness prematurely descending over the land. He looked skyward and saw the sun narrowing to a slender crescent—an event interpreted by the ancient Chinese as dragons attacking the golden globe. The Chinese believed that these raids on the sun could be foreseen by royal astronomers and that any dire consequences might be prevented by shooting arrows at the sky, beating their drums, and generally creating pandemonium. This time, however, Chung K'ang's astronomers, Hsi and Ho, had issued no forewarning. But in spite of the failure to mount a counterattack, the sun once again shone within a few minutes.

The sun was saved, but not so the astronomers. For their failure to warn of the attack on the sun—known to modernity as an eclipse—the two were put to death.

The Chinese were not alone in their fear of the darkening of the day or the sudden waning of the moon in a cloudless sky. Indeed, the word *eclipse,* from the ancient Greek *ekleipsis,* means failure—something gone wrong.

"The day of the new moon in the month of Hiyar [April-May] was put to shame. . . . The sun went down in the daytime," reads the earliest known observation of a solar eclipse, etched on a tablet in the Syrian city of Ugarit in 1375 BC. People all over the world struggled to understand and explain them. The mysterious behavior of the sun and the moon was linked to disaster, deaths, and the displeasure of the gods. Before 400 BC, the Greek poet Pindar tried to understand eclipses. "Is it a signal of war or a portent of famine?" he asked. "Does it mean a heavy fall of snow, or is the sea to overflow the land, or are fields to be icebound, or is the south wind to bring rain, or is a deluge to overwhelm the world and drown all men?"

To ward off any misfortune eclipses might bring, the ancients relied heavily on ritual. The Chaldeans, more than 4,000 years ago, thought the disappearance of the moon was caused by an attack of seven demons, signaling the end of the world. At the onset of an eclipse, a ceremony was performed in hopes of staving off ruin: A Chaldean priest lit a torch, placed it on an altar, and chanted dirges for the safety of the fields, rivers, and great divinities. People gathered and removed their turbans, covered their heads with their robes, and shouted at the sky. It seemed to work: The sun always reappeared.

The early Mexicans sacrificed hunchbacks and dwarfs during eclipses, and the Indians of the Yukon turned their pots and dishes upside down so that the sickness from the sun would not collect in them. The Qagyuhl Indians of northwest America thought the moon disappeared because a sky monster was trying to swallow the planet. In response, they danced around a fire of smoldering clothing and hair, hoping to cause the beast to sneeze and expel the moon.

About 470 BC, the Greek philosopher and astronomer Anaxagoras correctly explained why eclipses occur. Yet more than fifty years later, in 413 BC, superstition superseded science, with dire historical consequences. It was the time of the Peloponnesian War between the city-states of Athens and Sparta. The Athenian army, camped on the island of Sicily, had suffered one setback after another. One day, as the Athenian commander, Nicias, was about to order his troops to withdraw, the sky suddenly blackened. Nicias interpreted this as a sign from the deities to stay his ground. He did so, and rival Sparta launched a furious attack, roundly defeating the Athenians. This disaster was the turning point of the war, leading to the eventual demise of Athens.

Over the following centuries, through the growing science of astronomy, people learned not only to understand eclipses, but to predict them. This ability could be a powerful tool, as Christopher Columbus, anchored in Jamaica and running short of provisions, discovered in early 1493. When the Jamaicans refused to furnish him with supplies, Columbus, aware of an impending lunar eclipse, threatened the recalcitrant islanders with divine vengeance. He predicted that on that very night "the light of the moon would fail." Indeed, the moon disappeared, plunging the island into blackness. The natives implored him to intercede, and he gladly restored their moon—in return for his ship's provisions.

ones that circled through the sky's middle reaches, along the Way of Enlil, since this was the avenue taken by the sun, the moon, and the planets. They discerned a total of eighteen such figures, including all the signs of the modern zodiac except Aries, the Ram. Each constellation took on an astrological character, depending on its physical shape and its role in mythology. The constellation later called Libra, the Scales, represented balance and judgment. Virgo, seen originally as a furrow in a grain field, stood for fertility. Scorpio, an autumn sign, pierced the sun with his poison stinger, leaving the sun feeble and dying.

This early Greek bas-relief depicts Fanes, the god of light, truth, and justice, surrounded by the zodiac signs and the symbols of the four elements—a coiled snake for earth, a drinking bowl for water, wings for air, and a lion's head for fire.

Eventually, seers divided the Way of Enlil into twelve evenly spaced, month-long segments, and they named each segment after its corresponding star group. It did not matter that there were more constellations than segments, or that some constellations sprawled across greater expanses of sky than others. Some were dropped, and the differences in size among the rest were ignored. And sometime before the end of the fifth century BC, the zodiac assumed its final form, with the twelve signs dividing the sky into equal segments of thirty degrees each. With a few minor changes, it would remain astrology's basic tool from then on.

By then the urge to scrutinize the night sky in an organized manner had spread well beyond the kingdoms of Mesopotamia. Among the most ardent surveyors of the heavens were the philosophers of Greece. Greek mariners since the time of Homer had set their helms to various astral signposts, and Greek farmers would harvest their grapes when

Orion reached its highest point. But the philosophers, many of whom lived in Greek settlements in Ionia, on the west coast of modern Turkey, had no practical end in view. The sky gods had no hold over them. Nor did they seek to divine the future; the Greek oracle at Delphi was judged sufficient for that. No, the philosophers were driven by simple curiosity—the sheer delight of puzzling things out. As a result, they built a theoretical framework for the universe that they observed.

One of the earliest Ionian thinkers, born around 630 BC, was Thales of Miletus. Well versed in Eastern mathematics (he is said to have brought geometry to Greece), Thales devised a new approach to cosmic study. He sought to sweep the sky clean of the ancient mythologies and to substitute physical laws. The world could not have been formed, as the Babylonians thought, when Marduk slew the dragon Tiamat and shaped the cosmos from her parts. Rather, Thales declared, it evolved through natural causes from one physical element—which he took to be water. Applying his physical laws, Thales became adept at analyzing and predicting the movements of heavenly bodies.

Various pupils of Thales continued to work at determining the master plan of the cosmos. Anaximander proposed a geometric picture of the heavens, in which the universe was contained inside a huge wheel of fire with holes in its rim that allowed the stars to shine through. Another pupil, Anaximenes, suggested that the stars and planets were like the heads of shiny nails that had been driven into orbiting spheres of a transparent, crystal-like substance. He

Atlas balances a celestial globe upon his
shoulders in this statue, copied in the
second century AD from a Greek original.
According to Greek mythology, Atlas
had to hold up the heavens after losing a
war against Zeus, god of the sky.

thought that air, not water or fire, was the primal element. But both men sought a rational explanation for natural events. And for all their lofty speculation, the students of Thales could be resolutely down-to-earth. Anaximander, for example, took time to draw a map of the known world, which was astonishing in its overall accuracy.

As these heady ideas swirled about in the intellectual debates of the philosophers, other schemes of thought rose up to confront them. The most influential by far originated with another Ionian—Pythagoras, known to every modern high-school student for his famous theorem on the geometry of right triangles. Pythagoras was a giant in his own day, a man of towering intellect, a tireless scholar and a traveler to distant lands. He journeyed to Egypt, then to Babylon, and he returned home steeped in astral lore. The cosmos, he decided, had been created by a single governing intelligence that expressed itself in numbers. All parts of the universe fit into a mathematically perfect system that was as sure as the multiplication table and as strict as the notes in a musical scale. The result was a numerical harmony, a cosmic hum, that resonated from the stars above to the earth below. Each planet, as it circled in space, produced a musical note, and together the notes vibrated in a single perfect chord: the music of the spheres. The wise individual, Pythagoras declared, should strive for perfection by attuning the self to this prevailing symphony.

Pythagoras believed that the earth was round, as did most of his contemporaries, and he also thought of it as a stationary body at the center of an orbiting cosmos. But there remained one glaring contradiction in this neat picture—the odd backward pirouettes of the planets. Pythagoras could not explain them. His disciple Philolaus offered a solution, one that in time would prove quite literally to be revolutionary. The earth was not stationary, he said; it, too, moved in orbit. Centuries would pass, however, before this strange idea caught on.

Other astral thinkers stuck closer to the prevailing wisdom. One Empedocles of Cos, mulling over the basic elements, decided there were four: earth, air, fire, and water.

Each sign of the zodiac would eventually come to be associated with one or another. His neighbor in Cos was the physician Hippocrates, honored as the father of medicine, who suggested that a patient's good health depended on a proper balance between four bodily fluids, or humors, which corresponded to the four elements. And no physician, Hippocrates maintained, could practice effectively without full knowledge of heavenly influences.

Thus the classical cosmos: an earth-centered universe governed by a divine intelligence, which exercised its powers through mathematical laws of nature. And no one did more to perpetuate this image than the philosopher Plato, perhaps the greatest of all Greek thinkers. Plato embraced the astral knowledge of his day and lifted it to the highest levels of mystical abstraction. To him there was only one reality—an unchanging ideal realm of divine spirit, which cast its light across all creation. Beside this, the physical world as perceived by the senses—trees, tables, flowers, mountains, even the sky itself—was mere illusion. Any exceptions to the cosmic ideal, such as retrograde planets, scarcely mattered to him. Perfection was all, the natural habitat of truth and beauty. Each human soul was a part of the divine spirit, and each had its own private star to which one day it would return. Plato's scheme would profoundly affect the doctrines of future religions, including Christianity, and also the mystical uses of astrology.

If Greek philosophy took inspiration, in part, from intellectual currents that wafted in from Babylon, a more thorough mingling was now about to occur. It came, like so many cultural marriages in that unsettled age, through the agency of military conquest.

In 334 BC an army of 35,000 Greeks and Macedonians—a tiny force for the task at hand—marched out of Europe and into Asia. Their leader was a blond youth of twenty-two years, bold, handsome, and driven by a dream of almost mystical glory. If any man was destiny's child, it was Alexander the Great. His sire, people whispered, was Zeus himself, or perhaps the Egyptian god Ammon. His mother had supposedly held back his birth, under the sign of Leo, until the planetary aspects were just right.

Alexander streaked across the known world like a meteor, in a blazing trajectory that reached through the Nile Delta to the deserts of Libya, across Palestine and Turkey, on through Babylonia and into the wastelands of both Persia and Afghanistan, and finally came to earth in the jungles of western India. His passage was brief. Within a decade he lay dying of fever in Babylon—an event foretold by the local seers. But his legacy endured for more than five centuries in a unified world culture—called Hellenism—that combined the traditions of Greece

On this vase fragment dating from the second century BC, Alexander the Great wears a headdress adorned with symbols of the heavens. In Alexander's kingdom, astrology flourished as never before; the leader allegedly used it to plan his legendary battles.

with those of Alexander's eastern domains. Alexander's court at Babylon "swarmed with astrologers, soothsayers, and prognosticators," one chronicler related. And under his successors the study of astrology flourished as never before.

The joining together of Greek theory and Babylonian astral lore produced a major transformation in both. While the cuneiform tablets supplied a centuries-old record of stellar movements, the Greek cosmic models offered a logical way to organize them. What had once been seen as the art of reading messages from sky gods now took on the trappings of a scientific study based on natural law. The planets and constellations were given Greek names, the Babylonian deities equated to their Greek counterparts. Each part of the human body, the Greeks declared, was governed by one sign or another. Virgo commanded the belly, for example, and Aries the head and face.

A fresher, more democratic outlook swept through the

dusty corridors of astrological study. No longer was it a monopoly of royal soothsayers employed to read omens for the king, but an enterprise open to anyone with the wit to use it. A new concept came into play: the individual horoscope, which evaluated a citizen's prospects from the position of the stars at the hour of birth. Efforts were already being made in this direction for the offspring of monarchs, but the results were sketchy at best. A horoscope drawn up for the son of a Babylonian prince in 410 BC mentioned that the moon was near Scorpio, Jupiter was in Pisces, Venus in Taurus, Saturn in Cancer, Mars in Gemini. Judging from the written record, however, it seems the prognosis never went beyond a general "things will be good for you."

Now people of all social levels wanted to know what the future held for them and were willing to brace themselves for even the most dismal news. One luckless fellow, born in 263 BC, learned that while his life would be long, it would also be increasingly hard. "He will lack money," the reading went, and "his food will not suffice for his hunger. The riches he knew in his youth will dwindle away."

In response to popular demand, a number of schools sprang up to spread the new discipline. Most made no distinction between astrological prediction and pure astronomy. One of the earliest was started at Babylon around 315 BC by a Greek-speaking native named Kidinnu. A master of both divination and mathematics, Kidinnu figured out the exact length of a lunar month, clocking it at 29 days, 12 hours, 44 minutes, and 3.3 seconds. (When modern astronomers came to make their calculation of the month's

Planets in Retrograde

Seen from the Earth, retrograde Mars seems to loop in the sky.

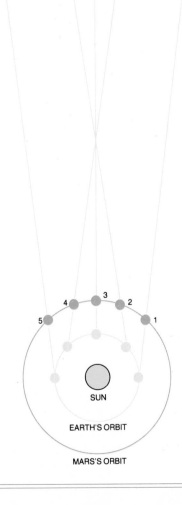

MARS'S APPARENT COURSE

When Babylonian astronomers first began observing the heavens, they were sometimes puzzled by the paths of the planets. The orbs did not always trace a continuous route across the sky; rather, they occasionally traveled a straight course for several weeks, then appeared to slow, come to a stop, and back up for several days before finally moving forward again.

Astrologers interpret this apparent detour, known as retrograde motion, symbolically as a time for individuals to review their pasts, to go back over ground already covered. Modern scientists, however, know that the planets do not literally move backward—they just appear to do so when viewed from the Earth.

Retrograde motion is observed at the time of conjunction between the Earth and a planet. In the case of the inferior planets—Venus and Mercury, whose orbits are closest to the Sun— retrograde motion occurs when a planet passes between the Earth and the Sun and overtakes the Earth in its orbit. For the superior planets—those outside the Earth's orbit—retrograde motion occurs when the Earth moves between a planet and the Sun and overtakes the planet, much like a faster car on the inside lane of a racetrack *(diagram, right)*.

One of the first astronomers to seek a physical explanation for this phenomenon was the Greek philosopher Aristarchus of Samos, who postulated about 300 BC that the Earth, the Moon, and the planets all revolved around a motionless Sun. However, his remarkable theories were summarily dismissed and forgotten.

Ptolemy, in the second century AD, rejected the heliocentric view of the universe in favor of an Earth-centered one. He attempted to account for the planets' periodic backpedaling by speculating that they moved in small circles called epicycles as they orbited in larger circles around the Earth. This theory permitted fairly accurate predictions of planetary motions and provoked little dissension from other stargazers until the sixteenth century, when Polish astronomer Nicholas Copernicus embraced heliocentrism. But Copernicus retained Ptolemy's concept of epicycles to explain the planets' backward movements.

It was German astronomer Johannes Kepler who finally established in the early 1600s that planets move in elliptical orbits around the Sun, and that because of an unknown force— later discovered to be gravity—the speed at which the planets travel increases as they near the fiery hub. Therefore, a planet's position relative to the Sun determines its orbital speed and sets the stage for periodic retrograde motion.

SUN

EARTH'S ORBIT

MARS'S ORBIT

Among the earliest surviving horoscopes is this Greek one, written on papyrus and calculated in Egypt on April 1 in the year AD 81. Composed by Titus Pitenius at Hermopolis, the chart begins by paying homage to the ancient Egyptians who studied the heavenly bodies and handed down their knowledge. Inscribed are the date and the time and the positions of the sun, moon, and planets in the zodiac. According to Pitenius's calculations, "the sun, the mightiest and ruler of all, moving from the spring equinox, had attained in Aries fourteen degrees and six minutes. . . . And the divine and light-bringing moon, waxing in crescent, had advanced in Taurus thirteen degrees."

length, they found him to be off by only .6 second.) Several decades later a Babylonian priest, Berosus, set up a school—the first in Europe—on the Greek island of Cos. Berosus cast horoscopes, circulated Greek translations of the Babylonian tablets, and offered an explanation for the phases of the moon. He achieved such fame that the people of Athens put up a statue in his honor.

Over the next few centuries astrology spread to the farthest reaches of the Hellenistic world. It took firm hold in India, which already enjoyed a native tradition of astral speculation. Ancient Hindu rites were scheduled to coincide with the spring and autumn equinoxes, and the earliest Hindu sages were thought to reside in the seven stars of the Big Dipper. Reflecting the age-old Indian propensity to think in majestic sweeps of cosmic time, the region's most famous astrological text, the Surya Siddhanta, was said to have been written in 2,163,102 BC. (Actually, the Surya Siddhanta probably was not written until long after the Hellenistic period—perhaps not until the fifth or sixth century AD.)

In this fertile environment the new astrology blossomed into full flower. The Indians adopted the twelve-part zodiac and many Greek technical terms. Even the Hindu gods learned to heed astral signs. The all-powerful Vishnu, it was said, became so alarmed by the baleful influence of Saturn that for a nineteen-year period he abandoned his heavenly throne and wandered about the forest disguised as an elephant. Then, resuming his former state, he boasted how cleverly he had avoided cosmic mishap. But Saturn, passing by, corrected him. "Why, sir," said the planet, "for nineteen years you have been eating nothing but grass, and leading a most miserable life indeed, tormented by flies and mosquitoes." One's astral destiny was inescapable.

The ancient Far East had still other traditions of astrological study. In China, the "Celestial Kingdom," the emperor had long been equated with the North Star, around which the entire universe was thought to revolve. Chinese astrologer-priests had been compiling records probably for even longer than their Babylonian counterparts, possibly from as early as the twenty-eighth century BC. The Chinese can be credited with recording the earliest verifiable eclipse, in 1361 BC. Celestial conjunctions were seen as having profound effects on human affairs, including the rise and fall of ruling dynasties. As the great Chinese sage Confucius declared around 500 BC: "Heaven sends down its good or evil symbols, and wise men act accordingly."

Greek armies had not penetrated to this distant shore, but a number of ideas that were common to both China and the West may have filtered from one region to the other along the trade routes through Central Asia. The Chinese used a twelve-part zodiac—although the signs do not divide the sky, but instead mark off sectors of the equator—and like the Babylonians they divided the day into twelve double hours. The emperor Wu, in the second century BC, built an observation tower that may have been inspired by the Babylonian ziggurats. A set of predictions made at that time resembled the great Mesopotamian omen text, Enuma Anu Enlil. Individual horoscopes may also have been a Western import. Some time after Greek and Babylonian seers began casting them, the Chinese did also, although for Chinese astrologers the decisive moment was not that of birth, but that of conception.

Still, given China's profound isolation from the rest of the world, huge differences were bound to remain. The Chinese saw the cosmos as a mechanical box containing many different compartments and intricately constructed around the number five. Along with the five planets there were five elements (wood, fire, earth, metal, and water), five geographic areas (the four compass directions plus a central point), five primary colors, five flavors, five basic musical notes. Beyond these, the two primal forces of Yin and Yang—one female and passive, the other male and active—governed all activity. Furthermore, all astrologers worked for the emperor, as part of a tightly controlled court bureaucracy. The position carried great prestige, but it also entailed some hazard. When the sun went into unexpected eclipse in 2136 BC, the chief astrologer and his assistant were routinely beheaded for not forewarning the emperor.

In contrast to this traditionally restrictive climate was the surge of freethinking inquiry that burst forth in Egypt in the third century BC. The hub of Western culture at that time was Alexandria, founded on the Nile Delta by the Conqueror himself and now grown into the greatest metropolis of its day. Its grand civic buildings included the world's largest library, where scholars could browse through some 700,000 manu-

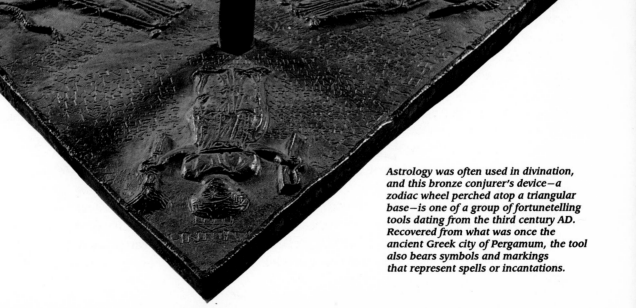

Astrology was often used in divination, and this bronze conjurer's device—a zodiac wheel perched atop a triangular base—is one of a group of fortunetelling tools dating from the third century AD. Recovered from what was once the ancient Greek city of Pergamum, the tool also bears symbols and markings that represent spells or incantations.

Fiery Messengers of Doom

In ancient civilizations, the appearance of a comet in the sky nearly always caused great consternation, for comets were almost universally thought to herald such disasters as floods, pestilence, and the deaths of rulers. Astrologers of the day made dire predictions based on the appearance of the long-tailed heavenly torches, and since a destructive event was fairly likely to be happening somewhere in the known world at any given time, those seers who linked comets with misfortune were more often than not deemed correct.

A Chinese text from the seventh century AD shows the portentous significance of comets. "When comets appear, whales die. . . . When a comet appeared in the constellation of the Big Dipper, all soldiers died in chaos. When a comet appears in the North Star, the emperor is replaced." In fact, it is a Chinese sentence, from the fifteenth century BC, that remains the earliest surviving reference to a comet. It reads, "When Chieh executed his faithful counselors, a comet appeared."

The word *comet* comes from the Greek word for hair, suggested by the comet's wavy luminosity. The Chinese called them broom-stars, among other names, and they still recount the story of a comet that appeared in the year 516 BC, in the kingdom of Ch'i. To avert what he considered inevitable disaster, the king of Ch'i commanded his ministers to pray. But minister Yen Tsu, who believed those who were innocent had nothing to fear from the dreaded intruder, countered, "How can you expect prayer to change anything? A comet is like a broom; it signals the sweeping away of evil."

Despite their dread of comets—or perhaps because of it—no other culture made such early, frequent, and valuable observations of the phenomenon as the Chinese. A treasure trove of cometary history was unearthed in the 1970s during the excavation of a tomb from the Han dynasty in the Hunan province. Archaeologists found an illustrated textbook, painted on silk, that

This detail from a Chinese silk atlas dating from the second century BC depicts eight of the twenty-nine comets chronicled by ancient Chinese astronomers.

showed twenty-nine comet types. Each was classified according to its appearance and meaning. A four-tailed one meant "disease in the world," a three-tailed one "calamity in the state." A comet with two tails that curved to the right presaged a "small war" but "the corn would be plentiful."

Scholars estimate that compiling such a catalog would have taken almost 300 years, given the average rate of one sighting every 10 years. And the Chinese records are detailed, listing the date, type of comet, constellation in which it was seen, subsequent motion, color, apparent length, and how long it stayed in the sky. The astronomers also made other observations; for example, they were the first to note that the tails of comets always point away from the sun.

But for all their data, the ancient Chinese did not know what comets really were. Some writers attributed them to disarrangements of Yin and Yang, whereas others said that comets came from the planets. It was left to the West to uncover in the mid-sixteenth century the true, harmless nature of these streaks of light.

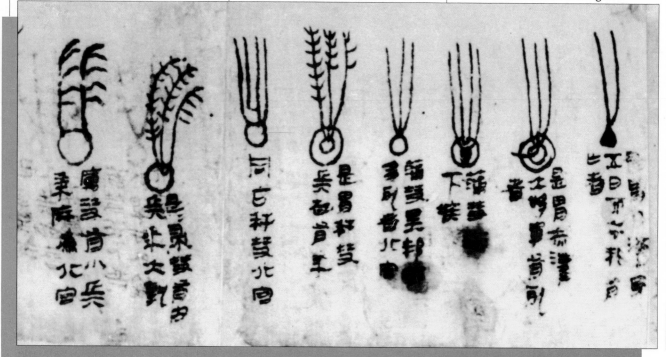

Set against a backdrop of constellations, the intertwined double helix of this creation image from the T'ang dynasty (AD 618-906) symbolizes genesis through the interaction of philosophical opposites: Yin, representing darkness, femininity, and the moon, and Yang, associated with lightness, masculinity, and the sun.

scripts. The geometer Euclid studied there, and so did Eratosthenes, who calculated the circumference of the earth to within 15 percent of its true size. Astrology, not surprisingly, received much attention.

Little work had been done in this field before the Greeks' arrival—despite claims from the Egyptians that their ancestors had been studying the heavens for some 500,000 years. Egyptian priests identified their gods with various heavenly bodies, to be sure. The moon was Osiris, a benevolent deity who was overshadowed in eclipses by his evil brother Set. The sun god, Ra, king of the cosmos, sailed through the sky by day in his celestial barge, and by night he battled the forces of underworld darkness. His earthly incarnation was the pharaoh. All three were descended from Nut, the primal mother, who comprised the entire dome of the night sky. When the Egyptians wished to ascertain the future, however, they relied for the most part on messages that came to them in their dreams. No one thought of consulting the visible heavens.

There was one exception. Egypt's main source of prosperity was the Nile River, whose annual flooding brought moisture and fertility to the desert soil. Knowing just when the flood would occur was of vital interest to everyone. And the best clue, as it happened, was in the stars. A week or so in advance, the so-called Dog Star, Sirius, would appear on the eastern horizon at dawn. Every year it was the same, as regular as the ticking of a clock. Once every 365 days, plus a few extra hours, the Dog Star rose with the sun. Shortly thereafter, the Nile also rose. As a result, the Egyptians achieved one of science's most important breakthroughs, a standard year length, while the

Greeks and Babylonians were still struggling to make their lunar months come out even with the solar year. Every Greek city had a different calendar, for example. And all the while, the Egyptians knew the answer, with a solar calendar of 365 days—a few hours short, but workable.

Needless to say, a proper calendar did much to advance both astronomy and astrology. The Egyptians divided their calendar into twelve standard months of 30 days each, for a total of 360 days. The other 5 days, thought of as being outside normal time, were given over to religious commemorations.

Alexandria would thrive as a center of astrological study for many centuries, with scholars grinding out long treatises on the more arcane aspects of the art. Horoscopes became increasingly sophisticated. Priests would embellish their temples, and aristocrats their tombs, with zodiacal insignia. And invariably, the works of foreign researchers would find their way into the city's vast library.

One overseas savant of note was Aristarchus of Samos, who picked up the far-fetched idea that the earth revolves around the sun. He also suggested that it spins on its axis, causing day and night—but no one paid much attention. Far more interest centered on the thoughts of Hipparchus of Nicaea, who in fact was an astral scientist of considerable ability. Hipparchus cataloged more than a thousand stars, and he hit upon the system of longitude and latitude for fixing geographic position.

Astrologers, however, were more interested in Hipparchus's studies of the zodiac. Hipparchus discovered that every year the zodiac slips ever so slightly behind the seasons. (Kidinnu had already learned this, but the information had

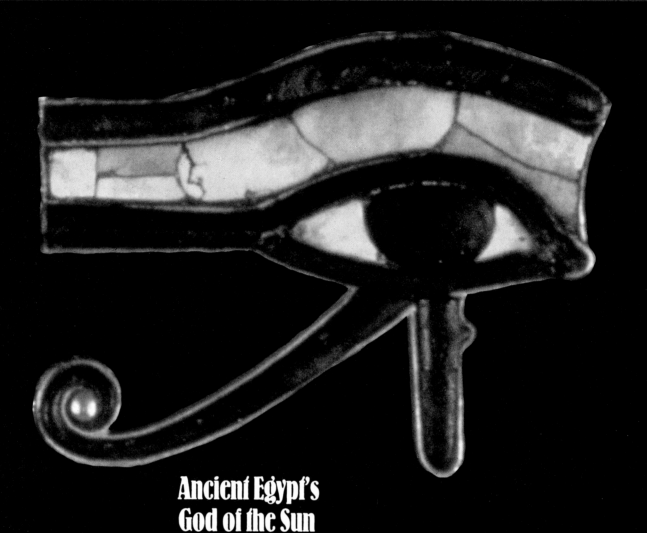

Ancient Egypt's God of the Sun

A pair of jewel-encrusted gold ornaments, from the tomb of the Egyptian boy-king Tutankhamen, who reigned about 1350 BC, depict the eyes of the solar deity, Ra. The right eye (above) represented the sun, and the left eye (opposite) symbolized the moon. The ancient Egyptians explained the true source of the moon's light in a text passage that reads in part, "Light of the night, image of the left eye . . . who rises in the east while the sun is in the west . . . received the light of the right eye."

Ancient Egyptians worshiped the sun, the fiery globe whose light and warmth, they believed, created and sustained life itself. The god they called Ra personified the sun, and he was credited with brightening a previously dark and cold world.

According to one legend, the omnipotent Ra simply willed himself into being; another version recounts Ra's emergence from the petals of a frail lotus blossom in the form of a scarab beetle, the symbol of birth and rebirth. Later, the story continues, the beetle changed into a boy, and when the boy wept, his tears became the earth's living creatures. The all-powerful Ra was said to have ruled then as the first king of Egypt. Each day, it was thought, Ra arose as a beautiful child. He climbed into a boat and, accompanied by gods, swept across the sky,

visiting his twelve provinces, which represented the daylight hours. When he reached the center of the sky, Ra was at his zenith, the pinnacle of manhood and strength. But by late afternoon, he was exhausted, becoming an enfeebled old man by sunset. At night, Ra entered another boat and was transported by the gods through the twelve perilous provinces of the underworld—the nighttime hours. There he battled serpents and demons who sought to exploit his weakened state. If there was stormy weather, those on earth always knew that an enemy had scored a victory; a total eclipse of the sun meant a rival had swallowed the boat, and day became night. But Ra always survived the battles and emerged from the shadowy underworld, passing once more into the morning sky.

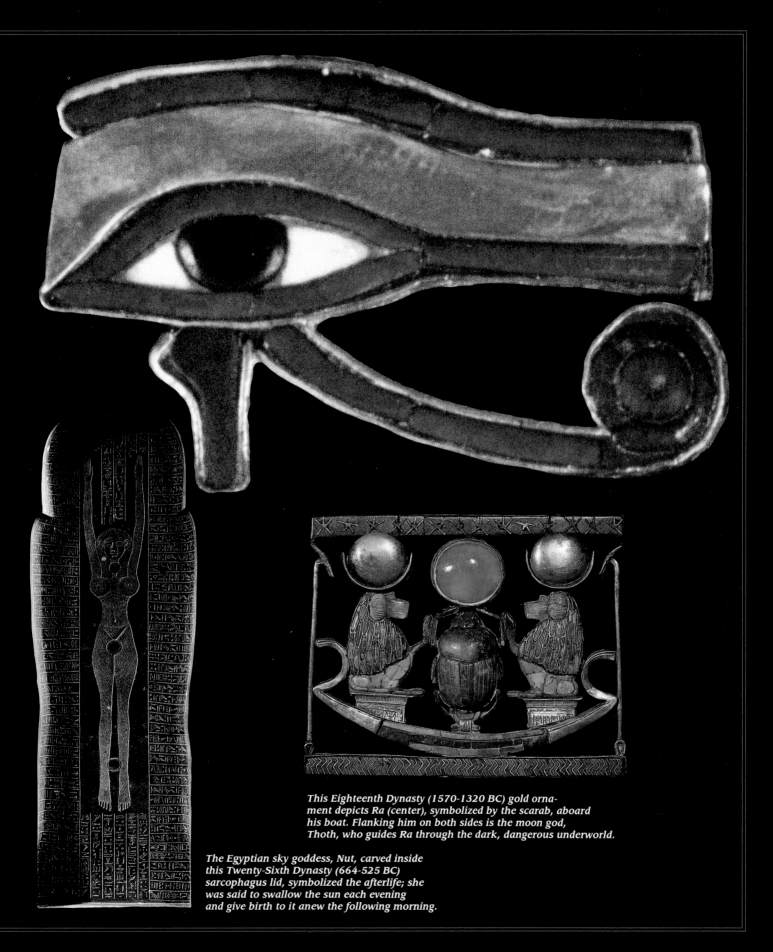

This Eighteenth Dynasty (1570-1320 BC) gold ornament depicts Ra (center), symbolized by the scarab, aboard
his boat. Flanking him on both sides is the moon god,
Thoth, who guides Ra through the dark, dangerous underworld.

The Egyptian sky goddess, Nut, carved inside
this Twenty-Sixth Dynasty (664-525 BC)
sarcophagus lid, symbolized the afterlife; she
was said to swallow the sun each evening
and give birth to it anew the following morning.

not filtered through to Hipparchus's era.) Some 2,000 years earlier, in Sumerian times, it was the dawn rising of Taurus, the Bull, that ushered in the spring equinox. By Hipparchus's era it was Aries, the Ram. The slippage, known as the precession of the equinoxes, occurs because of a slow but steady wobbling of the earth's axis *(pages 11-13)*—although Hipparchus did not know this.

What did become immediately clear was that the zodiac, the very cornerstone of astrological prognosis, is not fixed and eternal. Its shift is continuous so that, over the millennia, the birth signs change in relation to the time of the year. An Alexandrian Greek born on March 21, the day of the spring equinox, would have been an Aries. If twentieth-century astrologers adhered to the practices of the Alexandrian era, assigning the birth sign on the basis of the dawn-rising constellation, a child born on March 21 in this century would be a Pisces. Instead, however illogically, modern Western astrologers apply the signs as they appeared to the Alexandrians when the zodiac was originally standardized. Indian astrologers, on the other hand, accept the shift caused by the precession of the equinoxes and let the constellation rising at dawn determine the birth sign.

Even as Greek and Egyptian astrologers were refining their craft, the world's power center began shifting westward to the young, aggressive precincts of Imperial Rome. The early Romans had little cultural polish of their own, however, and they eagerly took up the ancient wisdom of the peoples they conquered.

Astrology came to their attention through the teachings of Posidonius, a Greek philosopher of the Stoic school who arrived in Rome sometime during the first century BC. The Stoics lived by a code of austere self-sufficiency, with a moral emphasis that appealed strongly to the Roman upper class. The idea was to adjust one's behavior as nearly as possible to the precepts of cosmic law—"to live consistently with nature," as it was commonly put. In other words, wise men and women submitted to their destiny. And what better place to learn what destiny had in mind than in the map of the stars? Posidonius enlarged this theory to include a mystic vital force that emanated from the sun and united the world in universal harmony. But it also behooved people to discover their own astrological fates.

Rome's intellectuals crowded in to hear Posidonius speak, and among his pupils was the great orator Cicero,

This photograph (left), a time exposure, reveals the circular paths of stars around the celestial North Pole. Observing that these northernmost stars never rose or set, ancient Egyptians reasoned that the orbs must belong to the realm of immortality. Egyptian tombs were often illustrated with the circumpolar constellations. A notable example is the painted ceiling in the burial chamber of Seti I (below), who ruled in the fourteenth century BC. At the center of the painting, a bull, representing the Big Dipper, is tethered to a post—symbolizing the celestial North Pole—held by a hippopotamus. A human figure clings to the golden lines leading from the bull to the mooring post.

perhaps the most persuasive voice in the Roman Senate. Cicero had been an adamant foe of astrology, but on hearing Posidonius, he became an immediate convert. Anyone with sense, he declared, could see that the stars "have divine power and intelligence." But eventually, he began to waver. For one thing, the astrologers backed the losing side in a civil war that divided Roman loyalties in the mid-first century BC. They made other mistakes as well, such as telling Julius Caesar he would live to an old age. Finally Cicero denounced the art, attacking it as "incredible mad folly which is daily refuted by experience." A newborn child, he argued, was probably more influenced by the weather, which it could at least feel, than by the signs of the zodiac.

Many other prominent Romans were equally skeptical. Julius Caesar took a dim view of all divination—although if he had followed the soothsayer's advice, he would have avoided the Senate on the ides of March, and thus escaped assassination. But most citizens were believers. When a comet streaked through the sky just after Caesar's death, people said it was his soul ascending to heaven.

Caesar's successors tended to regard astrology as serious business. The emperor Augustus issued a coin with Capricorn on one face, that being the sign in which the moon appeared at the moment of Augustus's birth. In his later years, he was terrified that some enemy would circulate a false horoscope predicting his death, thus sparking a public uprising. So in AD 11, Augustus published his own version, and he outlawed death forecasts for anyone.

Next to take Rome's scepter was Tiberius, who became so entranced by astral divination that he learned to cast his own horoscope. Whenever he sought professional advice, he made sure he got the best. At one point he retired to a villa on Capri, possibly to escape the designs of a maleficent planet, and there he continued to interview prospective court astrologers. To test each seer's powers, Tiberius would ask, "Now what of *your* horoscope?" If the answer was not to his liking, he would have the unfortunate candidate flung off a nearby cliff. All in all, it was a no-win proposition. But then a certain Thrasyllus came up with the perfect response. Thrasyllus studied his chart, began to tremble, and finally announced, "I stand at this moment in the most immediate danger!" Tiberius was so impressed that he made Thrasyllus his chief astral adviser.

Thus began a brief family monopoly in one of Rome's most powerful posts. Thrasyllus's son Balbillus served three emperors—Claudius, Nero, and Vespasian. But unlike his father, who tried to rein Tiberius's more violent impulses, Balbillus seemed quite ready to encourage imperial bloodshed. Comets supposedly foreshadowed the deaths of great leaders, and when one blazed overhead in Nero's reign, Balbillus suggested that the emperor deflect heaven's wrath onto other heads. The upshot was a mass slaughter of many of Rome's most prominent citizens.

Titus and his brother Domitian, who ruled toward the end of the first century AD, acted as their own astrologers, and both followed Nero's example in using the stars to justify violent deeds. Domitian was especially fearful and suspicious. In his spare moments he would cast the horoscopes of potential rivals, ordering the death of anyone who showed undue promise of success or power.

Whatever dark use the state made of astrology, the empire's scholars continued to refine the theory and practice of stargazing. Around AD 14—the first year of Tiberius's reign—Manilius, a follower of Posidonius, published a lengthy summary, the *Astronomica,* in rhymed hexameters. The poem, which became a basic text, listed the magnitudes of the brighter stars, told how to construct a birth chart, and stressed the signs of the zodiac rather than the planets as the chief arbiters of character and destiny. A greater work appeared in the next century, compiled by one of astrology's giants, Claudius Ptolemy of Alexandria.

Little is known of Ptolemy the man, beyond the fact of his great learning. His habits were abstemious, it seems, and his clothing dapper. He liked to ride horseback, and by some accounts he may have suffered from bad breath. Aside from that, we know nothing other than the testimony of his extraordinary accomplishments—pioneering discov-

The Bright Star of an Emperor's Love

Astrology figured prominently in the life of the Roman emperor Hadrian, who ruled from AD 117 to 138. At his birth, astrologers predicted that he would ascend to the throne; his horoscope, which survives to this day, revealed great ambition and a preoccupation with power. Eventually, the ruler became his own astrologer, drawing up his horoscope, consulting it regularly, and allegedly even predicting the exact time of his death.

Astrology was also involved in Hadrian's greatest personal tragedy. For years he was devoted to a fetching young boy named Antinous, represented in the sculpture at left dating from the second century AD. Antinous, whom Hadrian described as a "virile Athena," was the emperor's constant companion until the young man's death at the age of twenty. As the story goes, an oracle had proclaimed that Hadrian's life might be spared only by the death of a loved one. Antinous is thought to have sacrificed himself—or to have been sacrificed, some say—by drowning in the Nile.

Hadrian was inconsolable—until court astrologers noticed an orb, "until then hardly visible in the constellation of the Eagle," which "flashed like a gem and pulsated like a heart." He believed the star had been born from the young man's spirit and named it for his love; it was eventually included in the constellation Aquila (inset).

151-8301

Dolton Public Library District

eries in mathematics, the most accurate surviving maps of the ancient world, and two seminal volumes on the stars. The first, the *Almagest,* contained all that was known about the purely physical movements of heavenly bodies. The second was the *Tetrabiblos,* and it dealt with the manifold influences of stars and planets on the lives of humans.

Ptolemy championed the belief that the earth stood solidly fixed at the center of a moving cosmos. Such a scheme was only reasonable, he observed, for if the earth spun, "the birds would have their perches whipped out from under them." Nonetheless, he said, the stars and other planets circled the sun in unchanging, mathematically perfect orbits, as Pythagoras had suggested so many centuries earlier, and they projected their powers in a manner that could be determined by rational observation. Natural forces, not divine intervention, controlled human fate. And if astrologers sometimes issued wrong predictions, it was only because of sloppy reasoning. "We do not discredit the art of the navigator for its many errors," Ptolemy pointed out.

Much of the *Tetrabiblos* sought to forge logical connections between various star groups and other natural categories of things. Like others before him, Ptolemy assigned each zodiacal figure to one of the four elements. Virgo was an earth sign, for example, and Gemini an air sign. These in turn he related to specific geographic areas. Europeans resided in the domain of fire and its associated signs—Aries, Leo, and Sagittarius. They were also strongly influenced by Jupiter and Mars. As a result, they tended to be independent, industrious, warlike, commanding, and magnanimous—although, according to Ptolemy, they were "without passion for women." Africans, controlled by the water signs (Cancer, Scorpio, and Pisces) and the planet Venus, were ardent lovers but less stable in character. They liked to adorn themselves with "feminine trinkets."

After laying down these general criteria, Ptolemy gave detailed instructions for casting personal horoscopes. Most important, of course, was the sun sign—the constellation on the horizon at daybreak, beyond the sun, during the month of an individual's birth. But the sign ascending above the horizon at the moment of birth—the rising sign, as it became known—was of vital consequence as well. The relationships of the planets also had to be taken into account. Where was Jupiter, for instance, and what was its geometric relationship to, say, Saturn when plotted on the chart? If two planets were on opposite sides of the chart, 180 degrees around the circle from each other, then they were in opposition, and that meant something entirely different from their being divided by an aspect of only 60 degrees. If these and other factors were marked down with care and skillfully assessed, Ptolemy claimed, a practitioner could not only decipher a person's character but determine that individual's likelihood of marital happiness and worldly success, and all manner of other prospects.

Thus were the main guideposts of modern astrology set into place. Other authorities in future generations would add a few refinements. In the third century, for example, a Roman named Porphyry devised a system of twelve astrological "houses" through which the signs of the zodiac move, each house being related to a particular aspect of human life *(pages 120-121).* But Ptolemy's *Tetrabiblos* would remain the virtual bible of astrology from that day to this.

As the decades rolled on, the predictive art gained an ever larger audience. Emperors and statesmen continued to consult their charts. Citizens from all walks of life took up the practice—inspired in part by the occult doctrines of various religious sects that began filtering into Rome from the far reaches of the empire. Between the first and fourth centuries AD, the worship of Mithras, an old Persian sun god, became fashionable, and followers would crowd into obscure temples bespangled with stellar symbols. There were setbacks, of course. The rise of Christianity came as a heavy blow to astrologers, for despite an apparent tolerance in biblical text—including the star that announced Jesus' birth—the church condemned all types of divination. But astrology simply went underground. And soon a new generation of celestial savants, from the ancient deserts of Africa and the Middle East, would raise the art of reading the stars to new levels of intricate refinement.

Powers of the Planets

Observing that they seem to steer independent courses across the firmament of fixed stars, ancient peoples believed the planets to be gods. Their appearance and behavior were reflected in the divine roles ascribed to them. The one tinged blood-red, Mars, was the god of war. The small planet that darted to and fro but never strayed far from the imperious Sun was the gods' messenger, Mercury.

The planetary gods lived out great mythical dramas that were reflections of human emotions and experiences. They loved and fought, betrayed and were betrayed, died and were reborn. Astrologers have believed for thousands of years that the planets' movements not only describe the gods' behavior and the events related in these myths, but also coincide with manifestations of the same archetypal elements in the lives of human beings. The positions of key heavenly bodies at the time of an individual's birth and at later crucial stages are thought to be more than symbolic; they occur in synchrony with forces that shape life in ways that can be advantageous if understood and painful if not properly anticipated.

Authorities in other fields—even some who have nothing but contempt for astrology—concede that the fundamental mythical themes, which have remained constant throughout history and in all cultures, are indeed extremely relevant to life. The famed psychologist Carl Jung held that the mythical archetypes are ingrained into the collective unconscious of the human species. Only people who understand themselves and the archetypes, he declared, can avoid the pain of blindly reliving the myths. Astrologers believe the planets offer a route to that understanding.

In astrology the term *planet* applies to the ten bodies in our Solar System that appear to circle the Earth, eight actual planets plus the Sun and Moon. The following ten pages describe the supposed character, special qualities, and general astrological significance of each planet. However, the meanings of specific planetary positions in a horoscope are revealed only through complex calculations that account for many factors *(pages 118-127)*.

The Sun

⊙

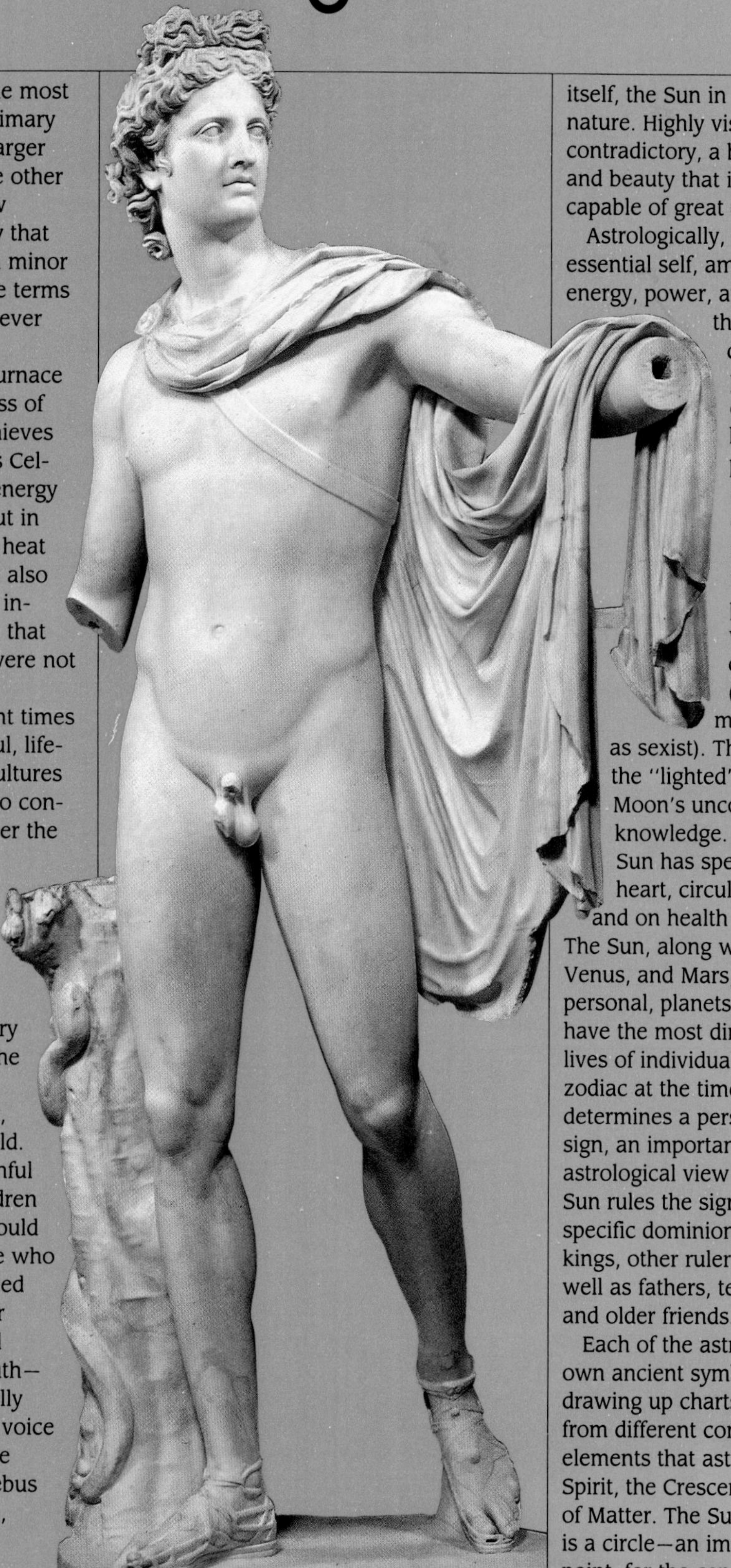

To ancient peoples the Sun was the most powerful figure in the skies, the primary source of light, warmth, and life, larger and stronger by far than any of the other heavenly bodies. Although we now realize through modern astronomy that the Sun is a fairly ordinary or even minor star, we also know that in absolute terms it is even more potent than it was ever imagined to be.

It is a gigantic, roaring nuclear furnace —a third of a million times the mass of the Earth—whose blazing core achieves temperatures of 15 million degrees Celsius. Its prodigious outpouring of energy is the source of all life on Earth. But in addition to providing the light and heat that sustain our existence, the Sun also spews a torrent of other radiation, including x-rays and ultraviolet rays, that could be fatal for humanity if we were not protected by Earth's atmosphere.

Mythologically, the Sun in ancient times was everywhere seen as a powerful, life-giving god, represented in many cultures with arms or rays reaching down to convey vitality to mortals. Kings all over the world claimed to be the Sun's descendants. The Egyptian sun god was Ra, who crossed the sky in a boat each day. Perhaps the sun god with the most enduring influence was the Greeks' Apollo, who traversed the heavens in a fiery chariot and later was adopted by the Romans for their own pantheon.

Apollo grew to manhood quickly, slaying a dragon while only days old. He became the ideal of virile, youthful beauty, fathering a number of children by both women and nymphs. He could also be a dangerous suitor to those who rejected him, however. Apollo turned the nymph Daphne into a tree after she spurned him, and he bestowed centuries of longevity—but not youth— on a woman named Sibyl; she finally shriveled until only a disembodied voice was left. The Greeks recognized the god's duality: He was at once Phoebus Apollo—Bright Apollo—and Loxian, meaning "the ambiguous one."

Like Apollo and the physical star itself, the Sun in astrology has a dual nature. Highly visible, it is nonetheless contradictory, a benevolent source of life and beauty that is at the same time capable of great destruction.

Astrologically, the Sun governs the essential self, ambition, spirit, will, energy, power, and organization. Among the traits it is said to confer are creativity, pride, generosity, and dignity. But it is also linked with egotism, pomposity, arrogance, and overbearing condescension. It represents dry, hot masculinity in a partnership of opposites with the Moon, which is cool, moist, and feminine (a traditional view some modern astrologers reject as sexist). The Sun is consciousness, the "lighted" part of the mind, to the Moon's unconsciousness, or intuitive knowledge. In the human body the Sun has special influence on the heart, circulatory system, and spine, and on health and vitality in general. The Sun, along with the Moon, Mercury, Venus, and Mars, is one of the inner, or personal, planets, which are thought to have the most direct influence on the lives of individuals. Its position in the zodiac at the time of birth, of course, determines a person's natal sign—the sun sign, an important element in the total astrological view of one's personality. The Sun rules the sign Leo, which is its specific dominion, and is personified in kings, other rulers and heads of state, as well as fathers, teachers, male partners, and older friends.

Each of the astrological planets has its own ancient symbol, or glyph, used in drawing up charts. Glyphs were created from different combinations of three basic elements that astrologers call the Circle of Spirit, the Crescent of Soul, and the Cross of Matter. The Sun's glyph, as seen above, is a circle—an image of wholeness—and a point, for the center or focus of life.

Even damaged, this sculpture of the sun god Apollo idealizes the quest for beauty and order.

The Moon

☽

The heavenly body closest to us has always been at once familiar and mysterious. Although it continually keeps the same face turned toward Earth, the Moon's appearance changes constantly as the sun-limned shadows of its prominences creep across its cratered plains. Throughout the ages observers have seen faces and figures there, all of them giving rise to legends.

But the most universally notable characteristic of the Moon is its regularity; it changes from new moon to full and back again every twenty-nine and a half days with unwavering constancy. Ancient peoples used it to keep track of passing time. To the Babylonians the Moon was Sin, god of the calendar and wisdom. The Greeks dreaded the unlit, new-moon period of each lunar cycle when Selene, one of several goddesses identified with the Moon, was taken down into the underworld for three days.

Since remote times people have credited the Moon with power over nature's processes. That the Moon causes tides has long been known, of course, and by extension it was thought to affect body fluids. Its long-supposed links to menstruation—the average length of a menstrual cycle nearly matches the lunar cycle—may be one reason most ancient cultures saw the Moon as female.

The most important moon goddess was Apollo's twin sister, the Greek hunter Artemis, known to the Romans as Diana. When her father Zeus, king of the gods, offered her gifts, she chose eternal virginity, with its unencumbered freedom, and a short skirt that made it easier to chase wild animals.

Armed with a silver bow, she roamed the mountains unfettered, reluctantly tolerating interruptions from women who invoked her aid in childbirth. She was the essence of woman as person, not woman as man's mate.

Another Greek goddess, Hecate, was associated with the dark side of the Moon. She was the queen of ghosts and other dark and hidden things, ruler of magic and deep wisdom.

Ancient astrologers had no way of knowing the Moon's true minimal size and unimportance in the cosmic scheme; they saw only that the orb was one of the two dominant objects in the sky. Thus they paired the Moon with the Sun in a female-male duality. Astrologically, the Moon represents the soul and the unconscious self. It is seen as feminine, watery, and emotional in opposition to the Sun's dry masculinity. The Moon correlates with fertility, maternity, the family, growth, death, and decay. In horoscopes it is associated with duality, light and dark qualities, rhythms, changeability, sensitivity, and memory.

The Moon rules Cancer, but since it moves so rapidly through the entire zodiac each month, astrologers think it also sets the tone for other signs. Physiologically, it is said to relate to the stomach, breasts, and ovaries, to lymph and other bodily fluids, and to the cerebellum.

The Moon's orbital plane is slightly inclined to the plane of the Earth's orbit, called the ecliptic (pages 11-13). Thus the Moon's orbital plane crosses the ecliptic every thirteen and a half days. The points where they intersect are called the North and South Nodes. Astrologers consider the nodes to have influence similar to that of planets.

The Moon's position at birth is said to reveal much about the relationship between child and mother. And a person born under a waxing moon is considered to be "younger," more reactive and excitable, while someone born beneath a waning moon might be "older" and more reflective. The Moon has several glyphs, among them the crescent of the new moon (above).

Diana—Artemis to the Greeks—rides in her lunar chariot in this fifteenth-century bas-relief.

Venus

♀

In what is surely only a coincidental analogy to the dangerous allure of the goddess, the conditions that make the planet Venus so dazzling to earthbound viewers would be fatal to any unprotected human transported there. Venus's atmosphere, mainly carbon dioxide, is massively heavy and traps solar radiation that drives surface temperatures up to 460 degrees Celsius.

But the dense envelope of scorching gases, churned by winds of more than 200 miles an hour, is covered by thick sulfuric-acid clouds that reflect 70 percent of the sunlight that falls on them. This gives Venus the brilliance that makes it the third-brightest object in our heavens.

Since it sometimes appears in the sky in the evening and at other times in the morning, Venus was once thought in some cultures to be two different bodies, the Evening Star and the Morning Star. Perhaps the hours it keeps, which bracket the period humans favor for lovemaking, is why the planet has traditionally been associated with goddesses of love—Ishtar to the Mesopotamians, Aphrodite to the Greeks, Venus to the Romans.

Venus was born from the sea, full-grown and irresistibly beautiful. She was wed to the blacksmith god, Vulcan, but presented him with three children actually sired by the vigorous and aggressive god of war, Mars. Hearing that his wife was betraying him, Vulcan forged a net of fine bronze threads and secretly rigged it to his marriage bed. He then announced he was going on an island holiday, but returned a few hours later to catch Venus and Mars snared in the net.

Vulcan unwisely called in the other gods to witness his wife's infidelity. There apparently was some snickering as they gathered around the entangled pair. The sun god Apollo nudged Mercury and said he doubted that Mercury would mind being in Mars's place, net or no net. Observing Venus's glorious nakedness, Mercury replied that he would not mind at all, even if there were three nets. The god of the sea, Neptune, his own heart stirring, undertook to guarantee that Mars would make restitution to Vulcan, paying the cuckolded husband what Vulcan had laid out as a bride price. If Mars defaulted, Neptune said generously, he himself would pay the bride price—and take Venus off Vulcan's hands.

But Vulcan was still smitten by Venus, and he kept her. The episode gained him nothing but some new rivals. Venus later bore children by both Mercury and Neptune and spread her favors to a number of others, gods and mortals. She was the embodiment of natural sexuality, unrestrained by shame or ambivalence, and the love and lovemaking that she promoted were sources of joy for humans. She inspired passion as a form of worship. But like other archetypal deities, Venus also had a dangerous side. The urgent yearnings she stirred caused

people to sacrifice family and duty. She was called the "dark one" because of tragedies resulting from the passions she inspired. A jealous Mars, hearing that Venus preferred the handsome mortal Adonis to himself, took the form of a wild boar and gored Adonis, killing him. An ascetic named Hippolytus offended Venus by declaring that he would have nothing to do with sex. She punished him by making his stepmother fall in love with him, for which he was killed by his father's curse. Venus could also be a devious and demanding goddess. When two mortal lovers failed to do her homage after she enabled them to marry, she caused them to offend the earth goddess Cybele. The unforgiving Cybele turned the newlyweds into a lion and lioness fated forever to draw her chariot.

Still, Venus is chiefly associated astrologically with things admirable and desirable: love, beauty and the love of beauty, appreciation of the arts, the feminine nature in women and men, harmony and unison, peace and reconciliation, and the enjoyment of pleasure. Venus's influence is felt in all kinds of relationships, in business and social ties as well as in love and sexual bonds.

It is thought that when Venus is in the right place in a horoscope at birth, an individual will be gentle, warm, sentimental, graceful, and artistic. Negative Venus influences are said to make a person vulnerable to laziness, indecisiveness, an excessively romantic and impractical attitude, carelessness, envy, and jealousy. A male born with Venus in certain positions was traditionally believed threatened by death at a woman's hands; later interpretations suggest he might instead be destined to domination by women. In the astrology of politics, Venus rules victory in war.

Venus rules two signs, Taurus and Libra. Its special correspondences to the human body include the throat and the kidneys, as well as physical beauty. Venus's glyph—a circle above a cross to indicate the ascendance of the spirit over matter—has come to be recognized as a universal symbol for the female.

Beautiful Aphrodite, known later as Venus, dries her hair in this ancient Greek sculpture.

Mars
♂

Mars's reddish hue, which probably is responsible for the character of the gods associated with the planet, results from corrosion. Crystalline rocks on the surface have been broken down and oxidized. It was natural for ancient peoples to link the shimmering red ball in the night sky to ill-tempered deities whose traits suited that color.

Thus the Babylonians said the planet was Nergal, god of war, with dominion over blood, fire, and heat. To the Greeks, the reddish orb was their war god Ares, a quarrelsome, arrogant deity who was admired for his unquestioned bravery and widely hated for his enjoyment of bloody conflict. Accompanied by two aptly named sons, Phobos and Deimos—Fear and Panic—he plunged wherever carnage was promised. (The planet Mars's two moons are named for that terrible pair of offspring.)

The Roman god Mars assumed many of the characteristics and myths attached to his precursor Ares but enjoyed a more revered status than the Greek deity. He held sway over agriculture as well as war and was the second-highest-ranking god in the Roman pantheon, after Jupiter. March, the first month of the old Roman year, was named after Mars. During that month his priests wended in procession into the countryside, chanting hymns, stamping their feet in a ceremonial three-step dance, and setting a cadence by banging sacred, antiquated spears against temple shields. The ritual marked not only the spring advent of the agricultural year but also the annual resumption of military campaigning, which was normally suspended during the winter months.

The human impulses represented by the Ares-Mars archetype have been among the most powerful determinants of history. They are evident, of course, every time armies clash in battle. But the archetype is also at work in all accomplishments that require great effort, courage, vigor, and tenacity—the stuff of rugged individualism—be they feats of athletic excellence or outstanding achievement in areas such as exploration, engineering, seafaring, social reform, or even business or scholarship. Our own century has been driven by the Mars impulse perhaps even more than most eras—witness its horrendous wars, the financial empires constructed by its indomitable entrepreneurs, and the deeds of its heroes on the frontiers of such fields as medicine, human rights, technological innovation, and space travel.

Not surprisingly, the planet Mars in astrology represents, on the one hand, roguery, anger, uncontrolled and aggressive self-assertion, thrusting personal ambition, and lust for power, and, on the other hand, it stands for assertive creativity, courage, and the quest for achievement rather than for power.

Mars rules the signs Aries and Scorpio. It is thought to signify men in general and husbands in particular and to be especially relevant to the careers of soldiers, police officers, and athletes, as well as such people as clerics and artists if their work requires, or is marked by, notable courage. An individual under the influence of the planet, it is said, may lack subtlety, refinement, and depth and may be pugnacious and prone to excitability, impatience, and wrath. But that person will never be too tired to bother, never afraid to challenge and change the existing order.

Physically, Mars is associated with red blood corpuscles, the muscular system, the adrenal glands, body heat, and sexual organs. The planet is often considered responsible for an aggressive sex drive.

In the glyph for Mars, the cross of matter is transformed into an arrow and drawn atop a circle to represent the ascendance of the material over the spiritual. It is generally viewed as a universal symbol for the male.

Radiating strength and virility, an Etruscan bronze Mars from the fifth century BC is poised for combat.

Mercury

☿

A diminutive planet, racing at a cockeyed angle on a highly eccentric orbit, Mercury well reflects its mischievous mythical and astrological heritage. Mercury, less than half the size of Earth, is the second-smallest planet in the Solar System, after Pluto. It is also the fastest planet, whipping around the Sun once every eighty-eight days. The Sun's closest neighbor, little Mercury is all but obscured by its huge protector's brilliance.

Perhaps because Mercury is so tiny and clings so close to the Sun, ancient mythology imbued the god Hermes—as Mercury was called by the Greeks—with some of the attributes of a wayward child. The love child of Zeus and the nymph Maia, a daughter of the Titan Atlas, Hermes grew into a small boy only minutes after his mother laid her newborn down to sleep. As soon as she turned her back, he tiptoed out and promptly rustled a herd of cattle belonging to his half brother, Apollo. The sun god was outraged, but Hermes charmed him and soothed his wrath by playing a tune on the world's first lyre, which he invented on the spot by stringing stolen cow gut across the inside of a tortoise shell.

As he grew, Hermes learned to put his quick wit to good use. He once rescued Zeus's lover, Io, from a hundred-eyed monster named Argus by playing his pipes so tediously that he finally put the beast to sleep. Perhaps because he was so resourceful, Hermes became the messenger of the gods, endowed with a winged helmet and winged sandals to speed him on celestial errands.

The Greeks considered Hermes the cleverest of all the gods. He was thought to have invented the alphabet, the musical scale, astronomy, and boxing. In addition, he was called the lord of travel and commerce and the patron of alchemy, the magic art of transforming base metals into gold.

The Romans welcomed Hermes into their pantheon as Mercury, who, along with his other duties, governed trade. The god's skills as an alchemist were extended by the Romans to the mastery of medicine. Thus Mercury carried the caduceus, a wand encircled by two entwined snakes and imbued with the power to heal the sick.

Just as the planet Mercury was long ignored by astronomers, so was it undervalued until recent times by astrologers. Mercury's influence, like its size, might appear meager, but astrologers now believe the planet is a powerful agent of self-knowledge. Like the liquid metal bearing its name, Mercury symbolizes fluidity overcoming rigidity. Thus Mercury is the champion of new beginnings, upsetting conventional attitudes, and blazing trails for invention and change. Mercury's message is one of personal transformation, a bridging of the gap between the self and its potentials.

The term mercurial refers to people with lively and changeable temperaments. Astrologically, people born under Mercury's influence are said to be experts at bursting other people's bubbles—pricking their pretensions and making them reexamine their attitudes. Of course, this talent is not universally admired, and certainly not by its victims. Although Mercury correlates with a tendency to be critical, argumentative, or sarcastic, the planet also denotes the gifts of great perceptivity, intellectual versatility, and skill at communicating knowledge. Mercury is the magician, the alchemist who magically transforms words into substance. The planet is said to figure strongly in our computerized age, with its advances in information and communications. Astrologers maintain that people whose charts feature a strong Mercury presence can be found in journalism, teaching, the travel industry, secretarial work, education, carpentry, engineering, and, of course, medicine.

Mercury rules the signs of Gemini and Virgo. It is also said to relate to the intellect, the nervous system, and the thyroid gland, as well as the senses of hearing, sight, and touch. Mercury's glyph is a cross surmounted by a circle capped by a semicircle, uniting mind, spirit, and matter, but giving primacy to intellect.

Caduceus in hand, Mercury seems poised for flight in this sixteenth-century bronze.

Jupiter
♃

Huge and majestic Jupiter, the largest planet in the Solar System, is an apt celestial metaphor for the king of gods. Over 300 times more massive than Earth, Jupiter proceeds at a stately pace around the Sun, circling it once every twelve years. Mammoth though it is, the planet is little more than a hot-air balloon. Composed primarily of hydrogen and helium, Jupiter is thought to have no solid surface. Rather, it is made up of layers of dense gas that give way toward the planet's core to liquid metals that finally condense into a tiny center of rock and ice. The horizontal bands of light and dark that stripe Jupiter are clouds in its atmosphere. In one place the bands are disrupted by a startling feature called the Great Red Spot, thought to be a massive storm that has lasted for hundreds of years.

Jupiter generates more radiation on its own than it receives from the Sun and thus forms the center of a miniature solar system of sixteen moons. A few of the satellites may be former planets captured by their giant neighbor's immense gravitational pull.

Lordly Jupiter was named after the Roman king of the gods, known as Zeus in the Greek pantheon. Zeus was ruler of Mount Olympus, the home of the gods. Legend has it that he came to power by overthrowing his tyrannical Titan father Cronus, an act sometimes interpreted as the triumph of human reason over animal instinct. Greek images show Zeus as a bearded man in a sky blue cloak, sometimes astride an eagle. The god holds thunderbolts emblematic of his power.

Although he existed on the most lofty spiritual plane, Zeus also had his carnal side. He was married to his sister Hera, the Romans' Juno; but he was a philanderer of Olympian appetite and stamina, cavorting with numerous divinities and mortals of both sexes. Even so, the Greeks regarded him as guardian of the social order, particularly the supremacy of men over women. The Roman Jupiter was, if anything, more revered than his Greek predecessor. He was the lord of day and—like

Zeus—the lord of lightning bolts, which were his direct messages to humanity. And Jupiter smoothly evolved from ancient myth into his astrological role, standing for masculine authority. He is the wise man, brightening the world with meaning rather than with lightning.

Jupiter is said to inspire us to reach beyond our immediate circumstances, spiritually and materially. The planet is therefore associated with religion and philosophy, benevolence, compassion, justice, law, and honesty, as well as wealth and social status. People whose horoscopes feature Jupiter prominently are supposedly established and respectable. But as conscientious individuals, they will flout conventions in the name of higher principles. They are said to operate on so grand a scale that they may run to extravagance if unchecked. Moreover, they have a tendency to overgeneralize, to throw around broad concepts without examining their fine print. This can make them blindly—and dangerously—optimistic.

Pastors, philosophers, scientists, doctors, philanthropists, judges, lawyers, teachers, and chief executives are believed to be influenced by Jupiter. The planet supposedly conveys an aristocratic demeanor and facility with languages, traits appropriate to superb diplomats.

Jupiter rules Sagittarius and Pisces and oversees the circulation of the blood. The glyph that represents him, a half circle rising over a cross, is symbolic of the mind's triumph over matter.

Thunderbolts and eagles symbolize power in this third-century rendering of mighty Jupiter.

Saturn

ħ

Ominous Saturn is the most distant planet from Earth still visible to the naked eye. It is also the sixth planet from the Sun, and astronomers once believed it was the Solar System's outermost planet, a cold, solitary pariah in deep space—alone, but an awesome presence nonetheless. Saturn is the second-largest planet, after Jupiter.

The Greeks identified Saturn with Cronus, chief of the race of giant gods called Titans who ruled before the Olympians. Fearful of a prophecy that one of his children would dethrone him, the grisly Cronus ate each child right after it was born. But his wife Rhea saved the infant Zeus by offering Cronus a stone in the baby's stead, and Zeus grew up to fulfill the augury. Cronus ended up as a bitter outcast, whom the Greeks portrayed as a stooped Father Time.

The Romans grafted Cronus onto an agriculture god they inherited from the Etruscans. The result was Saturn, a god of time and farming. His festival, the Saturnalia, was held every December to celebrate the winter solstice.

In the long run, Saturn never entirely shed its ancient negative associations. The word saturnine means gloomy and taciturn. Still, astrology finds the planet a complex and vital constricting force that stabilizes Jupiter's expansive optimism. Saturn may indicate adversity, but often it is in the service of a more realistic perspective.

Saturn is considered to be an intermediary between the inner, personal planets and the outer, "transpersonal" planets, those that govern the wider

environment beyond the self and an individual's interaction with it. As regulator, Saturn represents authority. Its position at birth is said to determine the relationship between child and father. It also represents internal authority, or conscience and self-control. Failure to heed the limitations they impose is said to mean possible conflict with established social order.

Saturn's influence can inspire or devastate. In positive circumstances, it confers persistence and endurance, prudence, thrift, and managerial skills. Saturn's strong presence in a birth chart may denote a person who is fond of routine and possibly is destined for a career in the military, government, business, or religion. A negative Saturn influence, however, warns of repression, selfishness, cruelty, deviousness, and greed.

Saturn's orbit of the Sun takes twenty-nine and a half years. Its first full circle through a person's horoscope, as one approaches the age of thirty, is thought by astrologers to signify a time of change, an opportunity for reassessment and transformation.

Saturn rules Aquarius and Capricorn. It is also said to govern the body's aging process and such predations of time as rheumatism, hardening of the arteries, degeneration of organs, loss of teeth, and ailments of the gall bladder and spleen.

Saturn's glyph, like Jupiter's, incorporates the cross and half circle. But in Saturn's case the cross is paramount, making matter ascendant over mind and bringing intangibles down to earth.

Armed with a sickle, Saturn glares at an infant in this Renaissance bas-relief.

Uranus

♅

In 1781 a self-taught English astronomer named Sir William Herschel gazed through a telescope and discovered a planet beyond Saturn. Called Uranus, it was the first planet to be added to humanity's concept of the Solar System in recorded history. Uranus is more than fourteen times as massive as Earth. It is thought to be composed of minerals and gases, possibly deriving its greenish hue from methane gas in its atmosphere. Uranus reels drunkenly around the Sun once every eighty-four years, heeling so far on its orbital plane that it virtually rolls along on its equator. It rotates in the opposite direction of every other planet with the exception of Venus.

Uranus was named after the Greek god Ouranos, a tyrant whose son Saturn castrated him and then cast him out of the heavens. But astrologers observing the new planet saw little despotism in it. On the contrary, they said, Uranus seemed to act as a disrupter of the old order. Obviously, its very discovery upset the eons-old notion of a seven-planet system. Moreover, the discovery roughly coincided with the French and American revolutions.

Astrology has concluded that Uranus would have been better named Prometheus—the name means "forethinker"— for the Titan who gave humans the gift of fire, the source of all human progress *(page 142)*. In Promethean terms, Uranus signifies creative energy and the breaking of old models of belief and action.

As the first of the outer, or transpersonal, planets, Uranus is believed to wield influence beyond the individual, infusing entire cultures and eras with rapid and profound change. Heralding disruptive transformations, the planet is, astrologers say, an icon for the final third of the twentieth century.

A major Uranian presence at birth supposedly denotes an individual determined to change society rather than conform to it. He or she is apt to be inventive, rebellious, unorthodox, freedom-loving, progressive, original, and resourceful. Workaday incarnations of the Uranian-Promethean spirit include electricians, inventors, and technicians.

But Uranus is not without its negative side. People influenced by the planet may be so bent on disruption and reform that they can be antisocial, even in a good cause. Their need to be different from others sometimes makes them rebels for rebellion's sake, and their restless energy can find outlet as sarcasm, brash impulsiveness, and moodiness.

Uranus rules Aquarius and the brain, especially the pituitary gland. The planet's glyph is a cross atop a circle, flanked on each side by a half circle. The symbol signifies spirit ruled by mind and operating in materiality, synthesizing attributes of all the planets.

A Roman bas-relief shows Uranus, wearing the cloak of the sky, driving his four-horse chariot.

Neptune

♆

Neptune's existence was forecast before it was observed. In 1843 the English astronomer John Couch Adams predicted the planet's location based on his observations of mysterious fluctuations in the orbit of Uranus—behavior that could not be explained solely by the gravitational influences of Jupiter and Saturn. Three years later a German astronomer, Johann Gottfried Galle, made the first telescopic sighting of Neptune, spotting it remarkably close to its predicted position.

Cold and sluggish Neptune takes 162 years to orbit the Sun. It is thought to have a mass more than seventeen times that of Earth and to be made of ammonia and other frozen gases. It has two moons. The larger one, named for Neptune's son Triton, orbits backward.

The prototype of Neptune was worshiped by the Greeks as Poseidon, god of the sea and all waters. Poseidon shared cosmic dominion with his brothers Zeus, who ruled the heavens, and Hades, who reigned in the underworld. Although he lived on the ocean floor in a golden palace, Poseidon was primitive and unruly and would rise up in the form of earthquakes and tidal waves. But the god of the sea could be nurturing as well as destructive. Poseidon was a god of male fertility, his waters the father of crops. The Greeks also venerated him as a tamer of horses. As the Romans' Neptune he was worshiped primarily as the lord of irrigation.

Modern astrology associates Neptune's ocean kingdom with the forces of the unconscious mind and his horses with the power of raw instinct. Astrologers believe Neptune is the bridge leading from the conscious mind to the collective unconscious, that theoretical storehouse of shared memory and understanding common to all humans. Mystics believe the collective unconscious is a source of human creativity and renewal. But storming its bastions can be risky, they say, since unconscious thoughts surfacing abruptly can result in mental disruption, or even insanity.

Still, Neptune's mythical ocean is said to convey enormous empathy and a capacity to understand the depths of human personality. People with strong Neptune influences are thought to be blessed with the potential to rise above their own concerns in order to serve family or society. They are also apt to be dreamers, a trait that adds to their possible success as spiritual and artistic leaders, actors, filmmakers, and poets. And given their mythical connections, they may be seafarers, deep-sea divers, or explorers for offshore oil.

For all its virtues, Neptune has its dark side; its power is believed to exaggerate evil as well as good. Violent as an earthquake, its influence erupts to cause people to do things they are unprepared to control and might later regret.

Neptune's trident, astrologers say, bears the tines of obsession. The planet is said to lead those who are misguided or ill-prepared for deeper knowledge to use drugs and alcohol in the errant hope of satisfying their spiritual yearnings. It is associated with hospitals and other institutions, and its influence is said to figure in the careers of chemists and anesthesiologists—both, in their way, givers of dreams. People who exhibit Neptune's negative aspects may fall prey to delusions and fanaticism. If so, they are capable of using any means to reach their irrational goals.

Neptune rules Pisces and has dominion over the brain's pineal gland, spinal fluid, and amniotic fluid, that inner sea that supports unborn infants. The planet's glyph, a trident composed of an inverted cross and a semicircle, is an astrological warning that only the spiritually adept can safely approach the deeper knowledge represented by distant planets.

Fierce Neptune straddles his son Triton in this 1620 marble by Gian Lorenzo Bernini.

Pluto

☳

Almost four billion miles from the Sun, Pluto is a dark, chill sentinel in deep space, its orbit defining the outer planetary boundary of the known Solar System. From this distant outpost, the Sun appears not as a fiery and life-giving god, but merely as one of uncountable bright stars, cold and far away.

Discovered in 1930, Pluto is the smallest planet—smaller than Earth's moon—and it has no known atmosphere. It has one satellite, named Charon after the boatman of Greek myth who ferried dead souls across the river Styx to Hades. Pluto circles the Sun only once every 248 years, in an orbit so elliptical that it sometimes cuts inside Neptune's path.

Pluto is the Roman version of the Greek god Hades, whose name means the "unseen one." Hades' underground kingdom, which bore his name, was the realm of the dead. Its gates were guarded by the three-headed dog Cerberus, who ate mortals and ghosts who tried to escape. On a rare foray outside his dark realm, Hades fell in love with the daughter of the earth goddess Demeter, Persephone, and carried her off to be his wife. In her grief Demeter let the Earth lie fallow, thus creating the seasons of late fall and winter.

Although feared, Hades was also revered—mostly for his wealth: Food grew from his soil, and precious minerals glinted beneath it. His statues were sometimes bedecked with jewels and produce.

As they have with Uranus and Neptune, modern astrologers have struggled to clarify the significance of Pluto. Since it is the outermost transpersonal planet, it is believed to have broad and deep influence, heralding drastic changes that affect entire populations. It also supposedly governs the most profound, universal, and yet personal of human myster-

ies: death, rebirth, and transformation. Pluto has aspects that seem especially meaningful to the twentieth century, the era of nuclear threat—and of the plutonium that echoes the planet's name. Pluto, astrologers say, represents the power of such minute matter as the atom. Befitting its satanic aspects, Pluto was discovered in an era of economic upheaval and world war. But on a more hopeful note, the planet is said to represent evolution, the winnowing of the weak and outworn— destruction as prelude to building, death leading to rebirth.

Pluto is also considered to be a source of revelation about higher realities. It is similar to Jupiter in its call to action in the name of principle. Those born under Pluto's influence may feel impelled to root out injustice. Pluto corresponds to useful dissatisfaction, the sort that spurs one toward self-improvement. Those who heed its message, say astrologers, may benefit by learning from tragedies and pitfalls and by seeking new beginnings.

But the planet's explosive power can be subverted. Those who fail to recognize and accept the negative aspects of their own personalities, for example, tend to crusade against what they perceive as evil in others while ignoring their own faults. In such cases, the crusades can have violent and disastrous results. At their very worst, people with heavy Plutonian aspects in their horoscopes can be criminal or sadistic, wholly without morals or scruples. The planet figured prominently in the horoscopes of the depraved Roman emperor Caligula, as well as Adolf Hitler and Joseph Stalin.

Pluto is co-ruler with Mars of Scorpio and Aries. It influences the male and female generative organs, the immune system, and genetically related diseases. Several glyphs have been proposed for the new planet. The most commonly accepted one is a cross surmounted by a half circle cupping a full circle, to depict spirit being forged in the crucible of matter.

Lustful Hades carries Persephone off to the underworld in this Bernini marble.

CHAPTER 2

The Ascent of Astrology

When a thirteenth-century Italian nobleman named Guido de Montefeltro went to war, the first person he consulted was not his general, but his astrologer, Guido Bonatti. Indeed, it might be said that Bonatti was chief of staff for Montefeltro, who frequently engaged in battle on behalf of Michael VIII, the Byzantine emperor, against Pope Martin IV, in their decades-long struggle for control of the eastern and western churches. If action seemed imminent, Bonatti would clamber into a church tower, consult his charts, and then, at three carefully calculated moments, signal by ringing a bell: once for Montefeltro's men to don their armor, again for them to mount their horses, and finally for them to gallop against the enemy.

Bonatti's reading of the stars was truly put to the test in 1282, when Pope Martin IV sent an army against Montefeltro's stronghold at Forli. Analyzing the horoscope of the opposing commander, which had somehow come into his hands, Bonatti saw disturbing signs of a victory celebration. He thereupon advised Montefeltro to withdraw from the town, leaving behind its women—who were evidently not unwilling to be used for so worthy a purpose—with instructions to entertain the foe with food, plenty of drink, and other amusements. Later, when the victory celebration foreseen in the horoscope was at its drunken climax, Montefeltro's force returned, fell upon the befuddled guests, and massacred them.

According to a contemporary historian, Bonatti's understanding of the heavens contributed to a number of Montefeltro's successes on the battlefield. Bonatti, who also advised a few other Italian noblemen and wrote a massive, multivolume collection of astrological information that would be used as a standard text for the next 200 years, had no doubts about the prophetic power of his calling. "All things are known to the astrologer," he said. "All that has taken place in the past, all that will happen in the future—everything is revealed to him."

Nor did Bonatti shrink from urging clerics to use astrology to predict everything from the most auspicious moment to begin construction of a church to their chances of promotion to the papacy itself. After all, Bonatti argued, even Christ had used astrology. When he asked his disciples, "Are

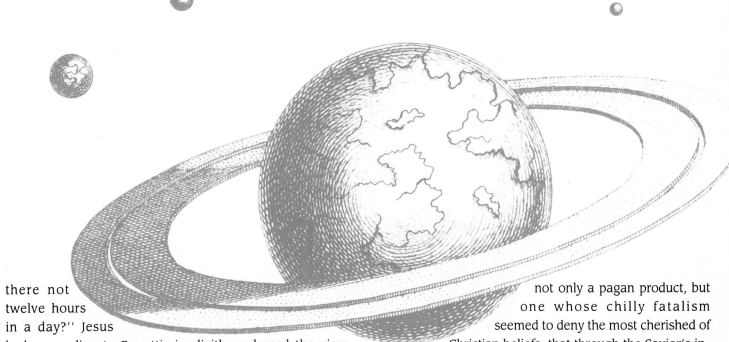

there not twelve hours in a day?'' Jesus had—according to Bonatti—implicitly endorsed the view that one could choose a time that was especially propitious.

For all his sweeping claims of prescience, Bonatti was haunted by a single error: He failed to predict a thunderstorm that spoiled Montefeltro's plans for an elegant feast. Nor did he foresee the time and manner of his own death, which came at the hands of robbers. And yet, in the prism of history, neither his failures nor his successes in predicting the future seem to matter as much as the fact that he was asked to make such predictions at all. His prominence was symbolic of the brilliant light into which astrology had emerged after the long eclipse that had followed the collapse of the Western Roman Empire and that had cast a pall upon the whole of European civilization.

Throughout the centuries of astrology's decline and subsequent revival, the fortunes of the celestial art had been inextricably linked to attitudes of the Christian church. As early as AD 313, Rome's great emperor Constantine, whose own path to power supposedly had been illuminated by a heavenly sign of the Cross, joined in promulgating the Edict of Milan, which granted tolerance to all religions. Although the decree in theory offered Christianity no more than equal status, such was the surge of this vibrant faith that within a few decades, and even as barbarians swarmed into the vast reaches of the Roman Empire, the church stood virtually alone as a beacon of institutional stability.

Yet Christianity was still young, insecure in the realization of its newly acquired power, and forever wary of the paganism that had undermined it so much. Astrology was not only a pagan product, but one whose chilly fatalism seemed to deny the most cherished of Christian beliefs: that through the Savior's intercession, people could achieve redemption and control their ultimate destiny by the exercise of their own free will.

Thus Ammianus Marcellinus, a fourth-century Roman historian and Christian, fairly bristled with scorn when he wrote, ''There are many who do not presume either to bathe or to dine, or to appear in public, till they have diligently consulted, according to the rules of astrology, the situation of Mercury and the aspect of the moon.''

Marcellinus's voice was just one among many in a rising chorus of the faithful against the pagan practice of astrology. Yet there were others, equally committed to the teachings of the fledgling church, who sought an accommodation between its beliefs and the dictates of astrological science. Among them was Julius Firmicus Maternus, both a Christian and an astrologer, whose *Mathesis,* probably written in AD 330-40, would become the last surviving major defense of astrology before Western learning descended into the abyss of the Dark Ages.

Even while admitting that astrology's ranks were filled with charlatans and self-styled magicians ''who stay in temples in an unkempt state,'' Firmicus insisted that most of its scientific tenets had time and again been tested and found valid. Then, drawing a fine line, he held that even though people's lives were undeniably shaped by heavenly bodies, those influences could be overridden by individuals exerting their own, God-granted power of self-determination.

Within that tidy argument lay a seed that would be nourished by later and more brilliant thinkers in making as-

A picture from a medieval psalter maps the church's concept of the cosmos: a flat earth with Jerusalem at its center, stars overhead, and a sun small enough to disappear nightly behind a mountain—all under divine control. The classical notions of a spherical universe and cosmic powers were considered heresy.

Old Greek myths about Pisces, written in Latin, appear within the outlines of the zodiacal fish sign in this tenth-century manuscript. Such rare classical works, copied and recopied by monks in the Dark Ages, conveyed knowledge of ancient astrology to medieval scholars.

point, he would write in his famous *Confessions,* a "wise, very skilled and very well esteemed medical man," after learning how much time Augustine was spending on astrological books, advised him "in a kindly and fatherly way to throw them away, and not to waste my time and energy . . . on such vain falsehoods."

It was no use. Augustine was hooked, and hooked he remained until—as he later asserted—a friend named Firminus told him a tale that proved the illogic of astrological calculations. Firminus's father, it seems, was an amateur astrologer who meticulously kept track of the positions of the stars. So intent was he on relating celestial movements to the lives of all earthly creatures that he even "took care with the most exact diligence to know the birth of his very puppies."

Seeking an opportunity to further his studies, he was naturally delighted to learn that one of his female servants was expecting to give birth to a child about the same time his own wife was due. As it turned out, the babies were born at exactly the same instant—which should, by the prevailing rules of astrology, have dictated that they had identical fortunes. Instead, however, the well-born son (who was none other than Firminus himself) spent his life in the enjoyable accumulation of riches and honors—whereas the child who had entered the world as a slave lived and died as a slave.

In fact, Augustine's example of the "astral twins" was no more than an ancient anti-astrology argument gussied up in contemporary clothing. But when delivered by the man who from AD 396 to 430 was the powerful bishop of Hippo in present-day Algeria, it had a compelling force. Moreover, both in his *Confessions* and in *The City of God,*

trology acceptable to Christianity. At the time, however, Firmicus's thesis was but a whisper that would soon be lost in the thunderous outcry against the stellar science. The voice raised loudest was that of Augustine, a future saint whose moral authority was all the greater because he had himself tasted of sin and then, through his own free will, chosen the path of Christian righteousness.

Augustine was born in AD 345 in Roman North Africa, the son of a well-to-do pagan father and a devoutly Christian mother. In his youth he had succumbed to temptations both of the flesh—he sired an illegitimate son—and of the mind, embracing the Persian cult of Manicheanism, which held that all matter is evil and must be overcome by the spirit through celibacy and asceticism. He had also cheerfully exposed himself to what he later condemned as "the lying divinations and impious dotages of astrologers." At one

which was written after barbarian Goths sacked the city of Rome in AD 410, Augustine assailed astrology as totally antithetical to the Christian faith. He dismissed the notion that the Star of Bethlehem was evidence of stellar influences on Christ's birth. To the contrary, he said, the "star that the Magi saw when Christ was born . . . was not a lord governing his nativity, but a servant bearing witness to it."

Augustine scoffed at the idea that human actions and decisions were beyond human control. How could it be, he asked, that an astrologer might beat his wife—"I won't say if he catches her being improperly playful, but even if she stares too long through a window"? Could she not reasonably fling his vocation back in his face by maintaining that her delinquency was all Venus's fault?

And, finally, when all else was said and done, Augustine laid down the law: "Those who hold that stars manage our actions or our passions, good or ill, without God's appointment, are to be silenced and not to be heard."

ilenced and unheard they were, not by official Christian proscription but by general Christian disapproval. Yet subsequent denunciations by astrology's opponents would seem to indicate that the practice continued long after Augustine was dead. For example, as late as the sixth century, the sagacious monk Cassiodorus found reason to reproach erring citizens who, "charmed by the beauty of the constellations and their bright splendor, seeking out most zealously the very causes of their own perdition, rushed blindly into the study of the stars' motions so that they might believe themselves able to foreknow events by unlawful calculations."

In a sense, the problem took care of itself. As western Europe sank deeper into the darkness of political chaos, barbarian clamors, feudal warfare, and disease, its educational system almost completely broke down. Science regressed, mathematics became little more than a matter of counting on fingers, grammar and rhetoric were taught at a level that would have been scorned by a twelve-year-old Roman schoolboy. Amid that sorrowful desuetude, astrology with all its lustrous intricacies became nothing more

than a faint and fading memory in the Western world.

But astrology's star would soon be rising in the East. There, within a century after the flight from Mecca in AD 625 of an Arabian merchant named Muhammad, who would be called the Prophet, a vibrant religion known as Islam had engulfed an immense expanse of territory that stretched from the fringes of T'ang China through northern India and the Middle East to the Mediterranean regions of North Africa, Spain, and southern France. As they settled the lands they had conquered, the Islamic Arabs—known as Muslims—drew heavily from the cultures that they ruled and took possession of much knowledge along with more tangible spoils.

And what Christian doctrine had condemned, Islamic thought commended; indeed, astrology's fatalism was congenial to Muslim ideas of predestination. By fortunate coincidence, the astrological hiatus in Christian Europe was counterbalanced by the accession to power of the Abbasid dynasty of caliphs, or earthly successors to Muhammad as rulers of Islam. The Abbasid caliphs traced their ancestry to Abbas, the uncle of Muhammad, and while they were cruel, capricious, and devoted to earthly pleasures that defied Muslim austerities, they were also enthusiastic patrons of the sciences. Astrology in particular struck their fancy.

In AD 762, the black banner of the Abbasids was raised at the new capital, built on the east bank of the Tigris at the site of an old Persian village called Baghdad. There, Caliph al-Mansur founded a school of astronomy and astrology; there, the famed Caliph Harun al-Rashid, a central figure of *A Thousand and One Nights,* presided in sumptuous splendor over a court and a city that attracted scholars—Jewish as well as Muslim—from throughout the Arab world; and there, Caliph al-Mamun endowed an observatory and, nearby, a House of Wisdom, where scientific and philosophical manuscripts were translated into Arabic from Syriac, Sanskrit, Persian, and, of course, Greek. Included in the works thereby preserved were Ptolemy's monumental *Tetrabiblos* and most of Aristotle's texts.

In their astronomy, studied not only for its own sake

The sign of Scorpio adorns a stained-glass window of the Chartres cathedral. Stripped of their pagan astrological meaning, zodiacal figures were often borrowed by Christian artists simply to symbolize segments of the calendar.

but also because it was necessary for astrology, the Arabs were very fussy about making precise measurements. To that end they refined the astrolabe, an instrument that could be used to calculate the height of celestial bodies above the horizon, figure latitudes, approximate the time, point the direction of the holy city of Mecca, or construct a horoscope. Although the astrolabe may have been invented as early as the first century BC and was certainly known to the Greeks, in the hands of the Arabs it became the most important observational tool before the advent of the telescope.

Despite the freewheeling ways of the Abbasid caliphs, their astrologers did, in fact, observe certain strictures imposed by Islamic law and custom. For instance, because orthodox Muslim artists were forbidden to depict human figures, the zodiacal symbol for Gemini, the Twins, became a pair of peacocks; Virgo, the Virgin, was represented by a wheat sheaf; and Aquarius, the Water Bearer, was downgraded to a mule bearing two baskets.

For the most part, however, the differences between Eastern and Western astrology were ones of emphasis. Generally disdaining the classical stress on long-term predictions, Muslims were much more interested in the here and now. For that reason, they favored astrological branches that would later become known as elections and interrogations. In elections, stellar positions decree whether conditions are favorable or unfavorable for individual activities ranging from launching an important business enterprise to the paring of toenails. Interrogations, computed according to strict and complex rules, enable the astrologer to advise on such matters as the location of a stolen article—or, for that matter, the identity of the thief.

Towering above the rest of the astrologers was a prolific writer named Abū Ma'shar, who not only was unsur-

passed in his own milieu but made an impression on later cultures in other places. But perhaps his greatest legacy was the adroit if murky manner in which he handled the old conflict, which had confounded astrology in Christian Europe, between fatalistic determinism and the ability of humans to make the individual decisions that govern their destiny. Such rationalization may have been necessary because Abū Ma'shar's royal patron, Mamun the Great, had rejected Muslim orthodoxy and adopted as the official religion of his caliphate the cult of Mutazilitism, which opted for free will.

According to the eminent astrologer, some things are immutable: fire, for example, can only be hot. But other matters are open to choice: Abū Ma'shar might be writing one day, but might—or might not—decide to do something else the next. Fire's heat was "necessary," and was ruled by the stars; the author's actions were "contingent," and were thus influenced by the planets. To round it all out, the power of the planets was of divine origin, and it was therefore susceptible to human reason.

Abū Ma'shar died in AD 886, just a year shy of his 100th birthday. By then, civil war, rebellion, corruption, and treachery had thrown the Abbasid dynasty into disarray and Baghdad's culture into decay. Yet during Abū Ma'shar's long life, events in Christian Europe had already begun to prepare the way for a renewal of astrology—by way of the Islamic outpost in Spain.

"These are the loveless days of the world's last age," lamented an English-born monk named Alcuin, describing the melancholy conditions he found upon going to the Continent as chief adviser and tutor to Charlemagne, king of the Franks and, from his coronation in Rome on Christmas Day, AD 800, until his death in 814, emperor of the West.

Charlemagne was an enormous man; not only was he exceptionally tall, but it is said that he daily devoured eight platters of meat and gulped down six bowls of wine. And he had a matching gusto for learning. Owing to the sorry state of European education at the time, he apparently was illiterate until well into his adult years, and although he eventually became an enthusiastic reader, he had trouble with writing until the end of his days.

Charlemagne was determined to improve the educational lot of his subjects, and to that enlightened end he had summoned Alcuin of York, perhaps the most renowned scholar of the time, to his side. Between them, they started a palace school whose sessions were regularly attended by the emperor himself. According to an admiring chronicler, Charlemagne was especially keen on astronomy and even had artisans fashion for his use a heavenly map made of silver. It was also said that the great monarch became a skilled astrologer.

Urged on by his royal sponsor, Alcuin established elementary schooling at Charlemagne's court and, at a loftier level, academies for the study of the seven liberal arts—grammar, rhetoric, logic, arithmetic, geometry, astronomy, and music—that would later constitute the curriculum of Western Europe's medieval universities. Most notable among those institutions was the school at the Abbey of Saint Martin, near Tours, where Alcuin himself lectured on, among other things, astrology.

However, because so little knowledge was actually available in the Christian Europe of their day, it is in fact doubtful that either Alcuin or Charlemagne knew more than

Muhammad reverently cradles a mysterious black stone that was later set into the wall of the Kaaba, Islam's holiest shrine and the center of the Muslim cosmos. Perhaps a meteorite, the stone was honored by Arabs as a heaven-sent object long before Islam began.

the barest smattering of astrology or any other science. Instead, their enduring achievement was to create an educational climate that would eventually spawn such scholars as Gerbert of Aurillac—and lead to the resurgence of continental science.

Of humble birth, young Gerbert went to a monasterial school in Aurillac and soaked up as much science as he could. But that, in the absence of the classical texts, was not enough, and when he tried to satisfy his restless curiosity he could turn in only one direction—toward Spain.

There, the most illustrious of the Western emirs, Abd el-Rahman III, had proclaimed himself caliph of Cordoba and Commander of the Faithful in AD 912. Under him and his heirs, the city of Cordoba had become a brilliant cultural center ("The ornament of the world . . . ," wrote one visitor, "young and exquisite, proud of its strength") whose library contained some 400,000 volumes at a time when most European institutions could count their manuscripts only in the dozens. From Cordoba, learning spread to other peninsular cities, where Muslim, Christian, and Jewish scholars lived in mutual respect and tolerance.

It was therefore to Spain that Gerbert went, accompanying a Barcelona nobleman who was traveling home from Rome. Although Gerbert went most specifically in quest of a deeper understanding of mathematics and astronomy, he soon found that astrology, in Arabian science, was very much a part of the same curriculum. During his Spanish sojourn, it is likely that he studied under Hasdai ibn-Shaprut, a Jew who, among other talents, related herbs to planets that

Early Muslims, like these mystic dancers known as whirling dervishes, accepted classical views of astronomy and astrology that Christianity rejected. The dancers' spinning motion symbolized the rotation of the universe.

he believed shaped their growth and benefits.

Upon returning to his homeland, Gerbert knew at least enough about astrology to impress his scholarly contemporaries, some of whom apparently muttered about his possession of magical powers. His acquisition of learning, however, would probably have been of little lasting consequence had it not happened that in AD 999 Gerbert of Aurillac became Pope Sylvester II. In his papal eminence, Sylvester installed an observatory in a tower of the Lateran Palace, fashioned an astrolabe with his own hands, and—although his interests lay primarily with the science of astronomy—thus provided tacit support for the resurrection of astrology in Christian Europe.

Although Sylvester's papal successors soon showed they were unready to follow in his footsteps, princely courts were more receptive, perhaps because their royal proprietors sought a hedge against the troubled times in which they lived. The eleventh century had got off to an uncertain start, with Christendom quailing in the face of widespread belief that the world would end in the first year of the new millennium; similarly, in 1066, humanity would tremble as Halley's Comet illuminated the skies with its fiery tail.

It was, then, hardly a wonder that Henry II, at the time of his coronation as Holy Roman Emperor in 1014, reportedly wore a cloak with Christian figures representing the ancient constellations and an overall pattern that showed astrologically significant relationships between the moon and the Scorpion, and the moon and the Crab. And it is said that William the Conqueror, after chancing the comet's

Mikkyō Buddhists invoked Mercury at this ritual hearth.

Oriental Astrology

Eastern peoples searched the heavens for portents as earnestly as did their counterparts in the Christian and Muslim worlds. And like the westerners, they melded astronomy and astrology into a single system that they reconciled with their religious beliefs.

The Mikkyō, or Esoteric, Buddhists, members of a mystical cult that spread from India to China and Japan, used burnt offerings and carefully prescribed rituals to take advantage of favorable planetary aspects and to avoid the baleful influence of unfavorable configurations. They planned their lives by the heavens. Days under lunar sway, for instance, were good for marrying, digging a well, or starting to build a house. Activities to avoid on such days included making clothes and setting out on a journey. Faithful attention to celestial influences would, the Mikkyō Buddhists believed, make the world a paradise.

omens in his invasion of England, followed the advice of his astrologer-chaplain in selecting high noon on Christmas Day, 1066, as the most propitious hour to be crowned.

Such astrologers were, however, laboring under a handicap. Few of the Arabic texts that would become the basis for the revived science had yet been rendered into Latin, and significant work did not actually begin until the early twelfth century. Among the early translators was an Englishman, Adelard of Bath—not to be confused with his French contemporary, Abelard, whose devotions were such that he gave to the child born of his star-crossed romance with Heloise the name of Astrolabe.

After traveling widely in Europe, Adelard of Bath returned to the England of Henry I and found it little to his liking. "Princes are violent," he wrote, "prelates wine-bibbers, judges mercenary, patrons inconstant, the common men flatterers, promise-makers false, friends envious, and everyone in general ambitious." Withdrawing into a scholastic shell, Adelard wrote extensively on mathematics, alchemy, and astronomy and, in the course of his studies, translated several Arabic works on astrology, including a set of tables that told how to cast a horoscope. Adelard also had an intriguing idea about the planets: They were, he thought, divine "animals" that fed on the humidities emanating from earth and water, which, by the time they arrived in the heavens, had been refined in a manner that made for a healthy planetary diet.

By the middle of the twelfth century, the flow of translations was well under way—the *Tetrabiblos,* the *Centiloquium* (a list of astrological aphorisms), the treatises of Abū Ma'shar and other Arabic astrologers, Ptolemy's other great work, *Almagest,* and much of Aristotle's legacy. Possession of the ancient texts naturally led to a proliferation of astrological practitioners, whose varied skills were soon put to a stern test when they calculated that in September 1186 all the planets would be in conjunction with Libra, an extremely rare celestial arrangement. Almost unanimously, the astrologers of the day predicted calamitous events. One, for example, entered into a trance, uttered thirty-three Latin

القول الثامن في برج الأسد الشمس نط والمشتري

بهذا الوجه يكون زدي اللون يعلون حمرة معتدل القامة غليظ مدكك الأكثر كبير اللحية جهر الصوت كثير الكلام صاحب جدل وحيله علمه خفي يستطيع أن يظهر خبرة وفي بصره وقال أنه تحصل له شمه وعلى ركبته وبا فذراعه شامات وقروع والله أعلم

The Sun in the sign of Leo and the planet Jupiter—pictured as a man—appear above smaller zodiacal symbols in a book by ninth-century Iranian scholar Abū Ma'shar. Renowned for introducing Greek astronomy to the Muslim world, Abū Ma'shar was also a skillful astrologer who advised princes and military leaders from as far away as India.

Crusaders during the following year.

Meanwhile, scholars of astrology were undertaking some serious work. The translations from Arabic had provided an abundance of material that needed to be sorted out in an orderly way, and among the first to set himself to the task was one Roger of Hereford. Roger defined four separate branches of astrology: electional, horary, natal, and mundane. Electional was, of course, the area of which the Arabs had been so fond. Horary, also followed by the Muslims, enabled astrologers to advise individuals about a wide range of personal problems, with the answers based on the state of the skies at the moment the questions were asked. Natal provided for the drawing up of birth charts by which the entire course of a person's life could be predicted according to the position of heavenly bodies at the instant of birth. Lumped together, the electional, horary, and natal divisions would be known as judicial astrology.

couplets about the impending doom—and died on the spot. Against the predicted catastrophes, warned another, there "is but one remedy, that the king and the nobles should take counsel: Serve God and flee from the devil, so that the Lord may turn aside these threatened punishments!"

In the spreading panic, prayerful church services were conducted, and some citizens even dug underground shelters to escape the anticipated storms. As it turned out, however, the fateful month passed more or less quietly, and not until much later did astrologers find an excuse for their apparent mistake. Looking over their shoulders, they explained that the Libra conjunction had in fact set the stage for the Muslim leader Saladin's crushing victories over the

Mundane astrology was of a different breed: It dealt not with individuals, but with groups. Shunning elaborate prophecies, it limited itself to interpreting natural or cosmic events through astrological cycles. In its most expansive form, designated as natural astrology, it concerned itself with the influence of conjunctions, eclipses, comets, and the like on such broad-scale earthly matters as the weather, agriculture, medicine, the outcome of wars, the rise and fall of religions, the fate of nations and indeed of civilizations. The English astrologer Roger of Hereford dealt largely with mundane astrology, and his interest led him to assign planets, paired with signs of the zodiac, to rulership of various cultures, peoples, and religions. For example: "Libra and

*Beneath a starry sky, a Hebrew teacher in fourteenth-
century Spain shows his students how to determine the positions of celestial objects
with an astrolabe. A Greek invention, the instrument was
probably brought to medieval Europe by Arabs.*

Saturn rule the 'land of the Christians' / Scorpio and Venus rule the Arabs/ Capricorn and Mercury rule India / Leo and Mars rule the Turks / Aquarius and the Sun rule Babylonia / Virgo and the Moon rule Spain.''

Through the distinction between judicial and mundane, or natural, astrology, some of the finest minds of the thirteenth century began to open the gates of the Christian church to the revived science. And by more than mere chance, many of those in the forefront of astrological thought were members of the young Franciscan and Dominican monastic orders, deeply steeped in the disciplines of meditative inquiry. Setting their style was Robert Grosseteste, an English Franciscan who became chancellor of Oxford University and later bishop of Lincoln, a scholar of fiercely independent mind who squabbled with secular and papal authority alike. On the one hand, he rebuffed attempts by Henry III to control ecclesiastical appointments; on the other, he criticized Pope Innocent IV for naming foreigners to lucrative positions in England; and for good measure, he assailed the Curia for general indolence and corruption.

Confronted by the question of free will that had already caused so much difficulty for Christian astrologers, Grosseteste had no trouble whatever in denouncing much of judicial astrology. Prayer itself, he insisted, would be meaningless "if the stars held sway, as astrologers pretend." For natural astrology, however, he had nothing but praise. There are, he said, "no, or few, works of ours or of nature, as for example the propagation of plants, the transmutation of minerals, the curing of sickness, which can be removed from the sway of [astrology]. For nature below effects nothing unless celestial power moves it and directs it from potency into act." Indeed, Grosseteste was so taken by the power of the stars that he declared natural astrology to be second only to divine worship in spiritual matters—and second to none as an intellectual discipline.

Carrying the argument in favor of astrology even further was one of Grosseteste's students—Roger Bacon, the gifted Franciscan monk who would much later be viewed as a father of modern science. Such were Bacon's powers of deductive reasoning, and so astonishing were the results, that he was suspected of practicing the black art of magic. In fact, Bacon made a distinction between magical quackery, which he excoriated, and scientific magic, which he embraced. Falling well within the favored category was astrology, and by accepting it in all its aspects, in its judicial capacity as well as its mundane role, Bacon ran afoul of the church's feelings about free will. For his outspoken opinions, Bacon was imprisoned for ten years.

Bacon's ideas were sometimes illusionary, but they were always interesting. Although the planets have no such qualities within themselves, he said, they nonetheless "have the ability to heat or to cool, to dry or to wet; just as wine is not naturally hot and dry . . . yet it heats and dries, and it makes drunk but is not itself drunken." And, in urging that the Christian church make positive use of astrology, Bacon suggested that it might well be employed to thwart the infidel Tartars or even to foresee and forestall the coming of the Antichrist.

For all the advocacy of the forceful English Franciscans, it was on the European continent—and largely through the voices of a pair of Dominican monks—that the breakthrough finally came in astrology's relations with the Christian church. Throughout much of their history, the Dominicans had been relentless in rooting out the heresies with which astrology was often associated. Yet somewhere along the way they had been charmed by the science they suppressed, and now, relying upon the reason of Aristotelian logic instead of Platonic mysticism, the friars reached for the rationale that would make astrology compatible with Christianity.

In that effort, one of the order's most eminent members, Albertus Magnus of Cologne, struck exactly the right note: "There is in man a double spring of action, namely nature and the will; and nature for its part is ruled by the stars, while the will is free; but unless it resists it is swept along by nature and becomes mechanical."

During a period when Albertus was lecturing in Paris,

At eight-year intervals, the ruler of the ancient Mayan city of Uxmal in northern Yucatan would see a portent in the early morning sky. The sovereign, always called Lord Chac—after the Mayan rain god—would stand in the central doorway of his palace just before sunrise and watch the rising of the planet Venus at the southernmost point of its long cycle. The palace's eighth-century architects had aligned the doorway to look out across flat terrain toward a landmark on the southeastern horizon—an eighty-foot-tall pyramid at Nohpat, some six miles away. Like clockwork, Venus would appear over the pyramid's apex once every eight years.

Manuscripts and stone carvings bear testament to the information that the master astronomers of the Maya

Master Astronomers of Ancient America

The stone face of the rain god Chac (above) bears the Mayan hieroglyph for Venus—two balls under a wavy line. The Maya looked to Chac for success in agriculture and to the bellicose Venus for triumph in warfare.

amassed about the heavens. Their records are especially rich in observations of Venus. Why they were so concerned with this particular planet remains a mystery, although it might have been because Venus is the third-brightest object in the sky, after the Sun and the Moon.

For modern investigators of the Maya, a puzzling hieroglyph proved a key clue to understanding Venus's importance. Called the shell-star hieroglyph, it was known to relate to battles among the jungle kingdoms. But, unaccountably, it included a rendering of two balls beneath a wavy line—a Mayan symbol for Venus. On a hunch, Yale anthropologist Floyd Lounsbury compared astronomical tables with the dates of Mayan military events whose records bore the

shell-star hieroglyph. He discovered that the battles coincided with significant positions in the cycle of Venus. Thus it seemed that—far from corresponding to the goddess of love, as in Roman myth and astrology— Venus was the Mayan counterpart of the Romans' Mars: a planet of war. In the Mayan world, battles and ritual combats, and the ensuing sacrifice of defeated warriors, proceeded in a Venusian rhythm.

Timing war according to celestial dictates gave Mayan society a unique character. With surprise attacks all but ruled out, the Maya could dispense with defensive moats and battlements for their cities and did not have to maintain constant vigilance. Their military fate was firmly governed by the cosmos.

In a mural (left) found in the ruins of Bonampak, warriors kill an enemy during a battle waged to capture sacrificial victims for a ceremony honoring the heir to the city's throne. Astrologers had selected the date of the encounter. The battle took place on August 2 in the year AD 792, coinciding with Venus's appearance as the morning star.

Beyond a throne of stone jaguars lie doorways to the House of the Governor, ancient home of Lord Chac at Uxmal. The central doorway aligns with the southernmost point on the horizon at which Venus rises before dawn. On the frieze above the portals are hundreds of images of the rain god Chac, each bearing symbols of Venus.

one of his students was a young man who would, during his lifetime, earn the title of the Angelic Doctor, and within a mere fifty years of his death would be canonized. Yet prestige and honors had not always been the lot of Thomas Aquinas. Stout of build and stolid in manner, he had been a butt of fellow students who called him "the Dumb Ox"—to which his mentor replied, "This ox will one day fill the world with his bellowings." And where Albertus had left off with astrology, Aquinas picked up and elaborated.

In threading the needle of conflict between astrologi-

cal mechanics and Christian theology, Aquinas held that the stars were the agents of God's will, and in that capacity they controlled a human's physical body—but not the soul, which was possessed of its own will, to be employed in direct communication with the Creator. "Because most men follow their bodily urges," he wrote, "their actions shall usually be subject to the influences of heavenly bodies." This occurred mostly where people were congregated in large groups—such as armies, cities, and nations—in which they were susceptible to being swept by common passions. In such cases, they were steered by heavenly bodies and were therefore fitting subjects for astrological prediction.

At the same time, strong-minded humans, acting as individuals, could overcome celestial influences by the power of reason and free will. Thus, wrote Thomas Aquinas, "the wise man is master of the stars." And there, in a single sentence, was the key that unlocked the door of Christian doctrine and led to the official acceptance of natural if not judicial astrology.

Yet even as Aquinas and his fellow theologians and philosophers were winning approval for their elegant proposals, others were earning their daily bread through astrology. For them, the practice of judicial astrology was a vocational necessity, and in any event they had long since learned that the church, whatever its official attitude may have been, was remarkably reluctant to prosecute transgressors. Over the centuries since the revival of the science, only a handful of astrological adherents had suffered penalty, and in one case it was inflicted posthumously. Gerard, archbishop of York, was denied burial in his own cathedral in 1108 because, according to one account, "he used to read Julius Firmicus secretly in place of his afternoon devotions"—and, compounding the crime, the astrological volume was found beneath his deathbed pillow.

But Gerard had been unpopular with other church leaders as well as with York's citizens (who acted out their dislike by stoning his coffin), and his astrological interests may well have been no more

On this moon card from a Tarot deck, two astrologers make calculations with the aid of a manual and calipers. For centuries fortunetellers have employed the Tarot's twenty-two Major Arcana, or mystery cards, some of which bear astrological symbols such as the moon, stars, or sun.

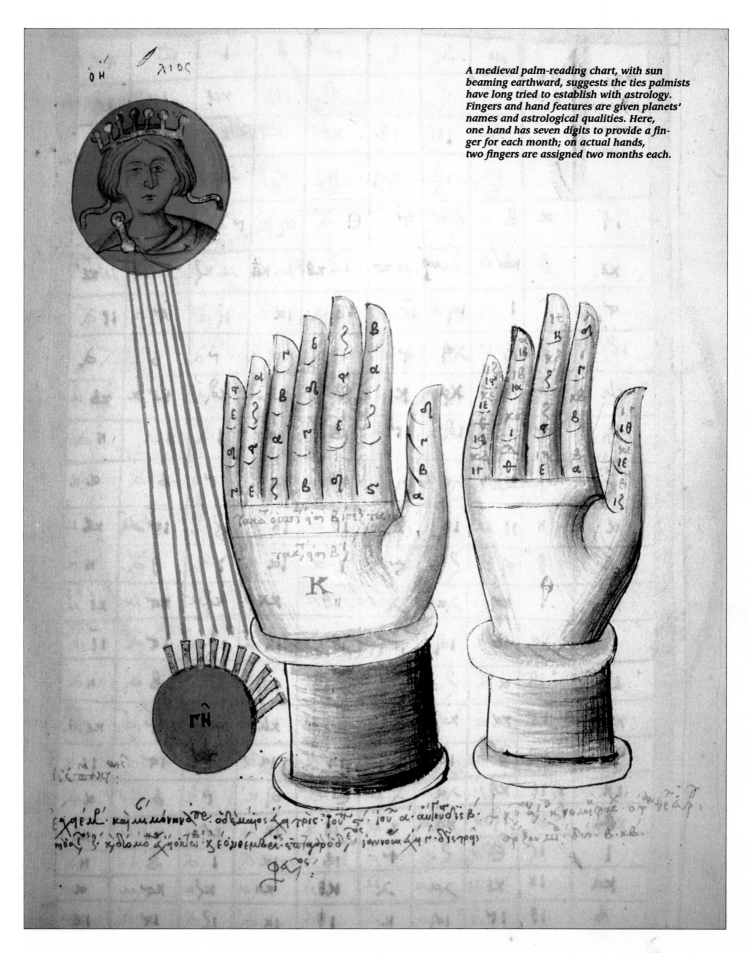

A medieval palm-reading chart, with sun beaming earthward, suggests the ties palmists have long tried to establish with astrology. Fingers and hand features are given planets' names and astrological qualities. Here, one hand has seven digits to provide a finger for each month; on actual hands, two fingers are assigned two months each.

than a handy excuse for reprisal. Similarly, the contentious Roger Bacon had trod on enough toes to make any number of powerful figures wish to put him out of the way, and incarcerating him for his astrological views had been perhaps no more than a convenient means to accomplish that end. In fact, not until the early fourteenth century would astrology be provided with its only martyr, the Florentine court astrologer Cecco d'Ascoli, who was burned along with his books. But even then, it would appear that political rather than religious reasons were mainly responsible for d'Ascoli's fate. In addition to his heresy in applying astrology to Christ's birth and crucifixion, he may also have offended one of his judges with his support for a political rival.

Those punishments, however, were isolated instances, and other astrologers had become accustomed to practicing judicial astrology with impunity. In the court of the Holy Roman Emperor Frederick II, for example, a Scotsman named Michael Scot was one of several resident astrologers. Described by a contemporary as "a scrutinizer of the stars, an augur, a soothsayer, a second Apollo," Scot was at any rate a peculiar fellow who was forever propounding unusual ideas for which he offered no explanations. For example, he put forth the notion that the fourteen joints in the fingers of the human hand signify that man's natural tenure on earth is 140 years.

Delving into natal astrology, Scot insisted that the instant of conception was every bit as important as the time of birth in determining the course of a person's life, and he detailed the ways the child may be affected by the relationship between the positions of the planets and the position of the parents at the point of conception. It is unknown whether Frederick obeyed his astrologer's every word, but clearly he was influenced: When the emperor married his wife, it was written that "he refused to know her carnally until the fitting hour should be told him by his astrologers."

Not surprisingly, Scot was taken by many to be a wizard, and it was rumored that he rode a demon in the guise of a black horse. That reputation was hardly diminished by the manner of his death, which he had prophesied would come from a blow on the head. To frustrate that fate, he went about wearing a steel helmet—a precaution that went for naught one doleful day in 1236 or so when Scot, accompanying Frederick to church, removed the helmet for the sake of proper religious manners. A stone promptly fell on his bared head, killing him instantly.

Although Scot plainly crossed the boundary between natural and judicial astrology, his only comeuppance came from the pen of the Italian poet Dante Alighieri. In the *Divine Comedy,* Scot was relegated to the fourth division of the eighth circle of the Inferno, with his head fixed backward in punishment for the sin of having gazed into the future. (One of Scot's companions there was Guido Bonatti, the astrologer who had doubled as a military adviser, but Dante probably sent him to hell because of his political rather than his astrological views.) The church evidently had no quarrel with Scot. In fact, it was not long before Aquinas's line between the two kinds of astrology became blurred, in practice if not in theory, both within and without the church.

As the Renaissance radiated throughout western Europe, astrology in all its aspects became recognized as a valid field of study, and only a few voices were raised in protest against its ascendancy. Among the vastly outnumbered critics, the most vociferous by far was Giovanni Pico della Mirandola, a rich, handsome, and brilliant young nobleman who was also incredibly argumentative.

As a youth, Pico had written no fewer than 900 theses on various controversial subjects—and offered to pay the expenses of anyone who would travel to Rome to debate him. Among the papers were at least a dozen about astrology, which he praised in extravagant terms, even to the point of describing astrological magic as "the practical and most noble part of natural science." Such claims drew papal fire, and so did Pico, who was briefly imprisoned for his work. The experience may have been instructive, because Pico soon became convinced of judicial astrology's fallacies—and when Pico della Mirandola changed his mind, he did so in a major way. The result of his about-face was an

Health and Sickness from the Heavens

Many Renaissance physicians believed the human body was under astrological dominion from head to toe, each part linked to a sign of the zodiac—the heart to Leo, for instance, and the thighs to Sagittarius. The signs mediated the shifting impact of the planets, which had their own special anatomical associations. But when planets moved into unfavorable positions, illness struck.

The practitioner consulted two documents for a diagnosis—the patient's birth horoscope and a second horoscope, called a decumbiture chart, which detailed the planetary positions at the moment the patient fell ill. The physician then turned to an almanac to discover what disease would develop under these conditions and consulted an herbal to select a drug. Each herb was believed to draw upon the power of a particular planet and, for greatest potency, had to be harvested on the day governed by its planet. Solar-dominated saffron was gathered only on Sundays, and catmint on Fridays, when Venus ruled.

Astrology also dictated times for treatment. Excess blood could be drawn from the feet when the moon was in Aries, for example, but not when in Gemini.

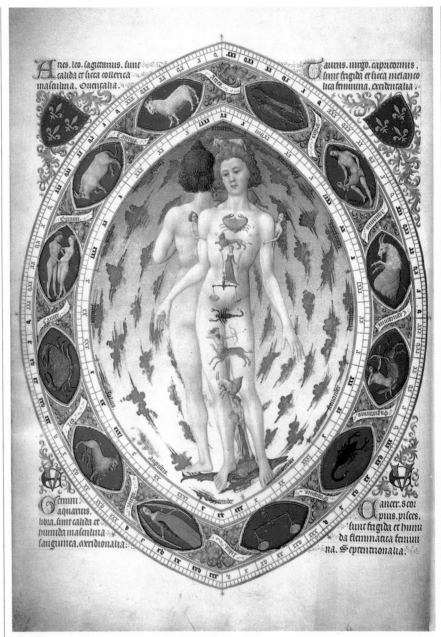

With his back to a mirror reflecting a cloud-dotted heaven, a figure from a fifteenth-century prayer book stands on Pisces and displays the other signs of the zodiac on the parts of the body they rule.

Chaucer gave his bawdy Wife of Bath (left) the birth sign Taurus and a tendency to explain her behavior by astrology. But in a more scientific mode, he detailed the construction of the equatorium (below)—a complex device used to determine planetary positions—in his Equatorie of the Planets.

A Starry-Minded English Poet

In 1392, Geoffrey Chaucer's ten-year-old son, Lewis, complained that he wanted to learn to calculate stellar positions but did not know enough Latin to read a treatise on the astrolabe. His father—already a famous poet though still writing *The Canterbury Tales*—obligingly translated the treatise, producing what is thought to be the earliest scientific work on astronomy in English. But Chaucer's knowledge of the heavens went beyond mere translating; he also probably wrote a treatise of his own, *The Equatorie of the Planets.*

And astral influence infuses his poetry. His characters measure time by the zodiac—the sun is halfway through "the ram," Aries, as the Canterbury pilgrims gather—and trace their fate in the stars. The blowzy, cheerfully unrepentant Wife of Bath blames her horoscope for her lecherous ways: "For Venus sent me feeling from the stars / And my heart's boldness came to me from Mars."

enormous, twelve-volume work that was apparently intended to include all the criticisms ever made of astrology.

Pico's science was sometimes shaky—among other things, he denied that the moon influenced the earth's tides. He was on sounder ground, however, in his assaults on the methods by which astrologers reached their disparate and often contradictory conclusions. In the process, he produced what may have been the first statistical study of astrological inaccuracy. "I spent a whole winter in my country house . . . ," Pico wrote, "observing the weather day by day and checking against the astrological forecast. May I be punished if I do not tell the truth: I made observations on over 130 days, and there were not more than six or seven

occasions when the weather agreed with the forecasts."

Yet Pico was wasting his breath. By the time he died in his thirtieth year in 1394, astrology had reached its apogee among the crowned heads of Europe. And although it took a bit longer for holy Rome to be converted, within a century popes were consulting their seers with all the zealousness of secular rulers. Far from restricting their interest to the relatively impersonal (and theologically approved) sweep of natural astrology, the Renaissance popes focused their attentions on the natal, electional, and horary branches by which their personal fortunes could be told.

For astrologers, the rewards for papal or royal patronage were considerable, but the job could be risky. In 1472

*Dante stands before the Mount of Purgatory, from
which souls must traverse nine concentric celestial spheres to reach paradise. He added
hell to Aristotle's cosmic model to accommodate Christian doctrine.*

one Perre le Lorrain, relying on the ill omens that invariably accompanied the passage of a comet, supposedly set a date for the imminent death of Pope Paul II. Being human, the pontiff did not like what he heard and promptly clapped Lorrain into prison, promising that the astrologer would be put to death if the prediction turned out to be wrong. When the fateful day arrived, Pope Paul appeared to be in bouncing good health, and Lorrain's friends visited him to offer their condolences. Undaunted, Lorrain insisted that his prophecy was correct—and lo and behold, the pope died before nightfall. Lorrain was released from prison and honored for his prophetic powers.

Franciscus Priulus, the pet astrologer of Leo X, devoted an entire book to the nativity of the pope and later revealed private secrets that Leo had believed known only to himself. Leo was proud of Priulus, boasting that his predictions of even daily occurrences were unfailingly accurate. Yet in his probing of the future, the astrologer must have seen something that drove him to despair. After futile attempts at suicide by trying to drown himself, jumping into a fire, slashing at his throat with a scythe, and hurling himself out of a window, he finally starved himself to death.

The Sun Rules Leo

The Moon Rules Cancer

Mercury Rules Gemini and Virgo

Venus Rules Libra and Taurus

Of all the popes, the one who was probably the most charmed by astrology was Paul III, head of the church during the Counter-Reformation. (Both Martin Luther and John Calvin, the leaders of the Protestant Reformation, had opposed the celestial science, although probably less out of conviction than because it was by then so closely associated with Roman Catholicism.) Paul's ascent to the papacy was foretold by an astrologer, Luca Guarico, whom Paul as pontiff naturally brought to the papal palace.

Guarico had ingratiating ways. He avowed that Luther would go to hell because he had been born under the sign of Scorpio. Later, when the pope called upon his astrologer to select the right time for laying the cornerstone of a new building in the Saint Peter's church complex, Guarico put on a fine show, appearing with an assistant decked out in a magnificent robe, who peered at the heavens with an astrolabe and announced that the propitious moment had come.

Appointed a bishop by the grateful Paul, Guarico left Rome, to be succeeded by astrologers who also aimed to please. One, Marius Alterius, delighted the earthy old pope by predicting that in his eighty-third year he would enjoy successes with women "which will overwhelm your spirit with singular pleasure." Furthermore, Alterius foresaw that Paul would live to be ninety-three. Alas, the pope died at a mere eighty-one, timing that had been foreseen by Guarico, who soon showed up in the French court of Henri II and Catherine de Médicis, where he created a stir with his warning that the king might face mortal danger in a duel around the age of forty-one.

Unfortunately for his enduring place in history, however, Guarico was eclipsed by the man who confirmed this prophecy—Nostradamus, the most renowned name in astrological annals. Whether he was an astrological scientist or a necromancer, a charlatan or a genius (and he was probably some of each), Nostradamus was undeniably endowed with extraordinary talents. Born in 1503 in Saint-Rémy, a small town in Provence, to a family of Christianized Jews, he spent much of his boyhood with his maternal grandfather, a man of scholarly bent who tutored him in, among other things, the classical languages, the medicinal uses of herbs—and astrology. While he was completing his studies at Montpellier, site of one of the finest medical schools of the day, plague struck the town, and Nostradamus pitched in to help the suffering victims.

Mars Rules Scorpio and Aries

Jupiter Rules Pisces and Sagittarius

Saturn Rules Aquarius and Capricorn

As even his enemies—and they were legion—would later admit, Nostradamus was a skilled physician, and for the next several years he followed the plague from place to place, attracting attention partly because he apparently possessed a palliative to the disease, partly because he escaped being infected himself. His immunity did not, however, extend to his wife and two small sons, who perished. Burdened by grief, Nostradamus for the next eight years wandered more or less aimlessly in France, Italy, and Corsica. It was evidently in that period that he honed his prophetic skills, which he exercised through astrology and other forms of divination, such as scrying, which involves gazing into crystals or other shining surfaces.

In 1555, Nostradamus published the first edition of his *Centuries,* a collection of quatrains that were riddled with anagrams, puns, and references so obscure that they amounted to a code known only to their author. The obfuscations were deliberate because, as Nostradamus explained, if he had set forth his visions as clearly as he saw them he would have been accused of consorting with the devil. One of them captured the interest of the French court because it seemed to confirm Guarico's warning that the king might be blinded or slain in a duel. And sure enough, in 1559 the forty-one-year-old Henri jousted with the captain of his Scottish guard, was pierced in the eye and the throat, and died.

Some of Nostradamus's prophecies concerned events that, according to their interpreters, were centuries in the future. The following verse, for example, is widely believed to describe the bloody fallout of the French Revolution, more than 200 years in the future: "At night will come through the Forest of Reines / A married couple by a devious route, Herne, the white stone, / The monk in gray, into Varennes, / The elected Capet—the result will be tempest, fire, blood—and cutting off."

Cloaked in murky obscurities, the quatrain must have been gibberish to the prophet's own generation. After the fact, however, many found the key to the puzzle in the reference to Varennes, a village whose solitary claim to fame is that it was where Louis XVI and Marie Antoinette were captured after their flight from Paris. Once that is known, the rest may be deciphered—more or less. Although no Forest of Reines has ever existed, *forest* may be a play on *fores,* the Latin word for door, and *reine* is French for queen. Hence the "Forest of Reines" may be the queen's door through which the royal couple had escaped from their palace. At the time they were seized, Louis was clad in monkish gray, while his queen *(Herne* may be an anagram for *reine* with one letter eliminated, as was permissible under anagrammatic rules) wore white. *Capet,* related to the Latin word for head *(caput),* was also the surname of Louis's royal predecessors, and Louis was the first head of the French state to rule not only by divine right but through election. Finally,

To alchemists, the sun in this late sixteenth-century illustration represented gold. Each "planet"—including the sun and the moon—was associated with a particular metal.

The Effects of Fire, Earth, Air, and Water

In medieval and Renaissance medical theory, an elaborate system of four-fold links joins people to the cosmos and determines their temperament and physical constitution. They are, in effect, microcosms made up of the four basic elements of the universe—fire, earth, water, and air. The human body, the theory goes, contains four liquids called humors that correspond to the elements—yellow bile to fire, black bile to earth, phlegm to water, and blood to air.

A perfect balance of humors would produce an ideal temperament and flawless health. But, according to the theory, everyone has some sort of excess that yields a characteristic temperament and a set of health problems. Black bile disposes a person toward melancholy, and phlegm to sluggishness; a quick or choleric temper is linked with yellow bile, and a buoyant or sanguine personality with blood.

Nor is a person's inborn mix of humors a closed system—the planets and stars can change the balance, for good or ill. A particularly dangerous influence is the powerful moon, which, according to the theory, governs water and can easily throw a phlegmatic's constitution out of kilter and turn that person into a fool, a drunkard, a glutton, or a wastrel.

A crescent moon, seen on the fluttering banner, rules the Renaissance painter Hieronymus Bosch's boatload of carousing phlegmatics. Their bad character is presumably caused by the moon's control over water, their special element.

in the "cutting off," the unfortunate king and queen were decapitated by the guillotine. Of course, it is somewhat easier to ascribe meaning to a vague quatrain once the events seem to have been perfectly played out.

Following his triumphs in the court of Catherine de Médicis, Nostradamus was the rage of high French society, whose members sought him out for every manner of prophetic advice. He also made considerable sums by producing annual almanacs for mass consumption. Yet despite his seemingly magical powers, he was of mortal flesh, and on the night of July 1, 1566, he uttered his last prophecy, telling a visitor, "You will not find me alive at sunrise." Within hours, Nostradamus was dead—leaving behind a legacy of forecasts supposedly projecting as far into the future as AD 3797, which his admirers are still trying to unravel.

Although English society was slower to accept astrology, British monarchs made use of talented European astrologers, and almost every chancellor under Henry VIII kept abreast of astrological developments. But it took an Italian, Jerome Cardan, to raise astrology to the rarefied level it enjoyed on the Continent. A scholar with many interests (he was, among other things, the first to suggest a touch system by which the blind might read), Cardan predicted that his sponsor, the sickly boy-king Edward VI, would live to at least fifty-five. When Edward in fact succumbed to consumption at only sixteen, Cardan courageously exonerated his science and assumed personal blame for the mistake. All the necessary data had been in Edward's horoscope, he insisted, but to interpret it correctly would have required an extra hundred hours—and, he said, he had been too indolent to spend the additional time.

Although Cardan had clearly failed, his celebrated presence was nonetheless enough to arouse the astrological interests of two young English scholars—

An ardent believer in astrology, Queen Catherine de Médicis of France summoned Nostradamus in 1556 to cast the horoscopes of her children.

Leonard Digges, who would go on to publish astrological almanacs, and, more important, the mathematician John Dee, who would one day become what the redoubtable Queen Elizabeth I described as "my Ubiquitous Eyes."

A precocious youngster, Dee had entered Cambridge at the age of fifteen and, by immersing himself in his studies for eighteen hours a day, had become versed in mathematics, navigation, astronomy, and optics. He also got himself in trouble by devising, for use in a stage production of Aristophanes' *Pax*, a mechanical beetle that flew so realistically that Dee was suspected of sorcery. Trailing controversy behind him like a demon's tail, Dee hastily departed for the Low Countries, where his knowledge of navigation led to an acquaintance with the great geographer Gerardus Mercator, best known for his system of projecting latitudes and longitudes in straight instead of curved lines. When he returned to England, Dee brought with him two of Mercator's globes and some navigational instruments.

In a seagoing nation whose very survival rested upon navigation, Dee's skills could hardly have remained unnoticed for long. But it was apparently his budding reputation as an astrological prognosticator that first captured the attention of Princess Elizabeth, who was then being held in confinement near Oxford while her elder half sister, Mary, occupied England's throne. At any rate, Elizabeth asked for and got a horoscope, in which Dee predicted that she would rise to a high place in the kingdom and would live to a satisfyingly old age. At the same time, Dee showed Elizabeth an astrological forecast he had made about the marriage of Queen Mary to King Philip of Spain: "Woe to the two nations: Woe and sorrow / Disaster by water: persecution by fire / And the queen shall childless die."

When word of his prediction got around, Dee found himself in jail, accused

Nostradamus (opposite) studied medicine and spent years consulting physicians and pharmacists as well as astrologers, alchemists, and magicians before turning to public prophecy in 1550. The seer observed the stars but not, as shown here, with the telescope, which was not invented until well after his death.

Predictions Véritables et Remarquables, Centuries de Michel de Nostradamus.

of the "lewde vayne practices of caculing and conjuring" against the queen. Dee was released after a few months, however, and his fortunes took a dramatic turn for the better when Elizabeth inherited the crown—and summoned Dee to select the most fortunate day for her coronation. (After consulting his charts, he settled on Sunday, January 15, 1558.) For years thereafter, her court was distinguished by the frequent presence of John Dee, a slender, handsome man with a "very faire cleare rosie complexion." Consulted by the queen on matters ranging from affairs of state to cures for her toothaches, Dee seldom failed to please.

Among his congenial predictions were the execution of her bitter rival, Mary, Queen of Scots, and the defeat of the Spanish Armada.

In addition to his services as an astrological forecaster, Dee was reportedly valuable to Elizabeth as a spymaster, communicating in code with a network of agents he had set up in the cities of Rome, Paris, Moscow, Geneva, Worms, Amsterdam, and Vienna. In particular, the intelligence collected by Dee about the arrivals and departures of foreign warships and cargo vessels was of vital importance to a commercial nation that was beset by hostile powers.

Unfortunately, there is little doubt that Dee also engaged in dark and illicit practices. He entered into a long relationship with one Edward Kelly, a rascal who had a pair of cropped ears to show for his encounters with the law. Claiming no gifts of his own as a scryer, Dee used Kelly as the crystal-gazing medium through which he supposedly conversed with angelic guides, the most talkative of whom was described as "a Spiritual Creature, like a pretty girl of seven or nine years of age." She called herself Madimi, a name that Dee subsequently bestowed upon one of his own daughters.

In Elizabethan England, such involvements could only stir up violent controversy. The great martyrologist John Foxe, for one, denounced Dee as "a caller of Divils," and though the wounded astrolo-

Political Astrology, Renaissance Style

Throughout the ages, astrology has been exploited for propaganda purposes. Few made more effective use of the old art than Cosimo de' Medici, the sixteenth-century leader of Florence's most powerful family.

Cosimo was born in 1519 when the sun appeared in Gemini and when Capricorn was rising over the horizon. When only eighteen, he crushed a rebellion and used the occasion to claim astrological kinship to three other illustrious victors. His propagandists noted that Alexander the Great, Emperor Augustus of Rome, and Cosimo's contemporary and protector, the Holy Roman Emperor Charles V, all shared the Florentine's rising sign. Moreover, Augustus had seized control of the Roman Empire by defeating Antony and Cleopatra in 31 BC on August 2, the same month and day as Cosimo's triumph. Thus did Cosimo wrap himself in the colors of great political and military power and also flatter his emperor.

Nor did Renaissance infighters ignore astrology in negative propaganda. Protestant reformer Martin Luther was probably born in November 1483, but Catholics bent on smearing him fabricated a new birth date—October 22, 1484. This coincided with an ominous planetary conjunction that gave astrological grounds for labeling Luther an antichrist.

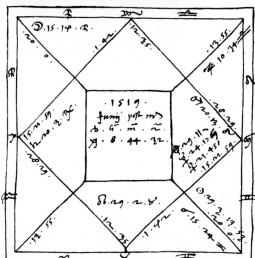

Shortly after coming to power, Cosimo de' Medici (top) commissioned astrologer Giuliano Ristori, a Carmelite friar and professor of mathematics, to prepare a horoscope (above). Cosimo's lucky goat—his ascendant sign Capricorn—became his emblem and appeared on many coins and medals like the one at left, which bears the Latin motto, "animi conscientia et fiducia fati," or "knowledge of self and faith in the stars."

ger replied that this was a "damnable sklaunder," the mounting criticism made him an embarrassment to the queen. Still, Elizabeth was loyal enough to the man who had provided her with so many convenient predictions: She named him to such honorific positions as chancellor of Saint Paul's Cathedral and warden of Christ's College of Manchester, and it is said she sometimes visited him at his home in Mortlake. Her successor, however, was James I, son of Mary, Queen of Scots, and the new king had no earthly use for the prophet of his mother's untimely end. Stripped of his positions and ostracized, John Dee died at the age of eighty-one.

At least to some extent, the fame—or infamy—of John Dee, Nostradamus, and others before them in the line of astrologers since the mid-fifteenth century had been spread by publications printed with movable type, whose invention had removed the science from the exclusive realm of royal and ecclesiastical courts and had placed it in the province of ordinary citizens. Indeed, within two decades after the completion of Johannes Gutenberg's Bible, the first almanac (a word that is derived from the Arabic *al-manakh,* or calendar) was produced, in 1469, and by the sixteenth century, astrological almanacs were read as widely and as avidly as newspapers were in succeeding generations.

For the most part, the almanacs were aimed at the agricultural audiences that formed by far the largest segment of Europe's population at that time. Thus, for example, almanac readers could learn that root crops should be planted when the moon was low or below the horizon, whereas the time to plant fruit-bearing trees was when the moon was waxing. Not all of the almanacs took themselves completely seriously, however; one astrological scrivener, who called himself Poor Robin, made some conspicuously tongue-in-cheek predictions. Among his safer bets: "If Mars and Venus happen to

John Dee epitomizes the Renaissance intellectual who bridged the scientific and occult realms. He was Queen Elizabeth I's astrologer and delved into magic. But he was also an accomplished mathematician and navigation expert, who prepared geographical studies of England's newfound territories.

be in conjunction this year, you may chance to hear of some wenches being gotten with child about the season of the year yclept Haytime."

Nowhere were the almanacs more generous in their advice than in the field of medicine—which throughout its history was so closely linked to celestial influences (whence comes the word *influenza*) as to defy distinction. Although the association of the signs of the zodiac with various parts of the human body had begun in Greece and Egypt a few centuries before the birth of Christ, it was in Renaissance Europe that medical treatment became inextricably connected with astrology.

To physicians and astrologers alike, all terrestrial matter was composed of the four elements of fire, air, earth, and water, which corresponded to the planetary qualities of heat, cold, dryness, and moisture. The four humors by which humans were supposedly afflicted were associated with the elements: choler with fire, blood with air, melancholy with earth, and phlegm with water. From there, it was only a short step to follow the ancient Greek example and attribute to each sign of the zodiac the governance of certain bodily parts: Cancer ruled the breast and stomach, Leo the back and heart, Virgo the viscera, and so forth.

Obviously, an aspiring physician needed a thorough knowledge of astrology. "Medical studies without astrology are like an eye which cannot see," was the pronouncement of the renowned University of Bologna medical school, which required each student to take a four-year course in astrology. At the equally famous University of Paris, an astrologer named Jean Avis for forty years provided every member of the

medical faculty with an annual almanac; beyond that, the university urged that all physicians and surgeons be required to own almanacs for tracking the celestial movements that dictated the course of disease.

Once licensed, a physician relied far more on a patient's horoscope than on physical examination. First the sufferer was placed in a category related to one of the four humors. Then the doctor sought an afflicting planet: Diseases of the skin or bones might spring from Saturn ill-aspected in Capricorn, a sore throat was clearly caused by Mars in Taurus, while syphilis occurred in persons with a Jupiter-Saturn conjunction in Scorpio. The course of treatment sometimes ran from diagnosis to determining when

Elizabeth I, portrayed here in her coronation robes, buttressed her reign with the symbolism of astrology, as shown in the engraving opposite. Entitled—in Latin—Sphere of the State, it declares her to be Queen of England, France, and Ireland and Defender of the Faith, and it bestows on her the positive astrological qualities of the planets, including Jupiter's majesty (maiestas), Mars's bravery (fortitudo), and the mercy (clementia) of Venus.

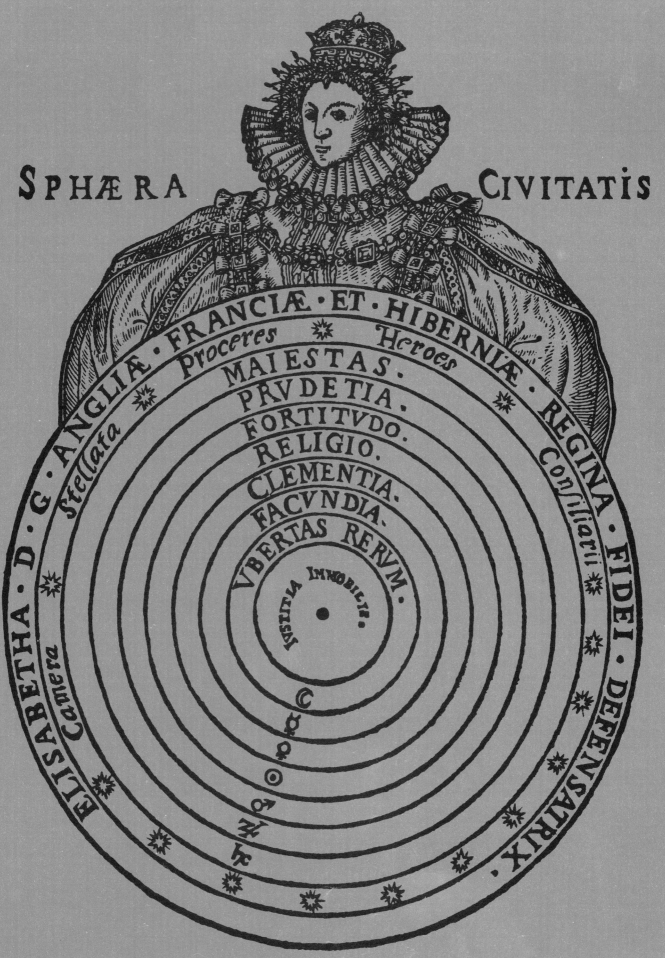

an invalid might arise from the sickbed, without the physician ever so much as seeing the patient.

During the sixteenth century, astrological medicine reached its apex in the career and astounding person of a physician who called himself Paracelsus but whose real name was a tongue-twisting Theophrastus Philippus Aureolus Bombast von Hohenheim. Born in eastern Switzerland, he was an inveterate wanderer who worked for a while in the Tyrol's mines and, though he probably never earned a doctor's diploma, served as a surgeon for the Venetian army. Wherever he went, he quarreled: He outraged physicians by refusing to take the traditional Hippocratic oath; he tossed respected volumes of medical learning into a public bonfire; he was forced out of Basel after roundly berating a judge who had declined to uphold his demand for a patient's fee.

In his belief in heavenly influences on health, Paracelsus was very much a man of his time. "Consider this carefully," he admonished. "What can a remedy for women's wombs accomplish if you are not guided by Venus? What can your remedy for the brain accomplish without the guidance of the Moon?" Yet at the same time, he held that some illnesses were generated from within, by negative emotions such as hatred or envy—an early recognition, perhaps, of psychosomatic disease. Furthermore, he maintained that the stars were but the servants of God, who had, in his wisdom, provided for every ailment a specific cure that went far beyond mystical mutterings about bodily humors. Paracelsus encouraged the medical world to seek those cures and so, in a sense, opened the way for modern medicine.

As the eventful sixteenth century entered its dying years, citizens of the West were touched in all their affairs by the science of the skies. They were ruled by monarchs who consulted astrologers on matters great and small; their spiritual lives were shaped by prelates profoundly persuaded by the advisers who found their answers in the stars; they marched to war according to the timing set by heavenly clocks; they survived or succumbed to ailments that were treated by physicians who looked not to fever charts but to horoscopic tables; they were instructed by almanacs as to when they should arise in the morning, when they should bathe, when they should hunt or fish or plant, when they should travel, and when they should marry.

Perhaps not least, the common coin of language and literature was indelibly stamped by astrological references. It was no happenstance that William Shakespeare, who tailored his history to suit highborn patrons but wrote to please the vulgar folk who jostled in the pits of Elizabethan theaters, packed his plays with astrological allusions in the full—and fulfilled—expectation that they would be understood by one and all. One of the many mysteries surrounding Shakespeare is whether he himself was a believer; it is in *King Lear,* after all, that the illegitimate Edmund derides the use of astrology as "the excellent foppery of the world."

But Edmund was a villain and untrustworthy. Elsewhere in that same tragedy, Shakespeare speaks of astrology with unequivocal respect. "It is the stars," muses one nobleman. "The stars above us govern our conditions."

FAMOSO DOCTOR PARESELSVS.

The Swiss physician Paracelsus claimed each person
had an astral body that was a conduit for planetary influences.
But he was a sensible medical practitioner and
pharmacologist notable for his treatments of ulcers and syphilis.

Reading the Sun Signs

Believers and skeptics may debate forever whether astrology is anything more than outworn superstition. Still, millions of people swear by it. Perhaps astrology owes its appeal to a universal trait: egocentricity. Astrology purports to tell us about what interests us most—ourselves.

Because of its life-giving quality, the sun is believed by astrologers to be the heavens' most powerful predictor of character. Thus the sun sign—determined by the sun's place in the zodiac at the time of one's birth—is the astrological designation almost everyone knows. Many people see their characters perfectly delineated in traits ascribed to their sun signs. Perhaps this is so because astrology expresses some mythic truth. Or it could result from the ease of fitting one's personality into the vague, elastic terms of most astrological language. A person who broods may be described as a typical Taurus, as might a jolly extrovert. In this way, conflicting qualities often rest comfortably within a single sign. Over the years, however, astrologers have come to some general agreement on what each sun sign means; these presumed meanings are presented in the following pages.

---

*Symbolized by the four basic elements of
earth, air, fire, and water, the world is ringed by zodiacal signs
in this illustration from a fifteenth-century encyclopedia.*

Aries

March 21 ♈ *April 20*

The great wheel of the zodiac begins its cycle on the vernal equinox, which is the first day of spring, as it rolls into Aries—sign of the Ram.

Astrologers liken those born under Aries to the season of spring itself, a time of awakening, emergence, shedding of restraints, impulses toward life. Arians are vital, instinctual, and young—the zodiac's perpetual children, youths in search of identity. As such, Rams are likely to be joyful, dynamic, assertive, outspoken, and brave. They celebrate life. The frenzied joy in the paintings of Arian Vincent van Gogh expresses the Rams' passionate love of life. On the other hand, they may also be intolerant, impatient, impulsive, and overemotional, deficient in the capacity for self-reflection and concentration, and inclined toward taking impulsive and ill-considered risks. Enormous energy is Arians' great gift. Channeling it outward, past self-absorption and toward enlivening the world around them, is the great challenge confronting Rams.

Arians hate constraint, boredom, apathy, and ambiguity. Nuance escapes them; shades of gray confound them. They are most comfortable with emphatic contrasts—black and white, yes and no, good and bad. Subtlety is foreign to their natures.

Confrontational, provocative, and at times even outrageous, they delight in testing limits and breaking rules. They despise pretense in others; if it exists in themselves, they simply fail to recognize it. They tend to prompt conflict and to revel in it, but their fights are usually over principle and their roles are heroic. Arians are the zodiac's warriors. Wary of joining groups and following leaders, they are also quintessential individualists, and they care deeply for individual rights. Astrologers deem it no accident that the Declaration of Independence was written by an Arian, Thomas Jefferson.

But Arian personalities are marked by paradox. Although they cherish their individuality, they can be disturbingly authoritarian and hierarchical. They prize their independence, but they tend to define their identities through interaction with other people—and self-definition is all-important to them. Thus they care deeply about relationships, even while they roil and plumb them for every last scrap of informative feedback. Flirting is a pleasant approach toward connecting with others, but if flirting is not feasible, fighting will do as well. For Arians, any form of contact is better than none at all, and even combat becomes a kind of telling intimacy. Of course, the point of combat for them is to win—on all fronts and at all costs. Competition adds zest to life; it helps slake their thirst for life. Not surprisingly, contentious Arians tend to have difficulty forming lasting romantic attachments. They are sentimental but apt to be domineering. They are passionate, to be sure, but their passions are inconstant. Their tolerance of boredom is minimal, their youthful attention span limited. The symbol of the Ram is as metaphorically significant as its season. It is the way of Aries to butt its way forward, scornful of obstacles, careless of consequences. The raw, erratic force of Arians can be destructive, astrologers say. Therefore, it is the task of those born under the sign of the Ram to direct their power toward mature and constructive ends. They must master the slow process of self-education if they are to bring to fruition the projects that they begin with such elemental enthusiasm.

Aries and Spring, a fresco dating from the early 1470s, adorns the Palazzo Schifanoia in Ferrara, Italy.

Taurus

April 21 ♉ *May 20*

In the fullness of spring, the inchoate energy of Aries resolves into the orderly pursuits of Taurus, the Bull. Taureans are as prudent and tenacious as Arians are careless and flighty. Methodical and faithful, even ponderous, Taureans peacefully tend and nurture spring's garden, bringing forth harmony from chaos. The glyph, or picture-word, symbolizing Taurus represents not only the Bull's head, but the womb—Mother Earth, spring's fecundity, sexuality in the service of procreation.

Taureans are the zodiac's sensualists. They revel in tastes, textures, colors, aromas, sounds. They love good food, comfortable living, aesthetic pleasures. All beauty delights them. But in a deeper sense, their sensuality brings them into close attunement with nature itself. They appreciate its loveliness; they are the wise stewards of its maternal beneficence. Astrologers believe Taureans were born to value, learn from, and care for the physical world—that they are materialists in the very best sense of the word.

Those born under the sign of Taurus are very talented at acquiring and consolidating wealth and power, which they seek mainly for the purpose of ensuring their own safety and survival and that of their offspring. They are not only earthy, but down-to-earth—practical, nurturing, home loving, conventional, conservative, moralistic. They tend to have great stamina and endurance, both mentally and physically. They also have a knack for focusing their energies toward a specific goal and moving relentlessly, if slowly, toward it. More often than not, Taureans get what they go after.

There is a negative side to Taureans' materialism. They may be possessive, controlling, and overconcerned with money, security, creature comforts, and convenience; they may even be prone to ostentation and avarice. In matters of the heart, they sometimes treat their partners as personal property, and they are capable of fierce jealousy and even violent anger. Depending on certain aspects of Taureans' astrological charts, they may be melancholy by nature, world-weary, brooding, and pessimistic, or they may be hedonistic and inclined to exaggerated extroversion and a lack of self-control. These unattractive traits are apt to come to the fore, however, only when Taureans misconstrue their true roles as custodians and nurturers. Stewardship must never be confused with ownership. If Taureans keep their balance and maintain their harmonious oneness with nature, they will flourish. If they stray from the path, they risk being consumed by greed.

Astrology holds that plodding Taureans lack agility and liveliness of mind. They are said to be bullheaded and fixed in their ways: stubborn, tunnel-visioned, inflexible, impervious to the opinions of others. But their slow and burdened mental gait should never be mistaken for stupidity. Unlike Arians, Taureans think things through. Their ideas are carefully conceived, planted, tended, and harvested like crops. Thus the sign of the Bull has produced some of the world's most profound thinkers, among them Karl Marx and Vladimir Ilyich Lenin, Immanuel Kant, Søren Kierkegaard, and Sigmund Freud. Even Taureans not gifted with single-minded genius often make reliable and conscientious workers because of their methodical and tenacious ways. Where others may swerve from a task or leave it undone, Taureans will persevere.

Anatomically, Taurus is associated with the throat and hence the voice. Many Taureans are noted for their musical talents, others for their distinctive vocal qualities. Some astrologers believe parents are well-advised to give Taurean children early musical training, since many of these youngsters have innate musical abilities. The great jazz musicians Duke Ellington and Ella Fitzgerald were born under the sign of the Bull, as were actors Lionel Barrymore, Joseph Cotten, and Orson Welles.

Taurus, the Bull, peers with penetrating eyes from the pages of a twelfth-century English book of psalms.

Gemini

May 21 ♊ *June 21*

After the heaviness of Taurus comes the airy agility of Gemini, the Twins. Taureans are bound to the earth, to the literal and concrete, but Geminis soar in the ether of abstractions, ideas, and—most of all—words. The Twins are the zodiac's wordsmiths, the lovers of language, the poets and bards, the verbal magicians. In the zodiacal quadrant where Gemini falls, Aries initiates life's energy, and Taurus gives it solidity and form. The Twins expand it, extend it, and turn it toward interconnection and communication. Astrology holds that they are the nerve synapses of culture, the facilitators who coordinate information and pass it along.

Gemini, ruled by the planet Mercury, weds a silver tongue to a quicksilver temperament. Twins crave experience, variety, mobility, change, company, banter, and intellectual play. They are endlessly curious and experimental. They loathe routine and fear stagnation. They are generalists; they can, and usually do, express cogent opinions on almost any subject, although their knowledge is apt to be superficial. Mentally quick, they nonetheless often lack the Taureans' capacity for deep, productive, singly focused thought. Befitting their sign, the Twins are skilled at seeing two sides, or all of the possible sides, of any question.

In love they are dubious partners, characteristically flighty and inclined to be overly intellectual, clinical, and cold. They may be sexually curious but are seldom truly sensual. Geminis prefer to keep their options open and their commitments light. For them, deep involvement is tantamount to entrapment.

The Twins are venturesome. A Gemini in a family is the member most likely to leave home in search of a larger arena for his or her talents and appetites. It is the Twins' bane that once they find their wid-er world they may feel achingly alone in it, despite their apparent extroversion. Given their charm, ready wit, and facility with words, they can easily present themselves as capable and confident. Only those closest to them are likely to see the insecurity that their confidence masks. The troubled actresses Judy Garland and Marilyn Monroe were both Geminis.

The Twins seldom take themselves very seriously. They are often actors, in life as well as by profession. They like to experiment with roles, discarding them as the glamour wears thin or new possibilities beckon. Gemini also boasts a number of diplomats and word-wielding politicians under its aegis—John F. Kennedy was one—along with a large number of writers, especially of long books. Thomas Mann and William Styron are among the many Gemini authors.

Gemini is the zodiac's adolescent. The advantage of this characteristic is that Geminis usually stay young in spirit throughout their lives. They retain their sense of humor and stay mentally flexible and open to new ideas. Nevertheless, the Twins fear age. Ironically, they often come into their own in their middle years, when they have learned to distill what is important from what is merely idly charming. Until they reach this point, they must struggle with the sign's particular demon: all talk, no action. Word-besotted Geminis are forever beset by ephemeral enthusiasms. For them, to discuss an idea is wonderful and magical, but to implement it is tiresome. They are the masters of the half-finished project, the thought abandoned short of fruition once talking stops and tedious work begins.

The Twins' manifest intellectual gifts often bring them great success with no real effort—but they are hard put to sustain it. Thus the chore of Geminis is to learn perseverance and cultivate depth. They must aspire to substance as well as style. They must take themselves, and their words, seriously.

Studded with golden stars, the Gemini Twins grace an illumination from the fourteenth-century manuscript, Tractatus Sphaera.

Cancer

June 22  *July 22*

With the coming of the summer solstice, the unfettered romp of Gemini is drawn earthward by the tidal pull of Cancer, the Crab. Cancer's ruling planet is the moon, linked in astrology to nature, gestation, motherhood, and the creation and preservation of life. Perhaps more than any other sign, Cancer represents the passive, receptive, but profoundly powerful and encompassing female force in nature—the all-nourishing, or all-devouring, mother. The Crab symbolizes the sea, cradle of all life.

As is typical in the ongoing dichotomy of the zodiac, Cancer's characteristics are mostly opposite from those of the preceding sign. Where Geminis are expansive, adventurous, and forward looking, Cancerians build boundaries, make homes, and gather things in for incubation, protection, nurturance, and mothering. Cancerians are family centered, tradition bound, tied to the past, fearful of the future and the unknown. Security is one of their major goals. While Geminis laugh at life, Cancerians tend toward melancholy and introversion. They are as restless and moody as the shifting tides. They find the real world threatening, astrologers say, and like to retreat into dreams and fantasies and to shelter themselves in the relative safety of the past.

Memory is one of Cancerians' special gifts. Geminis deal with experience by expressing it, Cancerians by remembering it. The taste and smell of certain biscuits were enough to call up the whole fictional world that Cancerian Marcel Proust created in *Remembrance of Things Past*. Cancerians love all things old; they cling to old possessions and old ways. They are wonderfully retentive; thus they make fine historians—caretakers and custodians of the past.

The symbol of the Crab is highly emblematic of Cancerian nature. Metaphorically, Cancerians have a hard outer shell and a soft interior. They need to feel safe if they are to put aside their brittle exteriors and expose their considerable vulnerabilities. They risk little and flinch easily. They are wary, defensive, and quick to withdraw into their shells. Like the crab, they approach the world obliquely, sideways. They tend to be exclusive in their social contacts; at the same time, they are particularly touchy about being excluded by others. And they never forget a slight. The Crabs' antennae are amazingly acute; another distinctive Cancer gift is great powers of perception.

Extreme sensitivity to their environment and to what others want or need makes Cancerians excellent business people. John D. Rockefeller and department-store magnate John Wanamaker were born under the sign of the Crab. Cancerians are also good resource people—the ones who always seem to know where the best goods can be had or the best services rendered. And they share their information generously—up to a point. Cancerians keep score. They expect their kindnesses to be returned. If they are disappointed, they become withdrawn and hostile. It is then that the Crabs' pincers come into play, nipping at the vulnerabilities they sense in others.

According to astrologers, the complex mother-child relationship dominates Cancerians' emotional lives. The dynamic may play out in any number of ways, with the Cancerian taking the role of good or bad mother, good or naughty child. In the child mode, Cancerians hunger for love; there is never enough to satisfy them. But they feel always compelled to doubt it and therefore to test it, seeing how much a friend or partner can endure before withdrawing or withholding love. In this regard, the generally unaggressive Cancer can sometimes be the pushiest of signs—as history witnessed in King Henry VIII of England.

The Cancerian man is likely to be very much attached to his mother. In his adult life, he may be greatly in need of security, protection, tenderness, domestic harmony, ritual and routine.

The Cancerian woman gravitates toward traditional roles of wife and mother, seeking outlets for her strong maternal instinct and her love of hearth and family. She is talented at creating a homey, protective atmosphere, a place of refuge—whether actually at home or among her colleagues at work.

At their best, Cancerians of both sexes are among the most loving of people, profoundly intuitive, and quick to grasp and respond to the emotional needs of others. They inspire and nurture growth—of children, animals, plants, projects, homes, ideas, cultures. Cancerian Buckminster Fuller invented structures to house the families of the future. Cancerian Emma Goldman, tough revolutionary though she was, still was moved to provide chicken soup to her colleagues in the midst of the Russian Revolution. It is Cancerians' task to find the safe haven in which their sign's exquisite sensitivity can bloom and flourish. Otherwise, the Crab may find itself dominated by the prickly, grasping side of its nature.

Cancer's Crab, also from the manuscript Tractatus Sphaera, seems to evoke its sign's protective nature.

Leo

July 23 ♌ *August 22*

At the height of summer's fullness, there springs from the nurturing cradle of Cancer majestic and fiery Leo, the Lion—producer, director, and star of life's drama. In Leo's passionate theater, pageantry, ceremony, and celebration are the order of the day. The spotlight is the Lions' birthright and applause their due. They live to perform and to create on the grand scale. But they have a dilemma: How do they differentiate between creating high art and merely living high melodrama?

For young Leos, life is the medium for art. The play's the thing. They want to experience everything—or at least to imply that they have. They need a watchful audience to feed their craving for constant attention and admiration. More-mature Leos come to value their creativity enough not to squander it in vain displays or emotionally exhausting scenes. They learn that they are not only the actors, but the playwrights as well, with a responsibility to direct their theatrics into productive roles.

Leos are both impulsive and emphatic. They are at home with absolutes, edicts, and flamboyant proclamations. They tend to construct rather overdrawn personal dramas around the issue of authority. They are quick to confront and challenge a power figure, yet they are wholly amazed if they suffer wounds in the ensuing fray. Metaphorically, Leos struggle to emerge from the mothering domination of Cancer; at the same time, they are apt to retreat to the authority figure for reassurance when the world proves too harsh. However cocky in their headlong assaults on life, Leos sometimes feel that only a parent can fully appreciate their brilliance or soothe their injured pride. As assertive as Arians and as clever as Geminis, Leos, like Cancerians, enjoy building. But where Crabs seek an edifice for security, Lions want a monument, a material testament to their greatness, their uniqueness, and their majesty. Exuberant Leo represents the first strong emergence of ego structure in the zodiac. Despite occasional fragility, Lions are confident—in their own ideas, their methods, their talents, and their expertise. Hence they are likely to give plentiful free advice, whether or not it is sought. They want to lead, to excel, to be noticed, and to matter, and they expect others to follow. They want to be somebody in the social sense, as well as in the larger cosmic arena. Willful, larger-than-life historical figures abound under the sign: Napoleon Bonaparte, T. E. D. Lawrence ("of Arabia"), Fidel Castro, Benito Mussolini, Mata Hari. Lions are also industrial leaders, literary masters, and pacesetters of style: Henry Ford, George Bernard Shaw, Carl Jung, Aldous Huxley, Robert Graves, Herman Melville, Percy Bysshe Shelley, Dorothy Parker, and Jacqueline Kennedy Onassis. Of course, show business is the Lions' natural habitat. Director Stanley Kubrick and rock star Mick Jagger are Leos, as were Cecil B. DeMille, Sam Goldwyn, Alfred Hitchcock, Mae West, and Annie Oakley. Leos are not shy, and they are seldom averse to self-promotion. Where they are, they rule.

Leos at their glorious best are great-hearted, passionate, generous creatures. They love loyally and sincerely, and they withhold nothing of themselves, possibly because they cannot bear hypocrisy or deceit in others. Mature Leos are excellent romantic partners, especially if they find mates who command their respect.

As befits their regal natures, Leos are devoted to high ideals; they are honorable, conscientious, courageous, and daring. Lions live for the moment, savoring life to the fullest. But for all their virtues, these children of the sun, their ruling planet, must strive to overcome an imposing dark side. Leos who fail to dispel these shadows can be demanding, domineering, insensitive, and destructive. They risk drowning in egocentricity and materialism, lacking both the desire and the capacity for spiritual development. Leos must endeavor to avoid the kind of exaggeration that can debase their many gifts.

Leo, the Lion, prances confidently in this illustration from a French book dating from the mid-fifteenth century.

84

Virgo

August 23 ♍ *September 22*

The cycle of the heavens, astrologers say, reflects the cycles of earth. Thus the wheel of the zodiac turns to Virgo, the Virgin, as summer ends and time nears for the harvest.

Virgo is sometimes associated with Demeter, the Greek goddess of the harvest, who made the earth lie fallow for half of every year. However, astrologers say Virgo's original symbol was the Sphinx, the mythological poser of riddles. So too do Virgoans question, turning inward to seek larger meanings about causes and purposes in life and looking for worthy goals to pursue. Virgoans are the zodiac's critics, its analysts, its purists. They are the servants, custodians, and perfecters of culture. As for the Virgin, she is a symbol less of purity than of hidden wisdom. She is woman in the fullness of self-possession—the high priestess, the healer, the keeper of life's mysteries. Her wheat sheaves symbolize the disciplined fertility of the earth. Enigmatic, self-possessed Virgo beauties include Greta Garbo, Lauren Bacall, Ingrid Bergman, and Sophia Loren.

Whereas Leos aim for the full development of the ego, Virgoans seek complete realization of the mind. They are logical, practical, and methodical. Their intellect subjugates their instincts. They have strong senses of order and organization and a love of the technological and the minute. Virgoan Samuel Johnson clearly exhibited the sign's passion for detail in compiling his famous dictionary.

Virgoans are theorists, masters of extrapolation and deduction. They are also perfectionists. They want their environments, as well as their lives, to be tidy. After summer's bounty, Virgoans put all in order for the coming winter. They separate the wheat from the chaff. They plan, sort, classify, and store.

Virgoans are usually very serious people. They are indefatigable workers with a strict sense of duty. Their need to serve, to be useful, is so strong that they suffer greatly when it is thwarted. This characteristic, coupled with their capacity for critical insight, makes them adept healers. Because they are often blessed with superb manual skills, they also make fine technicians.

There is an innate refinement about Virgoans, but also a nervous sensitivity. They are worriers who tend toward pronounced mood swings. In their negative moments they can be pessimistic, depressed, or even destructive. Virgoans are blessed with powerful creative drives, but these are sometimes handicapped by their need to control and perfect. At worst, their order-loving natures can make them cold, introverted,

punctilious, moralistic, overly fastidious, compulsive about personal health and cleanliness, obsessed with organization, and mired in petty details. Virgoans may ask large questions, but they do not take large risks. Unlike freewheeling Lions, cautious and conservative Virgins prefer small-scale plans to grand strategies. They are rooted in the present and amenable to change only after meticulous forethought. They will not willingly court disappointment.

If Leos are profligate with their love, Virgoans are extremely thrifty. They are rather aloof and repressed, even puritanical, viewing passion with a highly suspicious eye. They are demanding in their choice of partners. If Virgoans do not find precisely the right person, they will probably prefer to stay unattached. Virgo women are likely to find more fulfillment in careers than in homemaking. They are especially suited to commerce, science, and teaching. Confined to the home, they may channel their frustration into obsessive housekeeping and destructively critical behavior. Another pitfall for all Virgoans is their tendency to rehearse for life rather than to live it. As they see it, they are never prepared enough to take full advantage when an opportunity presents itself. In fact, astrologers say, Virgoans do themselves a disservice by not realizing that their fine intellects, fully developed or not, are more than a match for most challenges.

Virgoans' real challenge is to expand their perspective beyond details, to see the larger order and underlying pattern of creation and to marvel at its abundance and diversity. Virgoans who accomplish this will know the goals worthy of service. They will then serve with devotion, and in so doing will temper intellect with reverence.

Associated with the Greek goddess of the harvest, Virgo holds stalks of wheat in this fifteenth-century illumination.

Libra

September 23 ♎ *October 22*

By autumn the zodiac has come half-circle, and nature is midway in her cycle of generation and repose. All things seem to be seeking balance. It is the time of Libra, the Scales, which is the sign of harmony and justice.

If the first half of the zodiac was concerned with the development of the self, the second half deals with the relation of self to others. This is especially true for Libra, in which relationships are all. Librans are emotionally rich, gifted with tact and delicacy, and skilled at making and keeping friends. Because they are wonderfully careful not to harm or give offense, they invite confidence and trust. Through others they seek confirmation of themselves. But for all their loving natures, Librans have a talent for emotional distance—as their sign denotes. It is the zodiac's only inanimate symbol. Librans are at once involved and objective. They can look coolly on matters of the heart. At their best, they have the virtue of compassionate detachment.

Still, Librans' whole beings are centered on connections—not only between people, but between humans and the things around them. Like Taureans, Librans love beauty, but more as a backdrop than as an end in itself. Librans want a lovely setting where graceful events can unfold. To the extent that they are artists, their palettes are social settings and people their media. Charming themselves, Librans value charm in others. They love gossip and parties and make wonderful hosts. The Scales' influence is particularly strong in women who preside over salons where people of note connect with one another. Moreover, guests at such salons are likely to include a number of Li-

bran wits. Examples past and present include writers Oscar Wilde, Truman Capote, and Gore Vidal.

But people born under this sign are also social in a more profound sense. When scales are out of balance, Librans feel compelled to right them. They prize social justice and will battle mightily for it; however, their tactics will more likely involve compromise than confrontation. Mahatma Gandhi and former first lady Eleanor Roosevelt epitomized the Libran love for both social justice and peace. But they both had contemplative sides, as most Librans do. Librans value solitude as an opportunity for gaining perspective on the past as well as the present. In aloneness, mature Librans center themselves and find balance.

Like all the signs, however, Libra has a less-attractive side. While fully evolved Librans are judicious, immature ones are judgmental. A fondness for meddling can make Librans a source of irritation to their friends. Librans display great certitude when it comes to telling other

people how to behave. Unfortunately, they are not as certain of their own paths.

Vacillation is probably Librans' greatest fault. The Scales, after all, have two sides, and Librans seem always beset by the tug of opposites. They want to be with people; they want to be alone. They need solitude for balance, yet they are very vulnerable to loneliness. They are usually active people, but they must fight natural tendencies toward indolence and languor.

Librans are very concerned with making the right choices—a real predicament for such equivocal creatures. For some, this results in chronic indecision. They may also be overly dependent on the opinions of others and easily swayed by stronger personalities. Fortunately, the acute intelligence characteristic of Librans usually rescues them, in time, from the quandaries their vacillation creates.

Emotionally, Librans are particularly vulnerable. They are so eager for friendship, and their appetite for involvement is so vast, that the slightest rebuff can cause them great hurt. They are apt to feel martyred and badly used, and in reaction, to become overly strict and critical. Moreover, Librans who are out of balance are so needy of love that they may accept any relationship, no matter how difficult or destructive, rather than be alone.

Librans need to fight the indecisiveness that threatens to sap their strength and dim their charm. They must care less indiscriminately for approval, and they must pay as much attention to their own development as they do to that of others. In this way, with all things in balance, Librans will be able to elicit the best in themselves and stimulate the best in others.

Libra, symbolized by Scales, strikes a balance in life in this illustration from a fourteenth-century manuscript.

Scorpio

October 23 ♏ *November 21*

Autumn advances—a time of impending hibernation. But even as the land is chilled, the seeds within it promise eventual reawakening. This is the season of Scorpio, one of the most complex of all the zodiacal signs. Life, death, and resurrection are inextricably linked in Scorpio. Powerful, instinctual Scorpios sting and destroy, but as their natures evolve, they also rebuild and create. It is significant that this sign has not one symbol, but three—the Scorpion, the Eagle, and the Phoenix.

Profound perceptions and violent urges characterize Scorpios. They are often impelled by overwhelming unconscious forces that can find no coherent outlet. When this happens, they may become bitter and depressed. Scorpio's essence is illuminated by contrast with Taurus, the opposite sign on the zodiac's wheel. Taurus represents life at its simplest and earthiest and symbolizes sensuality serving the cause of procreation. In complicated, multifaceted Scorpio, sexuality is expressed as eroticism, even aggression—a union of love and death, or life and death. This formidable and sometimes perverse sexuality is a potential pitfall for Scorpios. Giving it free reign, they risk wreaking havoc with themselves and others. On the other hand, repressing it can engender terrible anxiety and feelings of guilt. Scorpios both male and female are deeply seductive individuals, driven by their erotic needs. They tend toward fiery, ephemeral passions and are prone to fierce jealousy and possessiveness. They are not well suited to marriage, which, over time, they find tiresome. In friendship, as in romance, Scorpios sometimes do not know their own power. They may sting others without meaning to, then

turn their venom on themselves in remorse. They may incite more fear than affection, and they tend to have a few intense relationships rather than a large circle of casual friends.

Unlike calm, methodical Taureans, aggressive Scorpios court danger and revel in risk. They have great courage and strength of will, but also a taste for conflict and a need to dominate. Whereas Taureans are tied to tradition, Scorpios are unorthodox, nonconforming, even revolutionary. They joyfully trample tradition and desecrate convention on their way to constructing something new and altogether different.

Scorpios' fierceness, their passion, and even their dark and mordant wit find sublime expression in many fine writers and thinkers. These include Fyodor Dostoyevsky, Albert Camus, Dylan Thomas, Evelyn Waugh, and Kurt Vonnegut. Passion, perception, and revolutionary creativity shine in the art of Scorpio Pablo Picasso, and insight and unorthodoxy combine in the science of Scorpios Marie Curie and Jonas Salk.

Each of Scorpio's three different emblems contributes distinctive qualities to the sign's nature. Aggression and instinct dominate the Scorpion guise: The deadly arachnid is destructive, viciously competitive, violent, and cruel. The essence of the Eagle, on the other hand, is the shrewd insight most Scorpios possess. With their

Eagle's eyes, Scorpios see what others miss. They discern hidden motives; they ferret out secret flaws and vulnerabilities. And they are not above exploiting others' weaknesses to their own advantage in their thirst for power and mastery. Among Scorpios' most important tasks, astrologers say, are ridding themselves of the tendency to be judgmental and tempering their insight with compassion. Those who manage this difficult assignment manifest the virtues of the Phoenix, the redemptive third aspect of the sign.

According to the ancient Greek historian Herodotus, the Phoenix was a beautiful bird seen in Heliopolis, Egypt, where it was a sacred emblem of the sun. Just as the sun dies in its own fires at night and is reborn every morning, so the Phoenix was believed to undergo unending regeneration, consumed in flames on a pyre only to arise again from the ashes. Like the Phoenix, Scorpios are survivors. Emotionally, they may perish in the ashes of their own destructive nature. But they can also transcend and transform; they can bring forth from the ashes new and shining life. During this phase their intense perceptions will bend toward compassion and understanding rather than judgment. Their eroticism will reach beyond passion toward love.

Scorpios have the capacity for high spiritual development, but, astrologers believe, their path toward it is the most difficult in all the zodiac. They must be alchemists, transmuting dark instinct and selfish impulse into purified desire, striving to discipline themselves and to curb and channel their great power toward constructive ends.

The fierce and complex sign of Scorpio is depicted in this illustration from a seventeenth-century Turkish manuscript.

Sagittarius

November 22  *December 20*

As the Archer shoots an arrow into the air, so does Sagittarius harness the raw energy of Scorpio and direct it toward a goal. Sagittarians are the zodiac's explorers and teachers, its zealous advocates fighting to expand and preserve culture. Half man, half horse, the Sagittarian Centaur symbolizes the potential for unifying the animal and the spiritual components of humanity, bringing them into harmonious balance to create the complete individual. Sagittarians try to create unity from duality.

On the wheel of the zodiac, Sagittarius is situated directly opposite Gemini, and the restless Archer shares certain characteristics with the restless Twins. Both are curious, fascinated by ideas, and enchanted by informa-tion. Both are adventurers, hating all things routine or methodical. Both want to break parochial confines and be citizens of the world. But as the astrologer Dane Rudhyar once observed, "Gemini has tolerance but no real understanding; whereas Sagittarius can have understanding even when he is most intolerant." Archers crave variety, whether in people, countries, or cultures. But even as they quest for experience, they are seldom satisfied with what they find. For Sagittarians, the point in life is the voyage rather than the destination, the search rather than the discovery. The outcome never seems to match the richness of the process.

Still, Archers love to travel and explore, mentally as well as literally. Geminis are the flitting mental prestidigitators of the zodiac, but Sagittarians are the true philosophers. They are fascinated by systems of thought and ways of organiz-ing information. They delight in the diversity of different cultures and disciplines—even when they view them, as they usually do, with a skeptical eye. They are also the collage artists of the intellect; they can encompass many unrelated interests and neglect none of them. They are tireless in pursuing knowledge to its outermost boundaries and sometimes beyond. Sagittarians are apt to be workaholics. They are the scientists who never leave the laboratory, the composers and writers who labor late into the night. They burn to know and to communicate what they know. But their work cannot be regimented by the artificial constraints of time clocks or bureaucratic routines. The Centaur's gait has its own unfettered rhythm.

Learning is Sagittarians' passion; teaching is their gift. The curious Archers are researchers and investigators—amassing all sorts of information, sorting it, and reprocessing it to make it accessible to those less mentally gifted than themselves. Best of all, they are able to pass along not only their knowledge, but their love of learning.

Denied actual travel, Sagittarians are adept at taking rich inner journeys and at transmuting them into art. The mental traveler emerges as storyteller in the work of such independent, if reclusive, nineteenth-century writers as Sagittarians Emily Dickinson, Jane Austen, and Louisa May Alcott. Less-strictured Sagittarian men of the same and earlier eras turned their actual journeys into great literature. Mark Twain, Joseph Conrad, Jonathan Swift, and Gustave Flaubert were all born under the Archer's aegis. Perhaps the ultimate avatar of Sagittarius was poet-artist William Blake. Indulging the Sagittarian love for working in more than one medium, Blake used words and paint in his fiery assault against all that would confine or limit the human mind.

But despite their questing spirits, Sagittarians lack the vast energy and untamed force of Scorpios. Archers are innovative, but not revolu-tionary. For all their restless-ness, they have a deep-rooted regard for conventions and customs. They value respectability, prestige, security, and comfortable surroundings. They may travel far and wide, but they want a pleasant home awaiting their return. Evolved Sagittarians are serious, but also jovial—even, at times, a bit madcap. They are honest, reliable, and enviably imperturbable. Exuberant but seldom compulsive, Sagittarians are interesting and amiable companions and lovers. When they are able to overcome their tendency toward intolerance, Sagittarians represent humankind's greatest potential for harmony and balance.

Sagittarius, the adventurous Archer, prepares to shoot an arrow in this illumination from fifteenth-century France.

Capricorn

December 21 ♑ *January 19*

Capricorn begins on the winter solstice, the longest night of the year and the first day of winter—a time of brooding, dark, introspective power. Capricorn is ruled by Saturn, the planet of cold rationality, and Uranus, the planet of strong will. Thus natives of the sign are apt to be defensive loners, spurred by a single-minded ambition that can carry them to great heights. Their progress may be slow, but it is virtually certain.

Capricorn's totem is the goat. When astrological symbolism arose, it took into account the two kinds of goats—the domestic one, gloomily chained to its post, and the sturdy and free-roaming wild goat. The two are emblematic of Capricorns' dual natures. If they feel chained and duty-bound, they are dour and taciturn. They may be good and responsible individuals, but never joyful ones. On the other hand, Capricorns who discover their own paths have a feisty strength and harsh humor that will help them climb any mountain.

Finding the right mountain to climb can be Capricorns' dilemma. They may reach a summit only to find that somewhere they wandered astray from the real goal. But if the correct peak is in sight, Goats will retrace their steps with only momentary discouragement before cheerfully turning again to their relentless climb. Still, they will climb alone, and they may well be lonely at the top. Elvis Presley and Janis Joplin were both Capricorns.

Capricorn lies opposite Cancer on the zodiac's wheel, and Goats share with Crabs the tendency to draw energy inward and to build structures around themselves. But while Cancerians seek to create homes and nurture families, Capricorns want to build empires, create political states. Driven, reclusive Capricorns who molded others to their solitary visions included Mao Tse-tung, Joseph Stalin, and Richard Nixon. J. Edgar Hoover was a Capricorn, and so, ironically, was the gangster Al Capone. Howard Hughes was among the Capricorn builders of great business empires.

Capricorns are seldom impelled by a

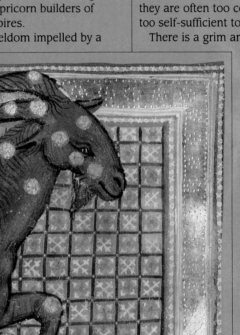

desire for money or possessions, nor do they take much pleasure in fleeting success or fame, however brilliant. They want durable power and lasting monuments. Their chilly rationality helps them keep control of their own emotions and of all situations that might distract them. They have a fierce work ethic and great managerial ability. They are capable of intense concentration and matchless determination. On the way to their goals, they are indifferent to obstacles or privations and are seldom swayed by the feelings of others. They press ahead at any cost.

Sensitive Cancerians are tied to the past, but Capricorns have no use for what is, for their purposes, dead and gone. They move inexorably on, permitting themselves neither regrets nor nostalgia. As lovers or spouses, Capricorns will probably provide material security, but at the cost of emotional drought. Capricorns make commitments only after weighing all the elements of a potential union. And they are often too cool, too solitary, and too self-sufficient to make loving partners.

There is a grim and gothic side to the sign of the Goat. It was Capricorn Matthew Arnold, for example, who wrote that there is "neither joy, nor love, nor light, nor certitude, nor peace, nor help for pain." The eerie writings of Capricorn Edgar Allan Poe also express this dark aspect. Even the Goats' humor is usually of the black variety, typified in the cartoons of Capricorn Charles Addams.

Capricorns are so insular by nature that they can get perilously out of touch with other humans. If this happens, their fate may be to seclude themselves atop their cold mountains like hermits. But it is not always so. The season of the Goat is not only the dead of winter; it is also the promise of spring. It is the glory of Capricorns that they can, from their hard-won summit, see sublime panoramas and inspire others with their vision. Heeding her solitary vision and her mystic voices, Capricorn Joan of Arc unified medieval France. And in modern America, Capricorn Martin Luther King, Jr., left behind the enduring monument of his dream of social justice. "He's allowed me to go up to the mountain," Dr. King proclaimed shortly before his death, "and I've looked over, and I've seen the Promised Land."

The slow and steady progress of Capricorn, the Goat, is portrayed in the fourteenth-century Tractatus Sphaera.

Aquarius

After reclusive and solitary Capricorn comes Aquarius, the most outgoing and receptive of all the zodiac signs. Aquarius lies opposite Leo, the sign that seeks full realization of the ego. The Aquarian dream is to merge that ego with the very cosmos. Aquarius, the Water Bearer, pours forth into culture the waters of new life. Aquarians are the mystics, the idealists, the reformers, the humanitarians, the innovators, the inventors—and, most of all, the communicators of their groups.

Aquarians are generous, flexible, freethinking, and curious about ideas that run counter to tradition. Given their humanitarian impulses, they are often strongly dedicated to the cause of human fellowship and are capable of total self-abnegation in the service of the common good. Many Aquarians strive to live more on the spiritual plane than on the material one. Nonetheless, their spirituality and profound insight are usually tempered by a degree of rationality. This fortuitous coupling produces great creativity, which may find an outlet in the service of an ideology. On the other hand, the restless and original Aquarian temperament may lend itself to many other interests, including science and technology.

Like Geminis, Aquarians are concerned with information and communication of all sorts. But while the Twins' favored form of expression is words, Aquarians love pictures—art, television, film. In their need to connect with the group, Aquarians always strive for speed and immediacy. The two wavy lines of their glyph sym-

bolize not only water, but fast-flowing currents of energy—or perhaps, in the case of Aquarian inventor Thomas Edison, electricity. It was Edison who invented motion pictures, the medium in which Aquarian directors D. W. Griffith and Sergei Eisenstein did their trailblazing work.

Aquarians push back boundaries and introduce new ideas. Aquarian Wolfgang Amadeus Mozart brought music to perfection previously unknown. Charles Darwin revolutionized thought about humanity's place in creation. Charles Lindbergh flew alone across the Atlantic when common wisdom held that such a feat was all but impossible. Aquarian writers Charles Dickens, Jules Verne, James Joyce, Gertrude Stein, and Virginia Woolf were all innovators in literature.

But as Aquarians go, Lindbergh—the Lone Eagle—was something of an anomaly, for most Water Bearers are not loners. Group-oriented Aquarians are usually very public people and natural politicians. Like Leos, they need applause, preferably from a worldwide audience. Successful Aquarians in public life range from Abraham Lincoln to Franklin D. Roosevelt, Adlai Stevenson, and Ronald Reagan.

A major Aquarian demon is oversensitivity to the group. This weakness can cause Water Bearers deep doubts about what their true feelings are. In turn, the uncertainty makes them fearful and even more dependent on the group. It is their task to look inward first, discovering their own thoughts before trying to assess the thoughts of others.

Another Aquarian risk is that of overindulging their mystical, nonconforming impulses. If they lack clear-headed rationality, they are capable of foolish, destructive attacks on tradition. Disloyalty, opportunism, and compromise are also potential Aquarian pitfalls. Water Bearers can be shallow, their genial exteriors masking an interior iciness. They may also be shortsighted and hampered by inertia. Just as Geminis think that to talk about a project is to finish it, so Aquarians think that to see a vision is to make it real.

At their best, however, Water Bearers are able to move from the abstract to the concrete. Beginning with imagination, Aquarians shape reality. And they work toward their most prized image, an all-inclusive and shining society in which each individual is a happy and productive contributor to the group.

The innovative ideas of Aquarius pour forth as water in this illustration from Tractatus Sphaera.

Pisces

February 19 ♓ *March 20*

Nearing full circle, the zodiac's wheel arrives at Pisces, the Fish. Those born under this sign inhabit the zodiac's twelfth house—the house of the ego's reunion with the infinite, the eternal. Pisces is said to be the most sensitive of signs—and the most vulnerable. Pisceans swim in the medium of dreams.

Pisces's glyph shows two fish, hooked together but swimming in opposite directions. The image is a metaphor for the Piscean character. One part of it swims wide, toward the edge of the universe, while the other dives deep, seeking some mystical substratum to reality. Ideally, there is a rhythm to the journeys: The Fish reunite and share their discoveries before setting out again on their separate missions. Lacking the rhythm, however, the metaphor signifies unbalanced extremes: the voyager wandering aimlessly and the unhappy introvert deep in the abyss.

The Fish as cosmological voyagers are exemplified by some of history's great students of the universe—Copernicus, Galileo, Albert Einstein. Einstein was, perhaps, Pisces at its most evolved—a complete human being, scientist and mystic, who joined intuition to rationality.

But not all Pisceans are so comfortable in the cosmos. Some are sensitive to the point of hypersensitivity—even, astrologers say, to the point of being psychic. (Edgar Cayce, the most famous psychic of the twentieth century, was a Piscean.) Piscean minds are so receptive that as children Pisceans may have trouble distinguishing their own thoughts from those of others. This confusion can spur a headlong retreat from reality as Pisceans seek to escape the clamoring mental static. They may then become withdrawn, submissive, anxious, and disorganized.

When it does not run to extremes, however, Piscean intuition is strong and redemptive, endowing the individual with intellectual and artistic gifts. On a larger scale, it instills profound understanding and compassion. And Pisceans are in touch with what the culture has forgotten or repressed—the magical, irrational world of unconscious longing and subterranean dreams. Pisceans have the ability to retrieve the dreams from the depths and return them to consciousness, revealing a cosmic unity that alleviates human alienation.

The Fish are the sign of wholeness. On the zodiacal wheel they lie opposite Virgoans, with their concern for minutiae. Unlike them, Pisceans are gifted with the ability to see the cosmos as a grand and meaningful design. Ironically, they may have trouble fitting into the external world. If certain negative aspects afflict their birth charts, they are prone to childishness, dreaminess, fear of responsibility, and feelings of discontent and victimization. Free of negative influences, however, they are cheerful and sensual and quietly appreciative of life's pleasures. Romanticism plays a large part in their lives. Romantic composer Maurice Ravel was a Piscean, as was master balladeer Nat King Cole. In love, Pisceans frequently act out their yearning for absolutes and perfection.

Pisceans are above all else visionaries; they often find it hard to live in the present or to interact with people less spiritually inclined than they. Many Fish have an acute tendency toward self-denial—and sometimes an almost messianic need to save. Indeed, they may be driven to share their spirituality—to save souls, for instance, whether the souls involved want salvation or not. Pisceans thus inclined would be wise to learn to impart their mystical vision of awe and wonder without forcing it on hapless friends.

The Fish mark the end of the progression of the zodiac from birth (Aries) to reunification with God or the cosmos, which astrologers liken to the sea.

These linked Pisces Fish appear in the calendar of the medieval Peterborough Psalter.

CHAPTER 3

New Views of the Zodiac

The sky was dark and clear on the evening of November 11, 1572, as a young Danish nobleman named Tycho Brahe walked toward his home and supper. Glancing up at the star-studded heavens, he spied a stunning new light, shining even brighter than Venus at its most brilliant. He stood rooted to the spot, unable to believe his eyes, calling on others nearby to confirm the luminous presence.

A gifted astronomer and mathematician, the twenty-six-year-old Tycho had recently completed years of study at the Universities of Copenhagen and Leipzig. Until that day, he had subscribed to the current belief that the stars existed in an immutable sphere of heaven—their numbers unchanging and their positions fixed in relation to one another. Upon seeing the new light in the sky, Tycho—and most other astronomers of the day—immediately embarked on a detailed study of what appeared to be a contradiction of that basic doctrine.

Using a new sextant he had just constructed at his observatory on the coast of Denmark, Tycho spent months recording the appearance of the light and its position in the sky. His observations, published the following year, proved that the object was immovable and was thus a star rather than a planet or comet. Evidently the heavens were mutable after all. (Future generations would identify the light as a supernova, a stupendous outpouring of energy as a massive star expired.)

But Tycho's interest in the object was not limited to its scientific significance; he also based a number of astrological prophecies on its arrival. Tycho predicted that the influence of the star would not be felt until after 1592, when Finland would see the birth of a boy who would grow up into a "valorous prince, whose arms would dazzle Germany, but who himself would disappear in 1632." This prophecy seemed to be fulfilled in the life of King Gustavus II of Sweden (also known as Gustavus Adolfus), who was born in Finland in 1594 and perished in 1632 after many military triumphs over German princelings in the Thirty Years' War.

Tycho Brahe was casting his eyes starward at an exciting time. The mid-sixteenth century saw the beginning of an age of incredible turmoil,

growth, and change in the twin studies of astrology and astronomy. An intellectual restlessness seemed to infect the brightest and the best in both fields, and the pursuits of these individuals would forever alter the way they and those practitioners who followed them looked at the world.

Some astrologers began seeking empirical methods to elevate their age-old tradition to the level of a science, while others chose to investigate the more mystical elements of the discipline. At the same time, ancient astrological assumptions were being increasingly undermined by the astronomical realities of the universe. Discoveries by scientists of the late Renaissance were revolutionizing humanity's vision of the stars and planets, and although astronomy and astrology had not previously been considered incompatible, more and more people had difficulty accepting the notion that celestial bodies influence life on earth. Like Tycho, however, a number of scholars in the scientific vanguard were themselves trained in both practices and tried to reconcile cosmological revelations with astrological tradition or to preserve some elements of astrology while discarding others that opposed new scientific findings.

The most jolting of the new findings had come from a Polish astronomer named Mikolaj Kopernik, best known today by the Latin version of his name, Nicholas Copernicus. A physician, mathematician, and church official as well as an astronomer, he also dabbled in astrology, becoming known at one point in his career as "the astrologer of Bologna."

But Copernicus is remembered foremost for his 1543 book, *De Revolutionibus Orbium Coelestium* (On the revolutions of the heavenly spheres), published as he lay dying. In this work, he boldly rejected the geocentric (earth-centered) model of the universe, accepted at the time, in which the sun revolved around the earth. Instead, he endorsed a heliocentric (sun-centered) scheme, holding that the sun stands at the center of the universe, orbited by the earth and the other planets.

A later generation of astrologers would find it easy to adopt this concept, once they realized it would not alter the positions of the stars and planets as seen from earth—the basis of astrology. "Whether (as Copernicus saith) the sun be the center of the world, the astrologer careth not," wrote one practitioner in 1603. But when the Polish scholar's notion first became known, it was regarded as a blow against all traditional thinking on matters related to the cosmos.

To be sure, Copernican cosmology was not a wholly revolutionary idea. The Greek astronomer Aristarchus had suggested a heliocentric model of the Solar System in the third century BC, and astronomers in ancient Babylon and the medieval Arab world had taken a similar view. But sixteenth-century Europe regarded this belief as an intolerable threat to the established order. Although Copernicus dedicated his book to Pope Paul III, the Catholic church outlawed his theory, forbidding any astronomical teaching that did not position the earth solidly in the center of the universe. So adamant was the church that in 1600 the renegade Dominican philosopher Giordano Bruno, a supporter of Copernican heliocentrism, was tried as a heretic and burned at the stake.

Copernicus's theory may have been suppressed, but it was hardly forgotten. Just a decade after Bruno's death, the Italian scientist Galileo Galilei began a series of astronomical observations that lent support to Copernican theory and laid the foundation for modern astronomy. Building his own

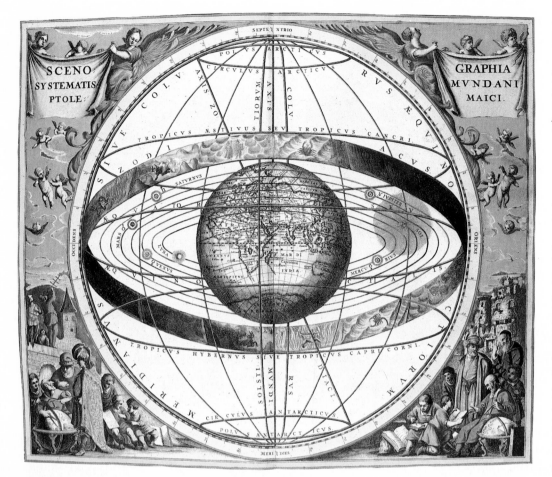

Formalized by the Greek astronomer Claudius Ptolemy in the second century BC, the idea of an earth-centered universe prevailed among Western astronomers and astrologers for nearly 2,000 years. The depiction of Ptolemy's system at left is from a "celestial atlas" published in 1708.

palled to discover that the tables of planetary movement available at the time were off by as much as a month in the date they assigned to this important event. Tycho found such inaccuracy intolerable from both an astronomical and an astrological point of view. For the rest of his life, he dedicated himself to painstaking measurement of planetary positions and other heavenly phenomena. Precision for precision's sake was

version of a new Dutch invention, the telescope, Galileo began to study objects in the sky. His startling findings, including the discovery of moons orbiting Jupiter, led him to conclude that the church-approved view of a geocentric universe was incorrect. The earth did not stand motionless at the center of solar and planetary orbits, he declared, but moved with all other planets in orbit around the sun. Soon Galileo, too, was brought to trial by the church, and in 1633 he recanted his heliocentric views under threat of torture.

But heliocentric thinking had already won important converts in parts of Europe where the Protestant Reformation had weakened church authority. One was Tycho Brahe, who favored a modified heliocentric approach. In his view, Mercury, Venus, Mars, Jupiter, and Saturn revolved around the Sun, while the Sun, attended by these planets, moved in orbit around the Earth.

Born in 1546, Tycho first became intrigued by astronomy at the age of fourteen, when he witnessed an eclipse of the sun. In the years that followed, he studied the work of the great Hellenic astronomer Claudius Ptolemy, eagerly read contemporary books on astronomy, and constructed primitive instruments that could measure the positions of stars and planets. In 1563, when he was only seventeen, he observed a conjunction of Jupiter and Saturn and was ap-

a way of life for Tycho, and he became known throughout Europe for his design of stargazing instruments that set new standards of mathematical accuracy for astronomers and astrologers alike.

As a young man, Tycho ventured an astrological prophecy that was to be vindicated more than a century later. Based on calculations concerning Leo and Cancer, "two of the zodiacal signs that are reckoned by Ptolemy 'suffocating and pestilent,' " he correctly foretold the coming of a great plague that would ravage Europe in 1665. He had less luck with a prediction, written in verse in 1566, declaring that an eclipse of the moon in October of that year portended the death of the Turkish sultan. Tycho was later distressed to learn that the sultan had actually died some time before the eclipse took place.

Probably the most significant celestial event in Tycho's career was the supernova that appeared near the constellation Cassiopoeia in 1572. When word of the young astronomer's findings on the star reached King Frederick II of Denmark in 1576, the monarch offered a splendid reward: He proposed to build a home and an observatory for Tycho on the 2,000-acre island of Hven, near Elsinore, and included in the package lavish annual grants to support the astronomer's studies.

Tycho gratefully accepted and chose an astrologically propitious date to begin construction of the complex. He outfitted the observatory with astronomical measuring instruments of his own design. Although he never peered through a telescope—the device was not invented until after his death—scientists still marvel at the accuracy of his observational work. The fame of the Hven observatory drew students from all over Europe, and Tycho enjoyed the life of a prosperous, productive, and respected scholar until 1596, when a new king, Christian IV, withdrew the Danish government's financial support. Tycho responded by abandoning his observatory and his native land. He moved to Prague in 1599, where he lived out the last two years of his life as court astronomer and astrologer to Emperor Rudolf II.

Tycho had mixed feelings about astrology as it was practiced in his day. In a letter dated 1587, he wrote, "I dislike spending my time on astrology and prophecies; these are worthless occupations. My taste is for astronomy." From the context of this complaint, it appears that Tycho

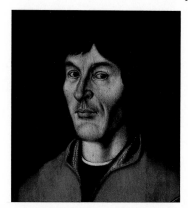

Polish astronomer Nicholas Copernicus (left), the first modern European to challenge Ptolemy's conception of an earth-centered universe, concluded that the earth and the other planets revolve around the sun. Copernicus published his description of a heliocentric universe in 1543, which touched off a long series of disputes between astronomers and powerful Church officials, who insisted that the earth stood immovable at the center of creation.

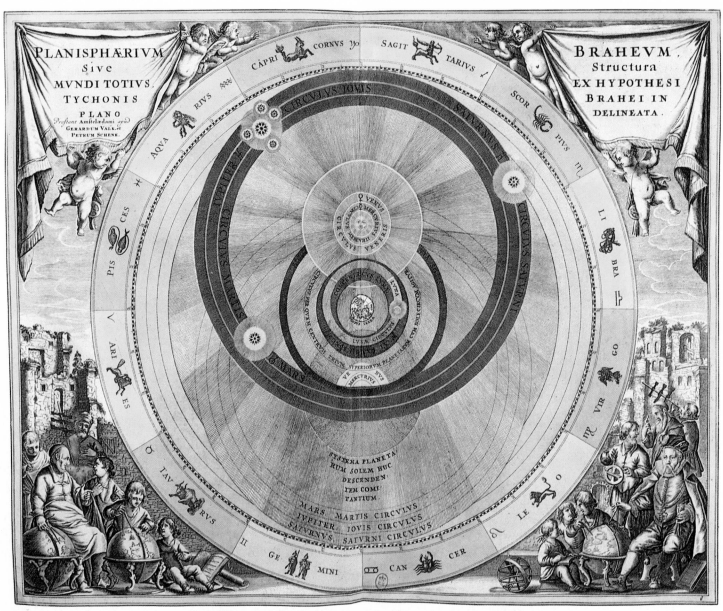

In this artful compromise between the Ptolemaic and Copernican systems, the sun revolves around the earth while the other planets circle the sun. The author of this view, Danish scientist Tycho Brahe (opposite), was a leading sixteenth-century astronomer.

was objecting to the burdensome duties of drawing up annual astrological forecasts for his royal patron and frequently consulting the charts to advise the king on one plan or another, or on the future of the dynasty. Certainly Tycho did not reject the value of all astrological work. He saw limitations to the study, but noted that although the predictions of his contemporaries were often wrong, some essential truths lay at the core of astrology. In a 1574 lecture at the University of Copenhagen, he warned, ''We cannot deny the influence of the stars without disbelieving in the wisdom of God.'' And while he understood that astrologers were fallible human beings, he still valued the art that they practiced. ''Astrology,'' he advised, ''is not a delusive science when

kept within bounds and not abused by ignorant people.''

In his post at the Prague observatory, Tycho was aided by a brilliant assistant twenty-five years his junior, the German astronomer and astrologer Johannes Kepler. It was a pairing that would revolutionize science, for in Kepler's capable hands, the data Tycho had spent a lifetime collecting would eventually prove Copernicus's theory of a heliocentric universe and pave the way for Isaac Newton's laws of gravitation, inertia, and motion.

Just as Kepler's mathematical work on the movement of the planets drew heavily on Tycho's careful astronomical observations, so did the young German's views on astrology echo his Danish master's combination of skepticism and

Tycho Brahe's specially designed observatory, built with royal funds in 1576 on the Danish island of Hven, set new standards for precision in astronomical research.

belief. Like Tycho, Kepler resented some of the astrological drudgery—producing predictions on demand for his employers, casting horoscopes for paying clients—that was expected of him at various points in his career. Forced at times to rely for his living on the practice of elementary astrology when he would rather have been devoting his energies to greater challenges, Kepler once complained, "Mother Astronomy would certainly starve if daughter Astrology did not earn the bread for both." He referred to astrology as a "dirty puddle" that any rigorous-minded mathematician would be reluctant to step in.

But these expressions of scorn were directed more toward the astrological practices of the day than toward the art itself. Kepler always hoped that a new astrology, one that existed as an exact empirical science, would one day evolve. Despite his discontent with astrology, however, Kepler prac-

A contemporary portrait of Tycho Brahe conceals a singular facial feature: Having lost a section of his nose in a duel, the versatile Danish astronomer fashioned and wore an artful copper replacement for the missing flesh.

ticed it with consummate skill, sometimes surprising himself with the apparent accuracy of his predictions.

Early in his career, before his association with Tycho, Kepler taught mathematics and astronomy at the Academy in Graz, a Lutheran secondary school in Upper Styria, in what is now southeastern Austria. With the job came the duty of compiling the school's annual almanac. In his first effort as an almanac prognosticator, Kepler concerned himself primarily with weather predictions and agricultural advice. However, in addition to forecasting a record cold wave, he ventured to predict a Turkish invasion of his country. Six months after these prophecies appeared in print, he wrote to a friend: "So far the almanac's predictions are proving correct. There is an unheard-of cold in our land. In the Alpine farms people die of the cold. It is reliably reported that when they arrive home and blow their noses, the noses fall off. . . . As for the Turks, on January the first they devastated the whole country from Vienna to Neustadt, setting everything on fire and carrying off men and plunder." Later in

Even as astronomers demystified the heavens, a seventeenth-century French nobleman, Count de Gabalis, was charting a novel way to search the skies for answers to earthly problems (right). His system was built around a triangle depicting the conjunction of the planets—the meeting of celestial bodies in the same degree of the zodiac. Questioners cast dice to get two numbers corresponding to the sets of roman numerals on the triangle; adjoining each set were two planets. A separate chart matched the combinations with the answers yes and no.

IOANNIS KEPPLERI,
Mathematici Cæfarei,
hanc Imaginem,

GENTORATENSI BIBLIOTHECÆ
Confecr.

MATTHIAS BERNECCERVS,
Kal. Ianuar. Anno Chr.

M DC. XXVII

In 1609, the German astronomer Johannes Kepler published his revolutionary findings that the planets orbit the sun in elliptical paths and that their speeds increase as they near the sun.

his career, Kepler cast the horoscope of the great German military leader Albrecht von Wallenstein and predicted "fearful disorders" for the country in March 1634. Wallenstein's assassination in late February of that year indeed brought about just the sort of political upheaval that the astrologer had foretold.

With successes like those to his credit, it is hardly surprising that while Kepler saw many faults in the practice of astrology, he defended its validity. He wrote a number of serious treatises on the subject. One of them included a warning to skeptical "theologians, physicians, and philoso-

phers" that "while justly rejecting the stargazers' superstitions, they should not throw out the child with the bathwater." Later he declared that "belief in the effect of the constellations derives in the first place from experience, which is so convincing that it can be denied only by those who have not examined it," and Kepler further concluded, "No one should regard it as impossible that from the follies and blasphemies of astrologers may emerge a sound and useful body of knowledge."

Kepler's own career is a classic example of an intellectual journey to useful knowledge. When he first began studying the orbits of the planets, he accepted the universal belief that heavenly bodies follow circular routes. This belief, based on the concept of the circle as a mathematically and spiritually perfect shape, had been shared by generations of astrologers and astronomers, from the geocentric Ptolemy to the heliocentric Copernicus. Kepler was fascinated by the ancient Greek idea that the circular orbits of the planets define a series of concentric spheres whose rotation produces the harmonious "music of the spheres."

For Pythagoras, the Greek mathematician and mystical philosopher who introduced the idea, this astronomical harmony was part of a complex system of numerical and geometrical relationships that expressed the essential truths of all existence. Inspired by the Pythagorean view of the universe, Kepler set out to demonstrate that the orbits of the planets were arranged according to a divine plan of geometrical harmony, with the distances between the planetary spheres precisely calibrated to accommodate the five solids in three-dimensional geometry that can fit perfectly inside a sphere.

In 1596, Kepler set out his theory in a book titled *Mysterium Cosmographicum* (Cosmic mystery). He described an eight-sided octahedron enclosing the orbit of Mercury, a twenty-sided icosahedron nested between Venus and Earth, a twelve-sided dodecahedron between Earth and Mars, a four-sided tetrahedron between Mars and Jupiter, and a cube between Jupiter and Saturn. Kepler did not believe that these figures literally existed in space, but he was

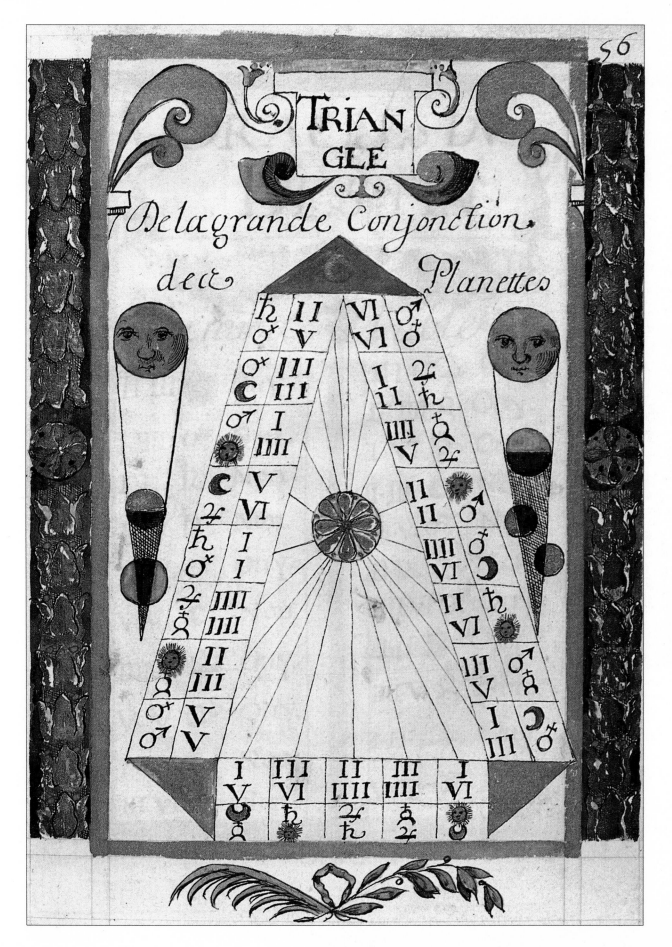

passionately devoted to the idea that the mathematical perfection he sought to impose on the Solar System was a true representation of the relationships among the planetary orbits. He believed, in fact, that he had been granted a holy vision of geometrical perfection in nature reflecting the spiritual perfection of the creator. "Geometry," he wrote, "existed before the Creation, is co-eternal with the mind of God, *is God himself.*"

Later in his life, Kepler looked back on his universe of nested spheres and perfect polyhedrons and dismissed it scornfully as an ignorant "astrological fancy." The march of scientific progress would have been slower, though, without Kepler's fancy. It was his effort to validate this vision of the Solar System that led him to plunge deeply into mathematical analysis of the data from Tycho's observations—an undertaking that gave birth to his famous laws of planetary motion. These laws supplied the first accurate picture of the Solar System, explaining that the planets move around the sun along elliptical paths. Like Tycho's studies of the new star of 1572, the insight rocked astronomy and astrology. The new star had demonstrated that the heavens were not unchanging; elliptical orbits replaced the perfect circles that had supposedly marked the

A contemporary of Kepler, the Florentine scholar Galileo Galilei affirmed that the earth revolves around the sun— a view Rome forced him to recant in 1633.

planets as divinely ordained signs that affected human life.

Astrologers, however, held that Kepler's reshaping of the cosmos was not a fatal blow, since astrological calculations are based on the positions of the planets relative to the earth, not on the shapes of their orbits. Furthermore, Kepler noted that planets move faster when they are closer to the sun, and he theorized that the sun controls their orbits with emanations of some unseen power, an idea that anticipated Newton's formulation of the law of gravity. The concept of one heavenly body controlling another by means of an invisible force seemed to vindicate the astrological belief in planetary influences. Kepler's work may have overthrown the old cosmology, but astrology continued to thrive in his new universe.

Kepler published his explanation of planetary motion in 1609, the same year in which Galileo constructed his first telescope and embarked on the investigations that would set him on a collision course with church authorities. Not yet a decade old, the seventeenth century was shaping up as an extraordinarily rich period in the history of astronomy. It reached its scientific climax in 1687 with the publication of Isaac Newton's *Philosophiae Naturalis Principia Mathematica* (Mathematical principles of natural phi-

losophy). In this book, the great English physicist and mathematician explained the powerful emanations suggested by Kepler as the gravitational force that holds the Solar System together and makes it possible to predict the precise influence exerted by one heavenly body on another.

Meanwhile, astrology grew increasingly estranged from science. The prevailing view among European intellectuals and savants was summed up in 1668 by the German astronomer and mathematician Tobias Beutel in his book *Arboretum Mathematicum.* "We know by experience that there are many instances when astrologers made correct forecasts," he wrote, "but there have been hundreds upon hundreds of failures. On the whole we should not trust horoscopes and no Christian man should fear or hope by reason of what his horoscope tells him." Soon many European believers in astrology went underground, often joining occult groups or secret societies such as the Freemasons and Rosicrucians, where interests in magic and things supernatural were freely pursued.

As part of popular culture, however, astrology's influence continued unabated, especially in England. From Shakespeare's plays in the late 1500s to Jonathan Swift's satires in the early 1700s, English literature overflows with references to astrological practices and beliefs. And one form of popular literature was singularly devoted to the subject: Astrological almanacs enjoyed sustained success throughout most of the seventeenth century.

Almanacs sold by the millions. Priced as low as twopence a copy, appealing to readers from all walks of life, these pocket-size guides at times outsold even the Bible. Most almanacs were built around three basic elements—a calendar highlighting religious holidays and other notable dates; a listing of the year's astronomical events, such as planetary conjunctions and eclipses of the sun and moon; and a prognostication setting forth astrological predictions

Soon after the telescope was invented in Holland, Galileo fashioned his own (above) and proceeded to make major contributions to the knowledge of the heavens. He studied the surface and phases of the moon, discovered moons orbiting Jupiter, and observed sunspots. The astrolabe shown below is believed to be the same one that was used by Galileo to measure the angles of celestial bodies above the horizon.

for the year. Around this core material, compilers included such widely varying contents as listings of markets and fairs, highway maps, gardening tips, and medical advice. Some guides, aimed at readers in particular professions, included specialized features: sample legal documents, stagecoach and freight-wagon schedules, tables of weights and measures for various commodities, and information on surveying, farming, seafaring, and other occupations. Such everyday matters as what to eat and drink, how much to sleep, and when to bathe were often included along with weather forecasts, tidbits of historical information, lists of the nation's nobility, poetry, fiction, humor, advertisements, and astrological advice on the best times for bleeding, purging, and other medical matters.

Sexual advice was a frequent almanac topic; astrologers offered married couples counsel on the ideal times of the year for sexual intercourse. Men were often advised "to be as a husband to thy wife" when the moon was in the sign of Sagittarius, and one almanac recommended "a lusty squab fat bedfellow" in the month of January, adding that December and February were also good months for intimate encounters. William Ramsey, a physician and astrologer, urged male readers of his almanac to avoid prostitutes during the summer months, when the danger of contracting venereal diseases was especially severe. Other astrologers offered

recipes for herbal contraceptives and aphrodisiacs (and for anaphrodisiacs for those times when the stars favored abstinence), and some sold charms known as sigils, said to endow the owner with magical powers of sexual attraction.

One astrologer, Richard Saunders, used his almanac to promote his belief in the improvement of the human race by scientific breeding. Noting that many farmers followed a livestock breeding schedule dictated by the stars and planets, he suggested that similar astrological scheduling of human reproduction could produce a race of "heroic spirits and famous worthies of valour and learning."

Almanacs did not always limit themselves to everyday domestic concerns. Some astrologers used their booklets to share their views on politics. During the English Civil War of the 1640s, for example, astrologer George Wharton was arrested for using his almanac to endorse King Charles I and the Royalist cause. After six months in prison, Wharton escaped and published another political almanac he had composed in his cell. Two of Wharton's colleagues, William Lilly and John Booker, supported the other side in the Civil War, predicting victory on the part of Oliver Cromwell's Puritan revolutionaries. The astrologers were once invited to join the troops, and encouraging passages from Lilly's almanac were often read to the soldiers before battle. A follower of Charles I was heard to lament that the

A precursor to the printed almanac was the so-called clog almanac, a stick of wood, brass, or horn that was notched with the lunar calendar. Such almanacs, widely used in Europe until the sixteenth century, were often hung near the hearth.

A Hand-Painted Almanac

Before the introduction of printing presses put almanacs into general circulation, the public often got their astrological and meteorological advice from xylographs—long strips of vellum, decorated with paintings or woodcuts, that were accordion-folded into tidy packages designed to be used year after year.

The early-sixteenth-century English xylograph shown here has thirty-six hand-painted panels, each of them four inches square; there are eighteen panels on each side. On one side *(left)*, twelve of the panels depict the zodiac signs. On the opposite side of the xylograph, twelve panels deal with the weather and what it may portend,

month by month. For March *(below)*, the author warned that thunder presaged a "grete battayle" and "lyttyll corne"—presumably a bad harvest—and illustrated both outcomes.

For each month there is also a calendar *(bottom)*, on which saints' days are highlighted. The red lines point to days of greater import than the black, in a system that designates the days of the week by the first seven letters of the alphabet. A fish is indicative of a fast day, the one in March immediately preceding the Annunciation of the Blessed Virgin. Still other numbers on the calendars could be used to calculate movable feast days such as Easter.

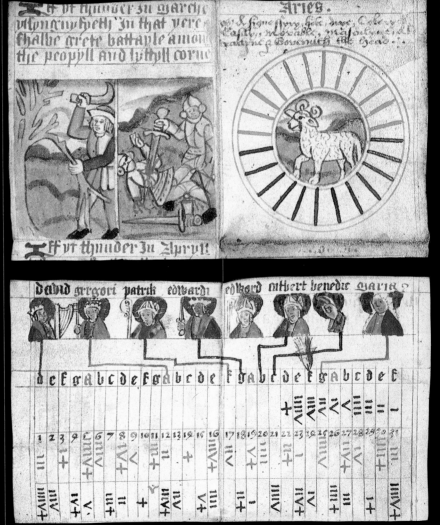

103

The seventeenth-century English astrologer William Lilly
displays a birth chart bearing the Latin words non cogunt—shorthand
for his view that "the stars incline, they do not compel."

two practitioners "led the commons of this kingdom, as bears . . . are led by the nose with bagpipes before them."

In addition to their multiple roles as political commentators, medical advisers, matchmakers, marriage counselors, and prognosticators, almanac writers often cast themselves as moral guardians and voices of social conscience. The virtues of hard work and the evils of idleness were recurring themes in their journals. It was common for astrological prophecies of disease, bad harvests, social upheavals, and other disasters to be accompanied by exhortations to the reader to repent and turn away from sin in order to stave off these signs of God's wrath.

An interest in maintaining the social order while at the same time promoting social justice led astrologers to offer moral advice to readers both rich and poor. On the one hand, the wealthy were urged to honor their obligations to the less fortunate, to practice charity and benevolence, and to remember that they were answerable to heaven for the uses they made of their earthly goods. "I tell thee, thy riches are not thy own, thou hast only a share of them for a short time," warned astrologer Vincent Wing. On the other hand, the poor were advised to accept their position in life and to remain courteous and submissive to those of higher social standing. "God keep us this year, and for ever, in due obedience to our superiors," wrote astrologer George Parker, echoing the reverence for wealth and position expressed by many of his colleagues. Little tolerance was shown for the greedy and corrupt, and almanac astrologers freely condemned landlords who oppressed their tenants, moneylenders who charged exorbitant interest rates, and merchants who hoarded commodities to drive up prices.

Religious disputes were also fair game. Many authors attacked Catholicism, a safe target in post-Reformation England, while others denounced the Anglican clergy or ridiculed Puritans, Presbyterians, and other nonconformists proliferating in English Protestant society. Some religious leaders struck back with charges that astrology was anti-Christian and that astrologers were setting themselves up in God's place by claiming to predict the future. Pope Sixtus V

had condemned astrology in 1585, and Urban VIII followed suit with a papal bull against the practice in 1631. In a time marked by bitter and sometimes bloody religious enmities, opposition to astrology was one thing on which Catholic and Protestant theologians could agree. Sermons denouncing astrology were common in English churches; William Lilly once remarked that he had been preached against from thirty London pulpits on a single Sunday. One Protestant clergyman warned that Christians should look at the world "not with an astrological, but a theological eye," and a group of clergy petitioned Parliament in 1652 to outlaw the practice of astrological prediction.

Despite the anti-astrology hostility of some religious leaders, however, many clergymen were believers in the prophetic power of the stars and planets. Several ministers published their own almanacs, using astrological forecasts of doom to encourage those who had strayed from the flock to return and repent; in 1628, William Laud, the archbishop of Canterbury, opened Parliament with a sermon that pointed to a conjunction of Saturn and Mars as an evil omen over the land. Astrologers sensitive to the religious climate of the times often took care to present themselves as good Christians, publishing declarations of faith and piety in their almanacs and reassuring readers that the stars were signs from God. Some defended astrology by pointing to astrological incidents in the Bible, including the Star of Bethlehem's guiding the Magi to the infant Jesus.

Dealing as they did with politics, sex, religion, and other topics of great public interest, astrological almanacs were in demand. Sales figures available for the 1660s suggest that one out of every three families in England bought an almanac each year. The guides also seemed to be popular with the colonists in America, where interest in astrology closely paralleled that in the mother country.

Almanacs provided "readier money than cakes and ale," observed Elizabethan satirist Thomas Nashe, but the chief financial beneficiaries of brisk sales were not the astrologers but the printers. Almanac authors were paid little

Published in 1645, The Starry Messenger was one of several works that landed William Lilly in political trouble. Lilly, who openly favored parliamentary rule, used astrology for political ends, making thinly veiled attacks on the crown in his prophecies and warnings. He was arrested on nine separate occasions for his views.

about which side to take in disputes between the king and Parliament. On one occasion in 1673, King Charles II himself consulted astrologer Elias Ashmole about the most favorable time to deliver an important speech.

While astrologers could be found in almost every village and town in England, the esteemed of the profession worked in London. Perhaps the seventeenth century's foremost practitioner was William Lilly, whose notebooks record some 2,000 consultations a year at the peak of his practice. Lilly is best remembered for a telling prophecy that appeared in his 1648 almanac, *Astrological Predictions:* "In the year 1665 the Aphelium of Mars, who is the general signification of England, will be in Virgo, which is assuredly the ascendant of the English monarchy, but Aries of the Kingdom. When the absis therefore of Mars shall appear in Virgo who shall expect less than a strange catastrophe of human affairs in the commonwealth, monarchy and kingdom of England. There will then, either in or about those times, or near that year, or within ten years, more or less of that time, appear in this kingdom so strange a revolution of fate, so grand a catastrophe and great mutation unto this monarchy and government as never yet appeared of which as the times now stand, I have no liberty or encouragement to deliver my opinion—only it will be ominous to London, unto her merchants at sea, to her traffique on land, to her poor, to all sorts of people inhabiting in her or to her liberties, by reason of sundry fires and a consuming plague."

Three years later, in 1651, his forecast of fire and plague still awaiting fulfillment, Lilly published a pair of symbolic illustrations—he called them "hieroglyphics"—dealing with the evils that lay in store for London. One of these illustrations depicted corpses wrapped in winding sheets and gravediggers at work. The other showed a group of citizens striving to extinguish a roaring fire as a pair of twins, the symbol of Gemini, London's zodiacal sign, plunged headfirst toward the flames. Once again the astrologer warned of impending disease and destruction.

True to the prediction in Lilly's words and pictures, bu-

for their work unless they were among the most popular prognosticators, and even then it was common practice for publishers to reap the better part of the profits by continuing to issue almanacs under the names of those elite authors long after they had died.

Far from being a labor of love, however, almanacs afforded astrologers a far-reaching vehicle for establishing their professional reputations, advertising their services, and attracting new clients. People consulted seers on a wide variety of subjects, profound and mundane. Many wanted the help of the stars in locating lost or stolen objects. Young lovers asked for astrological forecasts of their marriage prospects. Gamblers desired tips on horse races and cockfights and advice on the best times to win at dice. Invalids requested predictions about their chances of recovery. Families sought information about the fate of loved ones away at sea or at war. Doctors and clergymen inquired about their chances for professional advancement, and politicians asked for advice bonic plague ravaged the English capital in 1665, and the blaze known to historians as the Great Fire of London swept through the city the following year. So accurate was Lilly's prophecy that a committee appointed by Parliament to investigate the Great Fire suspected the astrologer of setting it himself, perhaps in collusion with some foreign power. The committee members summoned Lilly for questioning, but the seer satisfied them that his foreknowledge of the fire came only from studying the stars.

By that time, Lilly was a wealthy and celebrated public figure, a veteran of more than twenty years as an almanac publisher and private astrological consultant. He had cast charts and counseled clients at every level of English society, from penniless workers to members of the royal family. Lilly's likeness, adorning his best-selling almanac, had made his face one of the two most rec-

ognized in England, second only to that of the king. During the English Civil War, Lilly was consulted by Royalists and Puritans alike. King Charles I, although he deplored Lilly's sympathy for the Puritan cause, admired the astrologer's skill and once said that "Lilly understands astrology as well as any man in Europe."

Lilly was born in 1602 on a farm in Leicestershire, about a hundred miles north of London. Although his father was a member of the minor country gentry, the family was always in the midst of a financial crisis: When Lilly left home at eighteen to seek his fortune in London, he bade his father farewell at the Leicester jail, where the elder Lilly was being held for debt. Young William soon found work as a domestic servant in a well-to-do London household. He was apparently highly regarded by his employers; upon his master's death, he began receiving a small annuity, and a few years afterward he married the deceased gentleman's widow. With her death five years later came a substantial inheritance.

At the age of thirty, Lilly began studying astrology with a Welsh instructor known to history only as Mr. Evans. Lilly described his mentor as "the most saturnine person my eyes ever beheld . . . much addicted to debauchery, and then very abusive and quarrelsome, seldom without a black eye." But he added somewhat cryptically that Evans also "had the most piercing judgment naturally upon a figure of theft, and many other questions, that I ever met withal . . . he had some arts above and beyond astrology, for he was well versed in the nature of spirits."

Not until almost a decade after his studies with Evans did Lilly begin practicing astrology in earnest, and he waited until 1644 to publish his first almanac, *Merlinus Anglicus Junior* (The young English Merlin). In that maiden publication, Lilly gave favorable readings to supporters of both sides in the Civil War and professed himself a friend of both the monarchy and Parliament. Although he later became strongly allied with the Puritan cause and

Sarah Jinner, one of the few women astrologers in the seventeenth century, published several almanacs that combined medical advice with radical political commentary. As a pioneering feminist, she offered tips on birth control and generally praised her sex—although she denied a desire to "usurp the breeches."

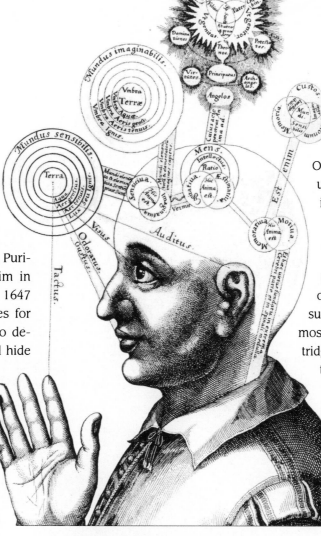

Spiritual forces enter the material world through seven planetary influences shown as spheres (left) in the complex philosophy of Jakob Boehme, a seventeenth-century German shoemaker-turned-mystic. Boehme linked the cosmos and Christianity; the sky was God, the sun Christ, and the light from heavenly bodies the Holy Spirit.

predicted the victory of Parliament and the death of Charles I, Lilly nevertheless made his astrological skills available to the Royalists. When the king was imprisoned by his Puritan enemies, Lilly assisted him in two failed escape attempts: In 1647 he accepted twenty gold pieces for casting an astrological chart to determine where the king should hide after breaking out of prison, and in 1648 he helped smuggle Charles some acid and a saw to use on his prison bars.

The enterprising astrologer emerged from the war with a considerable reputation and made a handsome living for many years from his almanacs and private practice. In 1665, Lilly settled into a country house in Surrey, where

In the view of Robert Fludd, a seventeenth-century English physician and mystic, the celestial world—which he called the macrocosm—is related directly to the spiritual and physical character of man, or the microcosm.

he devoted himself to the study of medicine. He received a physician's license in 1670 and continued to dispense astrological as well as medical advice until his death in 1681.

William Lilly's career coincided with England's golden age of astrology, and his death seems coincident with its decline. Over the next hundred years or so, the intellectual climate of the Enlightenment grew increasingly chilly toward astrology, and the formerly exalted practice moved to the margins of social acceptability, becoming little more than a disreputable form of fortunetelling. Physicians seeking to reduce the role superstition had played in their profession since the Middle Ages no longer consulted the stars when diagnosing disease, and serious astronomers ceased contributing to astrology, even if they did not abandon it.

Only a small core of believers continued to view astrology as a science; in general, skepticism and ridicule were the order of the day.

Jonathan Swift, the Irish-born satirist best known for his novel *Gulliver's Travels*, caught the mood of the age in 1707 with a savage and successful attack on one of London's most prominent astrologers, John Partridge. In an almanac of predictions for the year 1708—penned under the pseudonym Isaac Bickerstaff and bearing the subtitle *Written to prevent the people of England from being further imposed on by vulgar Almanack Makers*— Swift included a forecast of Partridge's death in the month of March. Soon after the appointed date, ''Bickerstaff'' announced the fulfillment of his prophecy and published a detailed description of the astrologer's supposed death. Although Partridge actually lived on until 1715, his almanac trade suffered: Many people believed the story of his demise. Some who knew that Partridge was still alive joined in the perverse fun by inviting him to his own burial and dunning him for funeral expenses. The episode succeeded in embarrassing not only Partridge, but the entire astrological profession, and it indicated the growing hostility astrologers would face as the century progressed. One historian observed that by the eighteenth century ''astrology had ceased, in all but the most unsophisticated circles, to be regarded as either a science or a crime; it had become simply a joke.''

Universities were gradually phasing the subject out of their curricula, and the prosperous astrological publishing industry dwindled as demand for textbooks on the subject

This *Rasi Valaya Yantra,* or ecliptic instrument (left)—one of twelve, for each of the zodiac signs—was designed to track the apparent path of the sun among the stars.

The most ingenious of Jai Singh's instruments is this huge concave bowl of stone sunk in the earth, across which two wires stretch, north to south and east to west. The shadow of the wires' intersection marks the position of the sun and the zodiac sign through which it is passing. Paths cut into the stone bowl made it possible for observers to move about and locate designated stars and planets in the night sky by peering through the cross wires.

The Maharaja's Giant Observatory

While European astronomers tinkered with their telescopes and astrolabes, the Indian maharaja Jai Singh II sought knowledge of the heavens on the grandest of scales. Born in 1686 and enthroned at the age of thirteen, Jai Singh studied mathematics and astronomy enough to be nettled by the inaccuracy of the astronomical tables he used—and he was powerful enough to do something about it. He built observatories at five of the principal cities of his realm, including Delhi and Jaipur, a city that he founded as a center of culture and learning. Begun in 1737, the Jaipur observatory was the largest and most accurate, and it remains the best preserved.

Believing that the brass instruments used in Europe were too small and unstable for precise measurements, Jai Singh built massively and in stone. His model was a fifteenth-century Persian observatory, but the instruments were largely of his own invention. There were numerous sundials, the giant of which—the Samrat Yantra, or supreme instrument, at Jaipur—was 90 feet high and 147 feet long. The device was said

The Nari Valaya Yantra, or circular dial (right), is another type of sundial found at Jaipur. The face of the sundial is divided into twenty-four hours of sixty minutes each; at the center, a style casts a shadow that marks the time.

to be accurate to within two seconds. Using other instruments, Jai Singh was able to predict with considerable precision lunar cycles, the position of various planets and stars, the eclipses of the sun and the moon, and the times of sunsets and sunrises.

Unfortunately, size is no guarantee of precision, and in many cases Jai Singh's measurements were no better than the measurements of the Europeans; moreover, the fact that his observatories were literally set in stone prevented him from making the corrections that are possible with smaller metal instruments. Nor did Jai Singh, whose astronomical references were mainly from the Muslim world, keep abreast of such important European developments as the invention of the telescope.

After Jai Singh died in 1743, a scholar wrote, "His wives, concubines and science expired with him on his funeral pyre." But his influence lingered for centuries. Until 1944, the Samrat Yantra at Jaipur—restored in marble in 1909—provided the city's official time. And to this day, Jaipur astrologers seeking to predict the coming of monsoons climb the stairs to the top once a year and search the heavens for clues.

all but disappeared. Occult enthusiasts at Cambridge University formed the Zodiac Club in the 1750s, but the society was short-lived. Practicing astrologers still made predictions and offered advice, but fewer of their clients were drawn from nobility or the scientists and savants of the day. Only ordinary folk regularly sought guidance from the stars.

The most telling sign of astrology's waning popularity was the decline in the sales of almanacs. By 1730, the last of the seventeenth century's elite astrological authors had died, and although their manuals were published posthumously for many years, only four almanacs were still available by the century's end. Of those four, only one, *Vox Stellarum* (Voice of the stars), had popular success. Originally issued in 1699 by astrologer Francis Moore—and offered by its publisher for more than a century after Moore's death in 1715—*Vox Stellarum* did more than merely endure. While other almanacs vanished altogether or scraped along with circulations of only a few thousand, *Vox Stellarum* sold more than 100,000 copies annually in the closing decades of the eighteenth century—an indication, perhaps, that the dismissal of astrology by Enlightenment thinkers had not completely abolished public interest in the subject.

The astrology revival suggested by the success of *Vox Stellarum* came only in fits and starts, however. Astrological notions were upended once more by a scientific discovery when, in 1781, German-born musician and astronomer Sir William Herschel announced the existence of Uranus, a planet unaccounted for in centuries of astrological calculations. Since then, astrologers have learned to incorporate that planet and two others, Neptune and Pluto, into their charts, even asserting that the discoveries resolved some old questions: The influences of the new planets, astrologers reasoned, accounted for previously inexplicable elements of an individual's character. But at the time of Herschel's revelation, any expansion of the Solar System threatened to topple an already tottering structure of traditional ideas.

Nevertheless, astrology rose from the ashes yet again. Perhaps spurred by a new preoccupation with ancient practices such as alchemy and magic, long popular in continental Europe, a growing contingent of English astrologers began moving away from the notion of astrology as a predictive science and embraced it as a branch of the occult. A small but enthusiastic group of practitioners advertised their services, and more women began to take up the trade. One adviser, a Mrs. Williams, would counsel only ladies at her home in London or, during the social season, at fashionable spas in the English countryside. But the most colorful astrologer of the time seems to have been Ebenezer Sibly, a patent-medicine manufacturer and physician who called himself an "astro-philosopher."

In an era when few astrology books were being written, Sibly was prolific. His works examined the occult sciences and such astrological traditions as the relationship between astrology and medicine. He claimed to have predicted the American Revolution, and he included in a 1776 volume titled *Celestial Science of Astrology* a "horoscope and symbolic representation of the independence of America." Sibly concluded that the new country "in time should have an extensive and rising commerce, an advantageous and universal traffic to every quarter of the globe and great prosperity among its people." In 1784, Sibly gained further recognition when he published the first volume of what would be a four-part work, *The Complete Illustration of the Celestial Art of Astrology*. The book, in which Sibly apparently plagiarized a number of seventeenth-century authors, contained horoscopes of prominent individuals and included a lengthy dissertation on magic.

Sibly's works may have whetted the appetites of astrologers hungry for publications that could fill the almanac void, for in 1791 a young journal called *The Conjurer's Magazine* was enthusiastically received. Originally designed to include amusing magic tricks, simple chemistry experiments, and a few short astrological features, the publication was soon reaching out to a more specialized audience. Its title was changed to *The Astrologer's Magazine* in August 1793, and the editor expressed his thanks to "our numerous Friends and Subscribers who have enabled us to contribute to the revival of Astrology." The revival was short-lived, as was the magazine, which folded the following year.

For several decades afterward, efforts to publish an astrology magazine met with little success, but in the 1820s the work of a young astrologer named Robert Cross Smith changed all that. Smith had come to London from Bristol to work as a builder's clerk, and he took up the study of astrology and the occult with the encouragement and financial assistance of a friend. In July 1824, Smith found employment in his new field as editor of *The Straggling Astrologer,* the first weekly publication devoted to the discipline.

Although the magazine had been on the market less than two months when Smith joined its staff, circulation was already sagging. To enliven the content and boost revenues, the enterprising young editor took the occasion of the publisher's vacation to announce in one issue an astrological technique for discovering "if the female you are about to wed be a virgin." The public's reaction to this titillating tidbit is not known, but Smith's publisher was outraged. Apologizing in print the next week, the well-meaning gentleman promised that in future issues "nothing offensive to the dignity of the fair sex will ever be inserted."

The magazine limped along for only a few more months, and by October of that year Smith was out of a job. His publisher, however, vowed to have another go at the astrology market and asked Smith to produce a new type of journal. Thus, in 1826, using the pen name Raphael—after a planetary angel who, according to Old Testament patriarch Enoch, presided over the spirits of men—Smith became the author of *The Prophetic Messenger,* a predictive almanac that pioneered the practice of giving astrological forecasts for each day of the year. While this newcomer to the almanac ranks did not approach the circulation of the venerable *Vox Stellarum,* which sold nearly 300,000 copies a year during the late 1820s, it steadily gained a following under Smith's direction. In fact, the almanac became so popular that numerous imitators began using the word prophetic in their titles as a means of stimulating sales. After Smith's death in 1832, one of his followers adopted his professional name and took over the editorship of *The Prophetic Messenger,* which continued publishing under a succession of "Raphaels" well into the twentieth century.

Smith's involvement in astrology stemmed from a larger interest in the occult, and during his editorial years he presided over a secret society, called The Mercurii, formed to study the subject. One of Smith's London acquaintances and a fellow member of the group was retired Royal Navy lieutenant Richard James Morrison. Morrison practiced crystal-gazing, but his main interest was astrology, fostered during a stint in the navy, when he studied celestial navigation and astronomy. After leaving the service in 1817 at the age of twenty-two, Morrison occupied the next thirteen years by writing occasional articles on astrology, performing some freelance intelligence work for the navy, and spending two years in the coast guard. He did not pursue astrology as a profession until 1830, when, taking note of Smith's success in the field, he launched *The Herald of Astrology,* an annual publication that he fully owned and operated. Under the name Zadkiel—after the angel who, according to Jewish rabbinical legend, rules Jupiter—Morrison penned the usual predictions and horoscopes and a host of general-interest articles.

In 1836, Morrison changed the journal's name to *Zadkiel's Almanack,* and he continued producing it for nearly forty years. Partially because of his military background and the fact that he was born of a distinguished family, Morrison sought to keep his identity secret. His anonymity was lost in 1860, however, when he published a prediction that painted the following year as "very evil for all persons born on or near the 26th August; among the sufferers I regret to see the worthy Prince Consort of these realms." When Queen Victoria's husband, Prince Albert, died as Zadkiel had foretold, the astrologer was vilified in the press. One newspaper demanded, "Who is this Zadkiel, and are there no means of ferreting him out and hauling him up to Bow Street under the statute as a rogue and vagabond?" Morrison subsequently sued one of his public detractors and won the case after a lengthy trial. The victory, however, was mainly sym-

Figures in Indian garb represent the constellations in this 1840 zodiac drawing of the western and eastern

hemispheres (left and right). It accompanied a horoscope commissioned by an Indian monarch for his son.

As a writer and editor of astrological literature in the early 1900s, Alan Leo made do-it-yourself astrology accessible to the general public.

bolic; the jury awarded him a mere twenty shillings in damages. Despite that additional slight to his reputation, Morrison remained until his death in 1874 one of the most influential astrologers of the Victorian era.

As the nineteenth century progressed, astrology and the occult became more firmly interwoven. While many astrologers still advocated a scientific approach to astrology, those who had revived and popularized it—Morrison, Smith, and Sibly, for example—had added a mystical element to its practice.

The mingling of astrology with other ancient traditions peaked in 1875 with the emergence of the Theosophical Society, a group formed to study theosophy, a religious philosophy grounded in mysticism. The society was started in New York by a Russian-born occultist and self-proclaimed spiritual medium, Helena Petrovna Blavatsky, and an American psychic investigator, Henry S. Olcott. Under their leadership, the group sought, through the study of ancient religions, philosophies, and sciences, to "obtain knowledge of the nature and attributes of the Supreme Power" of the universe and to develop the divine powers of man.

Madame Blavatsky, the charismatic widow of a Czarist government official, had traveled the world over and developed interests in Buddhism, Hinduism, and a variety of mystical traditions, including astrology. While stargazing was only one of the many esoteric disciplines that contributed to the doctrines of theosophy, it benefited immediately from association with this new cult. Theosophy was enthusiastically embraced in some intellectual circles of the day, and as a result, astrology regained a level of respectability it had not enjoyed since the days of William Lilly.

Although astrology was only a small part of theosophy, it became the consuming interest of one of Blavatsky's most influential followers, Englishman William Frederick Allen. A traveling salesman for a sewing-machine manu-

facturer, Allen first learned about astrology from an herbalist he was consulting for an illness. Allen became friendly with astrologers and soon took up the practice himself, using the pseudonym Alan Leo. In 1890, Leo joined the London branch of the Theosophical Society, and, with a fellow forecaster, began publishing *The Astrologer's Magazine*. Although the partners lacked journalistic experience, their monthly guide gained immediate popularity through a promotion that offered free individual horoscopes to subscribers. By 1895, Leo owned the magazine outright. He changed its title to *Modern Astrology* and was on his way to building an empire based on astrology. As his readership increased, he hired a small staff and eventually developed a thriving business that mass-produced individual horoscopes, provided simplified astrology courses by mail, and published a variety of books and periodicals on the subject.

Leo's writings were aimed at the general public, and though infused with occult jargon, they presented complicated information in a clear and straightforward manner. Suddenly astrology's advanced mathematical formulas were available for application by anyone of reasonable intelligence who studied the astrologer's unique guides.

Such entrepreneurial efforts brought astrology to the attention of a vast new public, influencing a fresh generation of prognosticators and their followers. Leo emphasized the theosophical, or spiritual, meaning of the horoscope—as opposed to its practical applications—and imparted an esoteric, occult flavor to the practice of astrology. While the scientific and mathematical elements of the discipline remained important to many practitioners, he helped establish a countervailing mystical tradition that reawakened interest in astrology throughout Europe. With his influence, those different approaches to the ancient tradition combined to lead astrology into the twentieth century.

Children of the Stars

Like many North American Indians, the Skidi Pawnee ordered their lives by the heavens. One of the Plains tribes, the Skidi believed they were descended from the stars. In their legends, a union of the Morning Star, probably Mars, and the Evening Star, Venus, had produced a maiden who, in turn, coupled with the son of the sun and moon. Accordingly, they spun an elaborate mythology about the lives of the celestial forebears that shaped their existence, from crop planting to the organization of their villages and even the interior design of homes.

Skidi dwellings were supported by four posts, for four stars most revered by the tribe, and faced east toward the rising sun. Each village was identified with a certain star; the villages may even have been situated according to the configuration of their stars in the sky. But compliance with the stars had its price: The tribe would sometimes sacrifice a young girl to the Morning Star to commemorate his trials in fathering the human race.

A Skidi Pawnee infant is strapped to a cradleboard crowned with a Morning Star design (left), and a Skidi chieftain's deerskin robe seems embellished with a firmament of stars (right). The ceremonial star chart shown above, painted on buckskin, depicts most of the constellations that were revered by the Skidi Pawnee; the chart was stored in a sacred bundle along with such items as corn, reeds, scalps, and buffalo meat, which the tribe believed had been transmitted to them by the star gods.

Casting the Birth Chart

Astrologers believe that an individual's personality traits and the general direction of life are revealed in the positions of the stars and planets at the moment of birth. The potential for creativity, for example, is thought to be determined at that instant. To interpret these possibilities and advise how such potential might be developed, astrologers depend on a tool called a birth chart. A typical format for such a chart, blank except for the twelve signs of the zodiac, appears on the opposite page.

A completed birth chart is a diagram of the heavens as they appeared on a particular date, at a certain time, and from a specific place. But such charts are not restricted solely to the moment of a person's birth. Because the planets' paths can be accurately predicted well in advance, astrologers can also draw up charts for future events—to determine whether a date and time set for a wedding, for example, would be astrologically propitious.

This celestial map differs considerably from a familiar geographical map. For one thing, its orientation is reversed—east appears at the left of the birth chart, west at the right. And the birth chart is constructed from a geocentric viewpoint; the Earth, symbolized by a small circle, is positioned at the center of the diagram and everything revolves around it.

The outermost circle of the chart represents the ecliptic, the apparent path of the Sun around the Earth. Imposed on the ecliptic is the zodiacal band. Each sign occupies a 30-degree area of the ecliptic, with zero degrees beginning at the first point of Aries. While the ecliptic has a total circumference of 360 degrees, when astrologers refer to a particular position on it, they cite the position within the sign—10 degrees Gemini, instead of 70 degrees around the circle as a whole.

Astrologers believe each zodiacal sign has a distinct meaning *(pages 79-91)* that outlines a range of moods and behaviors within the individual. The essence of each sign is said to be reflected in the colors that form a color wheel around the chart. Scorpio, for instance, is deemed an intensely emotional sign, and Scorpios are thought to be interested in things that are deep, dark, or hidden. The sign's color is blue-green, the color of deep water, symbolizing those things that are concealed beneath the surface.

During the course of a twenty-four-hour day, a different zodiacal sign rises on the Earth's horizon every two hours. On the birth chart, the horizon is represented by a line bisecting the diagram horizontally. The point where the horizon and ecliptic meet on the left side of the chart, in the eastern hemisphere, is known as the ascendant; the sign appearing on the horizon is called the ascending, or rising, sign and is thought to describe the person's outward manner.

Once the rising sign is established, the other signs are plotted in their established order counterclockwise around the chart. The sign that is setting on the descendant western horizon is referred to as the descending, or setting, sign. This sign, according to astrologers, reveals the individual's attitude toward relationships or partnerships. (On the chart shown opposite, the sign ascending is the first sign of the natural zodiac, Aries; Libra is the descending sign.)

Bisecting the chart vertically is a line representing the meridian, or the line of longitude. The place where the meridian and the horizon intersect symbolizes the location on Earth of the individual's birth or of whatever event is being charted. The point at the top of the chart where the meridian meets the ecliptic is referred to as the *Medium Coeli,* MC for short, also called the midheaven. The midheaven is thought to govern one's profession and public persona. The corresponding point at the bottom of the chart is the *Imum Coeli,* or IC, which is said by astrologers to rule the home, family history, and the need for security.

Preparing a complete birth chart is a complicated process that requires guidance from a number of sources, among them astronomical tables designed to calculate the horizon and meridian lines and to discover the positions of the planets at a particular moment. Such computations can be mastered only with instruction, patience, and practice, or by using specially designed computer programs. Or, in the time-honored tradition, a skilled astrologer may be engaged to draw up the chart.

Usually included in the astrologer's fee is a detailed interpretation of the chart and its many elements. Most practitioners will also offer guidance for the resolution of conflicts and the use of innate talents. Some of the elements from which an astrologer gathers and interprets information for a birth-chart reading are detailed on the following pages.

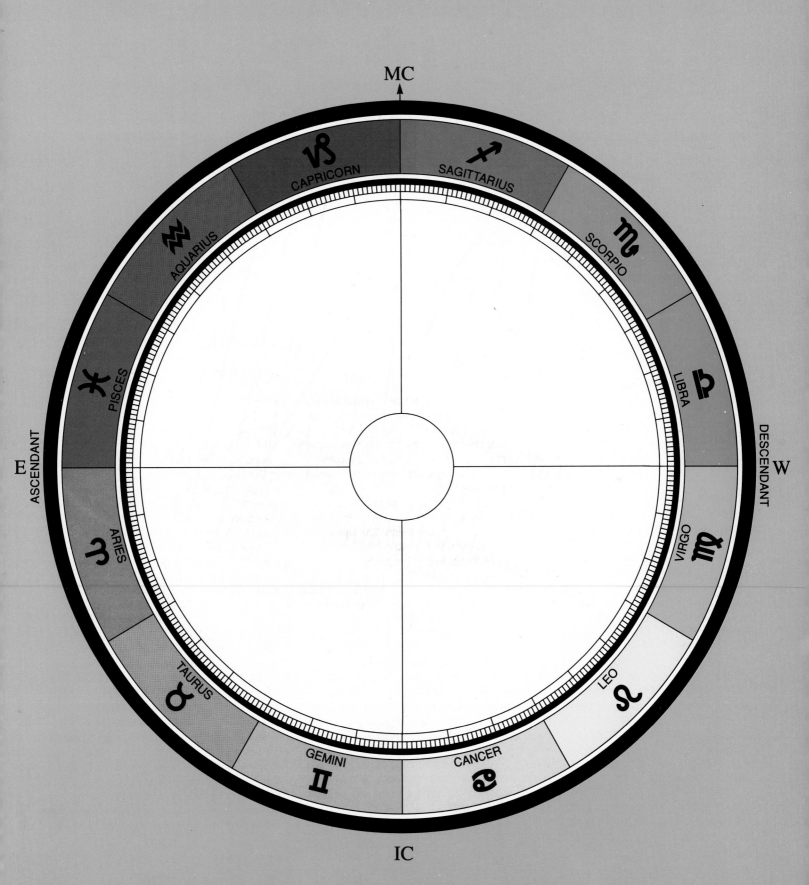

Houses of a Horoscope

The area of the birth chart between the Earth at the center and the surrounding ecliptic is divided into sections called houses. There are twelve houses, and unlike the twelve signs of the zodiac, which revolve around the chart, the house positions are fixed. In the chart opposite and in those on the following pages, the houses occupy twelve equal segments of 30 degrees each, calculated by what is known as the Equal House System. Any of about twenty other systems may be employed to determine the size of each house, but the Equal House is the oldest method—dating back to the time of Ptolemy—and the easiest to use.

The houses are numbered, starting from the ascendant—always the beginning, or cusp, of the first house—and proceeding counterclockwise. The descendant is always the cusp of the seventh house.

Each house represents an arena of everyday experience, such as career, family, and community standing. As the positions of the planets are plotted on the chart, a number of the celestial bodies will appear in certain houses, enabling the astrologer to determine the particular life situations in which the planets' influence supposedly will be felt. If no planets appear in a house, however, it does not mean misfortune for that area of life or a lack of importance or interest. People who have children, for example, do not necessarily have planets in the fifth house, which governs offspring. The lack of planets may simply mean their lives are not defined by children. In addition, the houses are said to correspond to the different signs of the natural zodiac. The first house is thought to be imbued with the characteristics of Aries, and so on. Although on any given individual's chart other zodiacal signs will typically fall within the houses and impart their own special qualities, astrologers claim that these natural traits are always present to some degree. The third house, for example, is said to govern communi-

cation and is influenced by inquisitive, logical Gemini. But, say astrologers, if someone's chart has the sign of Leo in the third house, the person would still be inquisitive; the style of communication would simply take on the essence of Leo, becoming more daring and flamboyant.

The areas of life thought to be affected by the houses, and the signs corresponding to each house, are examined below.

1 The first house, also the rising sign, corresponds to assertive, adventurous Aries. This house allegedly affects what is unique about an individual—temperament, disposition, appearance, and level of self-awareness—and influences all forms of outward behavior.

2 This house, relating to stable, conservative Taurus, reveals what is important or of value to a person. It governs moral values and money and possessions of all kinds, including attitudes toward them, how they are acquired, and how they are used.

3 The style and manner of communication, including speech and writing, are ruled by the third house, which corresponds to curious Gemini. Also governed are sibling relationships and short journeys.

4 The fourth house, influenced by nurturing and domestic Cancer, reveals an individual's home—both the childhood abode and the adult home. It represents how one seeks or views security and also has a bearing on parents, particularly the mother.

5 This house, governing creativity, corresponds to artistic, warm-hearted Leo. The fifth house also rules children, pets, all objects of one's affection, and pleasures such as holidays, the arts, sports, and gambling.

6 Work and health are said to be ruled by the sixth house, which is colored by the analytic sign of Virgo. Service to the community and attitudes toward subordinates are also included in this house.

7 The seventh house affects an individual's feelings about close relationships—not only emotional pairings but working partnerships as well. Libra's drive for connectedness influences this house.

8 The entire life process of sex, conception, birth, and death is outlined by the eighth house and influenced by the dedicated and intensely emotional sign of Scorpio. This house governs attitudes about reincarnation, magic, and the occult, as well as the money or investments of others and the inheritance of possessions or traditions.

9 The ninth house is the house of religion and philosophy. It relates to the wanderer, Sagittarius, and rules extensive journeys of the mind, spirit, and body and the desire to explore outside one's own culture. This house governs higher education, publishing, languages, and the law, and it also reflects the drive to organize information into systems.

10 Ambition and desire for a standing in the community are revealed in the tenth house. Influenced by pragmatic and aspiring Capricorn, this house also governs parents, particularly the father and his relationship to work.

11 The eleventh house influences a person's creativity in social situations and interaction with individuals and groups. Corresponding to freethinking Aquarius, this house rules general hopes and dreams as well as political activity.

12 The twelfth house relates to self-sacrifice, service to others, and the need for seclusion. It also encompasses all forms of confinement—in hospitals, monasteries, prisons, or other institutions—and privacy in terms of the unconscious, dreams, hidden problems, and secret enemies. The twelfth house is influenced by sensitive, vulnerable Pisces.

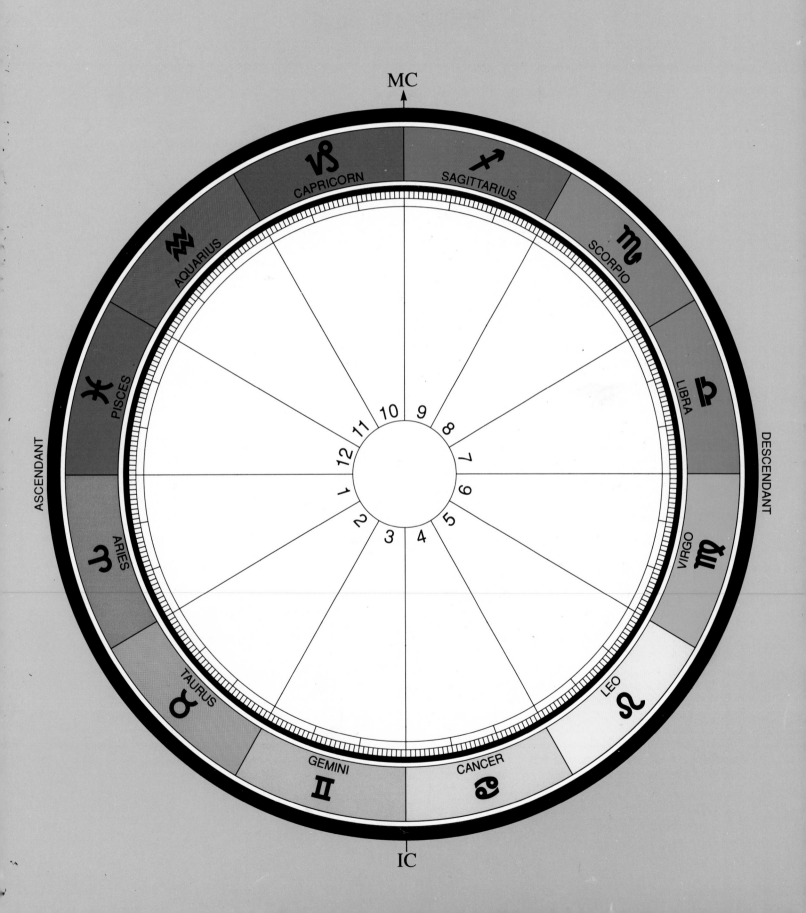

Refining the Signs

According to traditional astrology, each sign of the zodiac has certain intrinsic characteristics or tendencies. Some of these attributes are said to derive from the planets, since each sign is allegedly ruled and thus influenced by one or more heavenly bodies *(pages 34-37)*. Other traits are thought to be the result of the sign's connections to an element of nature (three zodiac signs, called the triplicities, are said to correspond to each of the four elements) or to one of three qualities (four zodiac signs, or quadriplicities, are thought to relate to each quality).

The elements of nature are fire, earth, air, and water. Each sign is associated with an element, beginning with the designation of Aries as a fire sign and continuing in turn counterclockwise around the zodiac: Taurus corresponds to earth, Gemini to air, Cancer to water, and so on *(opposite)*.

The fire signs—Aries, Leo, and Sagittarius—are described as enthusiastic, spirited, and impulsive. They are thought to be adventurous and innovative, yet impatient and at times impractical. Taurus, Virgo, and Capricorn are earth signs and are said to be practical, logical, dependable, and wary. They are also associated with the amassing of wealth, food, and creature comforts. Air signs Gemini, Libra, and Aquarius are associated with communication, reflection, and the application of ideas. They show a concern for possibilities, for what could be. And Cancer, Scorpio, and Pisces, the water signs, are thought to be sensitive, imaginative, private, and compassionate. They are said to show interest in the intangible and a concern with dreams and the unconscious.

When interpreting a birth chart, one of an astrologer's first tasks is to tally up the number of planets appearing in the fire, earth, air, and water signs. In some charts, planets may dominate only one element, but that situation is rare; most charts show a balance of two or three elements. A fire-water combination, for example, can be an intriguing mix of fire's enthusiasm and energy with water's imagination. Tempered by the presence of earth signs or communicated through air signs, this combination could be exceedingly powerful, according to astrologers. On the other hand, they say, those with a predominance of earth-water signs may be practical and affectionate but lack the intellectual or emotional sparks provided by air or fire signs.

Some astrologers will advise clients with seemingly imbalanced charts to literally make contact with the element of nature—to seek heat or sunshine, for example, to counter a lack of fire signs. They also may recommend association with other people whose charts are abundant in the desired elements. The earth-water person allegedly tends to be introverted and to be overwhelmed by details; associating with air and fire people might lighten this individual's mood and perhaps spark creativity.

As shown by the chart on the opposite page, each house is also related to an element. The influence of the houses is considered more subtle than that of the signs, although an individual lacking planets in earth signs, for example, might compensate for this deficiency with a planet in the second house, which is considered an earth-related house.

To add an additional level of information to the birth chart, each sign is also associated with one of three quadriplicities, or qualities. Said to influence the individual's relationship to the environment, the quadriplicities are known as cardinal, fixed, or mutable, and each imparts a particular essence to four signs. The cardinal signs—Aries, Cancer, Libra, and Capricorn—are considered exuberant, outgoing, and energetic; these signs initiate action and take command. The fixed signs—Taurus, Leo, Scorpio, and Aquarius—reflect stability, resolve, and resistance to change. They consolidate the ideas and actions of the cardinal signs. It is left to the mutable signs of Gemini, Virgo, Sagittarius, and Pisces—which signal flexibility, adaptability, and communication—to take those ideas out into the world.

The houses, too, are classified as either cardinal, fixed, or mutable. Cardinal houses supposedly represent the initiation of new plans or projects; fixed houses are stabilizing influences for the implementation of those plans; mutable houses provide the ability to follow through on the project. Planets are said to act assertively in cardinal houses, become more emphatic in fixed houses, and more variable in mutable houses.

When taken together, the elements and quadriplicities are said to reveal the true nature of each sign of the zodiac. Aries, for example, is fire-cardinal and channels its enthusiasm and energy into initiating and developing future possibilities; those born under this sign are entrepreneurs, leaders, and innovators. Cancer is water-cardinal; this sign exhibits its enterprise through emotions and intuition. Sagittarius is fire-mutable, and focuses its energies on communication, perhaps through broadcasting, travel, or teaching; Sagittarians may also, at times, find release in fiery outbursts. Taurus, an earth-fixed sign, gains its power through consolidation or stewardship of wealth or material goods. Leo, a fire-fixed sign, is said to reveal its power through passionate creativity.

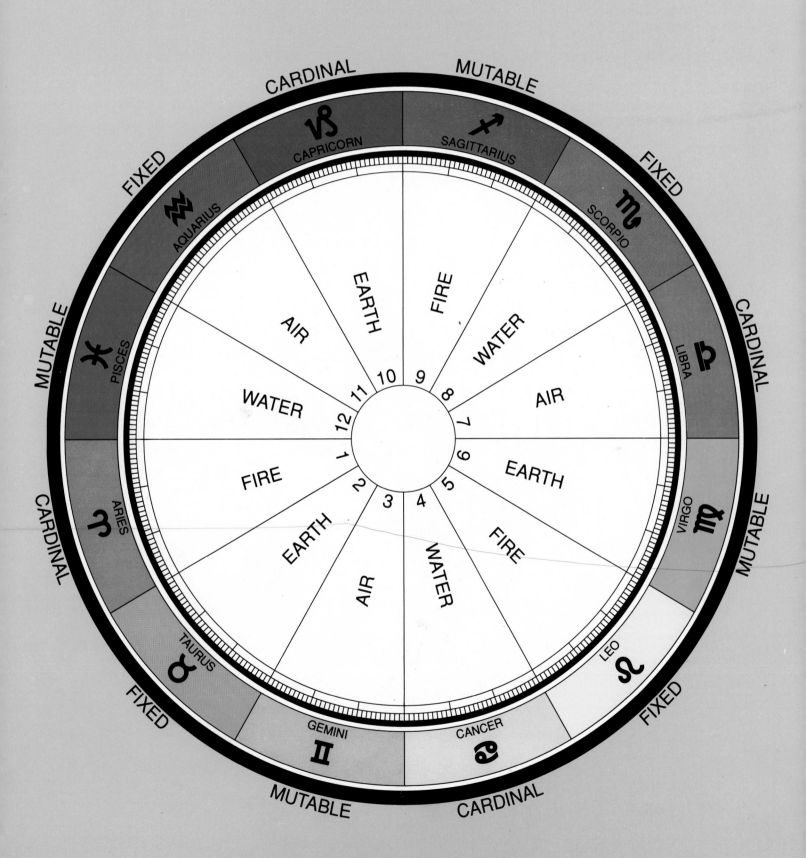

Plotting Planetary Aspects

Another major birth-chart component is the planetary aspects. Aspects occur when certain established distances, measured in degrees around the ecliptic, can be plotted between any two planets in a chart. Some of them, known as hard aspects, are said to reveal areas of stress; so-called easy aspects allegedly provide a helpful setting for developing potential.

The most powerful aspects to appear in a chart are the hard aspects of opposition, square, and conjunction and the easy aspect called trine. Planets in opposition, which are separated by 180 degrees, are said to signify difficulty; planets located 90 degrees apart form a square aspect, implying tension; and planets in conjunction, found within 8 degrees of one

another, are thought to represent internal conflict. A trine, occurring when planets are 120 degrees apart, signals harmony.

These four aspects and the situations they describe—as created by the positions of Mars and Saturn—are represented on these pages. For each aspect, the planets are shown linked by the color customarily used by astrologers when plotting charts.

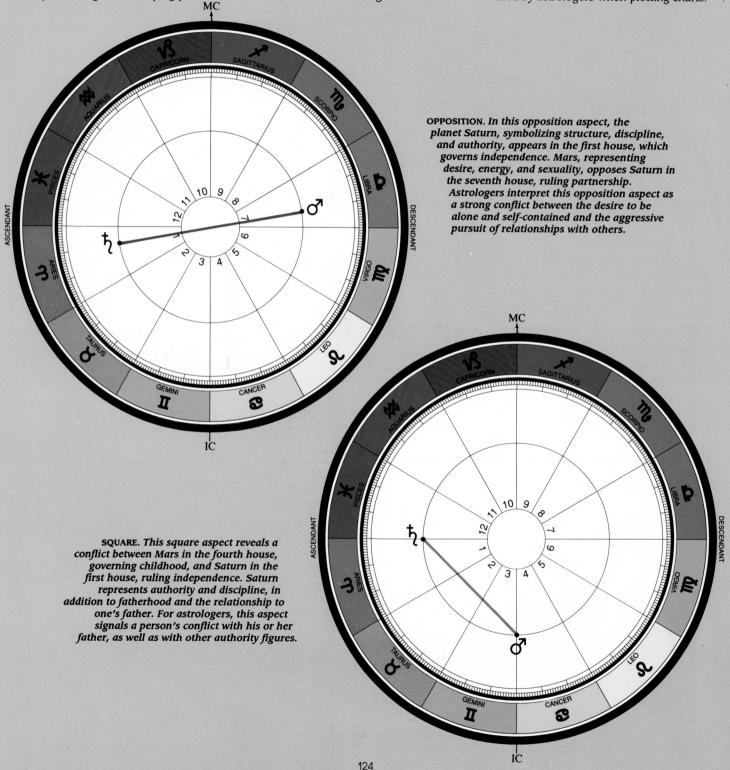

OPPOSITION. *In this opposition aspect, the planet Saturn, symbolizing structure, discipline, and authority, appears in the first house, which governs independence. Mars, representing desire, energy, and sexuality, opposes Saturn in the seventh house, ruling partnership. Astrologers interpret this opposition aspect as a strong conflict between the desire to be alone and self-contained and the aggressive pursuit of relationships with others.*

SQUARE. *This square aspect reveals a conflict between Mars in the fourth house, governing childhood, and Saturn in the first house, ruling independence. Saturn represents authority and discipline, in addition to fatherhood and the relationship to one's father. For astrologers, this aspect signals a person's conflict with his or her father, as well as with other authority figures.*

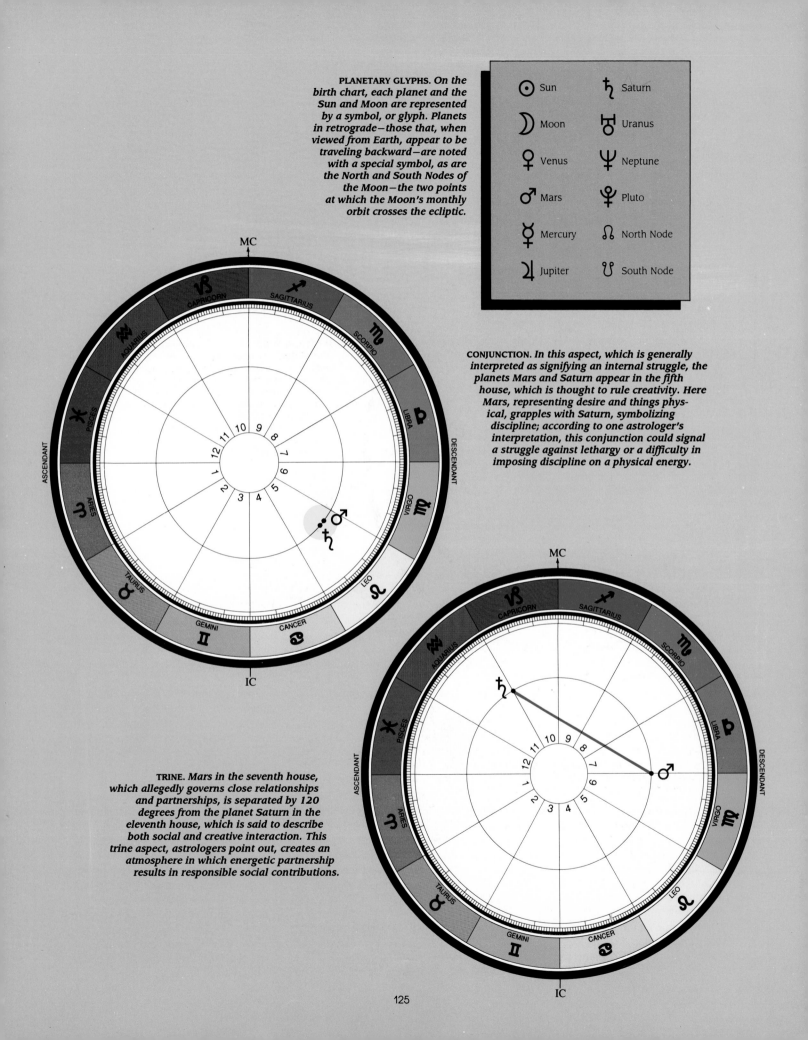

PLANETARY GLYPHS. *On the birth chart, each planet and the Sun and Moon are represented by a symbol, or glyph. Planets in retrograde—those that, when viewed from Earth, appear to be traveling backward—are noted with a special symbol, as are the North and South Nodes of the Moon—the two points at which the Moon's monthly orbit crosses the ecliptic.*

☉	Sun	♄	Saturn
☽	Moon	♅	Uranus
♀	Venus	♆	Neptune
♂	Mars	♇	Pluto
☿	Mercury	☊	North Node
♃	Jupiter	☋	South Node

CONJUNCTION. *In this aspect, which is generally interpreted as signifying an internal struggle, the planets Mars and Saturn appear in the fifth house, which is thought to rule creativity. Here Mars, representing desire and things physical, grapples with Saturn, symbolizing discipline; according to one astrologer's interpretation, this conjunction could signal a struggle against lethargy or a difficulty in imposing discipline on a physical energy.*

TRINE. *Mars in the seventh house, which allegedly governs close relationships and partnerships, is separated by 120 degrees from the planet Saturn in the eleventh house, which is said to describe both social and creative interaction. This trine aspect, astrologers point out, creates an atmosphere in which energetic partnership results in responsible social contributions.*

The Birth Chart of Sigmund Freud

Over the years many astrologers have constructed and interpreted the birth charts of numerous noteworthy individuals, seeking to understand the inner drives behind an outstanding person's actions and accomplishments. One chart often employed in such a way is that of Sigmund Freud, the Austrian founder of the psychoanalytic movement. Presented here is an interpretation by astrologer Caroline Casey.

"In looking at the elements, or triplicities, of Freud's chart, the majority of signs—four—are earth signs, which signal adamancy, form, and structure. Three air signs reveal intellect and imagination, and three water signs signal sensitivity and compassion. In terms of quadriplicities, or qualities, the chart shows four fixed signs and four mutable. Fixed signs underscore certainty and power, and set up structures for posterity; mutable signs are flexible and fluid. This combination usually signals a paradox, someone who has an absolute point of view, but might change it.

"A second important element in the chart is the point at which Aries appears on the ecliptic. Whatever house Aries occupies designates the area of life where the individual will be innovative. Here, Aries is in the sixth house, which rules work in the healing professions, service to the community, and attitudes toward subordinates. In this house we see Venus, which corresponds to how one relates to others. So we conclude that Freud relates, in regard to his work, the community, and his subordinates, in an Aries manner, in a maverick way, one that is dynamic and confrontational.

"Also present in the sixth house is the North Node of the Moon, representing life work and the direction it takes. Most important, you find Pluto conjunct Venus in this house. Pluto is significant as a co-ruler of Freud's rising sign, Scorpio, which suggests penetrating insight and judgmental tendencies. As a ruler of the ascending sign, the principles Pluto represents are construed as the individual's primary concerns; Pluto is the initiator into the realm of the unconscious. The planet also stands for death, rebirth, sexuality, and transformation. Freud, then, relates dynamically to others through his work about his primary concerns, of which sexuality is one.

"We now look for Mars, the other co-ruler of the ascending sign. Mars, representing aggression and sexuality, is also retrograde (represented on the chart opposite by the symbol ℞), suggesting its energy is even more deeply hidden. The planet appears in Libra in the eleventh house, which is the broad social world, implying sexuality as a social force. Then we see that Mars is the only planet in the eastern region of Freud's chart, a phenomenon called a singleton pattern.

"The planet in a singleton pattern is considered a key insight into people's lives, revealing what they concentrate on, how they do things, what they are meant to accomplish. Here Mars—aggression and sexuality—is singleton, but part of a major configuration called a T-square. The T-square consists of three important aspects—Mars square Saturn, Saturn square Jupiter, and Jupiter opposing Mars. Taking Mars square Saturn first, Mars is aggression, sexuality in the eleventh house, the broad social world. You find Saturn, which is restrictions, inhibitions, authority, and father, in the eighth house, which rules things hidden and things inherited. This is interpreted as sexuality struggling against the father in a way that is repressed or hidden—the basis for Freud's Oedipus complex theory.

"Saturn is also square Jupiter, which represents knowledge, religion, and expanded understanding. Jupiter is at 29 degrees Pisces, and Pisces deals with the realm of the mystical and occult. Mars opposing and Saturn square to Jupiter together suggest that Freud viewed Jupiter's domain as his enemy—the basis, perhaps, for Freud's view that religion was a guise for sexuality, conflicts with the father, the unconscious death urge, and so on.

"Next, we look for the Sun, which represents one's central self. Freud's Sun is in Taurus, an adamant sign, and in the seventh house, which rules one's impact on other people. The Sun is conjunct Uranus, which describes one who is unconventional, makes important discoveries, and has an awakening or transformational impact on others. The Sun is in sextile (a 60-degree easy aspect) to Neptune, which is the principle of dreams and visions, and Neptune is in the fourth house, governing the root of one's being—childhood, family. So the interpretation is that this man will ardently embrace an unconventional message that will have a transformational impact on others. He will gain access to this message by understanding the importance of dreams and visions."

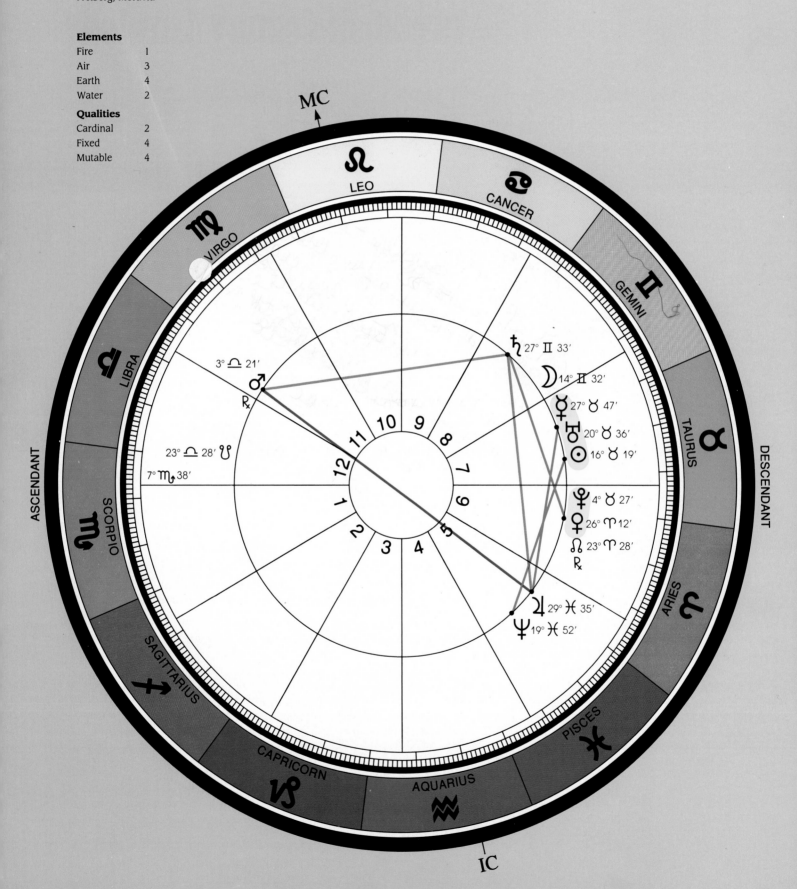

Horoscope
Sigmund Freud
May 6, 1856
6:30 p.m.
Freiberg, Moravia

Elements

Fire	1
Air	3
Earth	4
Water	2

Qualities

Cardinal	2
Fixed	4
Mutable	4

CHAPTER 4

Twentieth-Century Astrology

uring July of 1980, Ronald Reagan, then a candidate for president of the United States, remarked offhandedly to a reporter that he read his horoscope every day. Soon after the story was published, Reagan received a joint letter from several scientists, including five winners of the Nobel prize, who said they were "gravely disturbed" by the report. "In our opinion," they wrote, "no person whose decisions are based, even in part, on such evident fantasies can be trusted to make the many serious—and even life-and-death—decisions required of American Presidents."

The letter to Reagan reflected a sense of alarm among scientists over the expanding public acceptance of astrology. From early in the twentieth century, the old art had been steadily sloughing off the disreputability that had cloaked it for some 200 years in the West. The rehabilitation had been initiated by European spiritualists and astrologers, got a boost or two from an occasional profit-minded charlatan, and was promoted by governments for propaganda purposes during World War II. It was also helped by the serious consideration given to astrology by some respected thinkers and by the widespread publishing of horoscopes in newspapers and magazines.

In the cultural ferment of the 1960s, interest and belief in astrology soared, especially among the well-educated young. Astrology as a career and as a field of earnest study attracted increasing numbers of people who—although critics would call this a contradiction in terms—were of an intellectual bent. The public perception of professional astrologers changed from the old carnival-booth image to something that conferred a certain respectability in sophisticated circles, even a degree of cocktail-circuit cachet. And "What's your sign?" became a social watchword of the era.

Responding to this trend, more than 180 scientists—18 of them Nobel laureates—signed a statement in 1975 objecting to astrology as contributing "to the growth of irrationalism and obscurantism." The statement asserted categorically that "there is no verified scientific basis" for belief in astrology and "there is strong evidence to the contrary." To be sure, some of the nation's savants declined to go along with the blistering manifesto. The famous science-popularizer Carl Sagan, for example, refused to sign, not because he thought there was any truth in astrology but because he viewed the statement as an example of "the pretentiousness of scientific orthodoxy." And at least one scientist attacked the propriety of the whole exercise on the grounds that some signers may not have been familiar with astrology but were condemning it as unbelievable without bothering to study the subject.

From the viewpoint of astrology's critics, the situation had only worsened by 1980, when Ronald Reagan acknowledged his interest in the subject. Thus the letter of protest, which came from the Federation of American Scientists, a Washington lobby dedicated to acting on issues in which "the opinions of scientists are relevant." The presidential candidate's response was mollifying. "Let me assure you that while Nancy and I enjoy glancing at the daily astrology charts in our morning paper," Reagan told the offended scientists, "we do not plan our daily activities or our lives around them."

Reagan, of course, went on to the White House, and those trying to curb the growth of astrology's popularity moved on to other battlefronts, where their efforts were not notably successful. In 1978 a Gallup poll had revealed that 40 percent of Americans from thirteen to eighteen years old believed astrology worked; by 1984 the figure was up to 55 percent. In the latter year the Committee for the Scientific Investigation of Claims of the Paranormal, an organization of scientists, scholars, devoted skeptics, and debunkers, issued a call to the 1,200 U.S. daily newspapers that carried astrology columns to regularly publish a disclaimer. "The following astrological forecasts should be read for entertainment value only," the proposed text stated. "Such predictions have no reliable basis in scientific fact." As of the summer of 1986, however, only seven newspapers were known to be using the disclaimer.

But the biggest jolt to the anti-astrology forces came in 1988, when a White House insider revealed that the lives and daily activities of the Reagans were, after all, sometimes planned around an astrologer's charts. However sincerely Reagan may have meant his 1980 disavowal, a nearly successful attempt on his life by a gunman the following year reportedly convinced his wife that his safety depended on following the guidance of the stars. Since that time, presidential movements and other aspects of his schedule had been cleared in advance with Nancy Reagan's astrologer, a San Francisco woman named Joan Quigley.

"The President's schedule is the single most potent tool in the White House, because it determines what the most powerful man in the world is going to do and when he is going to do it," wrote Donald T. Regan, the former White House chief of staff who disclosed the astrological connection. "By humoring Mrs. Reagan we gave her this tool—or, more accurately, gave it to an unknown woman in San Francisco who believed that the zodiac controls events and human behavior and that she could read the secrets of the future in the movements of the planets." The fact that the president did not overrule the arrangements, wrote his former aide, "was regarded as sufficient evidence that he was willing to tolerate the state of affairs."

The sensational revelations cheered the president's opponents and critics, because—they thought—he was made to appear ignorant and superstitious. But the most important long-range effect of the news very probably was something altogether different: another boost in popularity for astrology. Here was perhaps the best-liked American president since World War II calmly declaring in the face of a gale of criticism that he would not proclaim disbelief in astrology because he did not know enough about the subject to judge it. Here was his widely admired wife, who plainly believed in astrology so strongly that she would fight powerful men of state to make sure heed was paid to the heavenly signals.

Meanwhile, television airwaves were crowded with sound—brief debates that pitted skeptics, who in some cases came across as stuffy and nastily aggressive, against astrologers, many of them attractive, media-wise, and smoothly articulate. At the same time, magazines and newspapers used the news as a peg for reports on the phenomenal growth in the astrology business, describing the work of financial astrologers, astrologers who specialize in psychological counseling, and Hollywood astrologers who read the stars for the stars. The editorial cartoonists and intelligentsia could jeer at the practice if they pleased; it seemed likely that the entire episode would only further enhance astrology's status, in a century that could already be characterized as the age of astrology's renaissance.

At the beginning of the twentieth century, astrology was little known in the Western world. In Europe, those who were aware of it at all mainly saw it as an adjunct of Theosophy, the popular Victorian mystical religious movement founded by Madame Helena Blavatsky. In Germany before World War I, for example, interest in Theosophy and astrology marched hand in hand. Not everyone who preached the word was a true believer, however.

One of the foremost heralds of modern German astrology was Hugo Vollrath. A student of Theosophy since his university days, Vollrath quickly saw that there was a potentially lucrative market for occult knowledge. He rushed to cash in on it by founding the Theosophical Publishing House in Leipzig. (Such was his sense of humor about his enterprise that he was said to wear a fez in his office, explaining that "it keeps my aura in place.") Later, Vollrath would perpetrate some out-and-out frauds, including selling phony mail-order lessons in the occult arts, but his initial efforts promoted the spread of genuine interest in astrology. He began in 1909 with an occult magazine called *Prana* and hired an Austrian named Karl Brandler-Pracht as its editor. Brandler-Pracht founded the German Astrological Society in Leipzig and edited a monthly astrological supplement to *Prana* called *Die astrologische Rundschau.*

After World War I, in the wake of military defeat and economic hard times, astrology was one of a number of avant-garde movements that flourished in Germany. A large number of well-educated Germans began to look to the stars for signs of better times to come. Many of the converts to astrology in the 1920s thought of astrology as a field of study that in time would be widely accepted as a science. And once they embraced astrology, the Germans displayed their traditional thoroughness. In the early twenties, their output of astrology manuals, tables, and almanacs far exceeded that of any other country in Europe.

As Adolf Hitler began to attract attention in the early 1920s, a woman named Elsbeth Elbertin capitalized on the Nazi's growing following to become the first nationally known astrologer in Germany. Elbertin included in the 1924 edition of her annual almanac, which hit the newsstands in July 1923, a forecast about an unnamed individual: "A man of action born on 20 April 1889 . . . can expose himself to personal danger by excessively uncautious action and could very likely trigger off an uncontrollable crisis," she wrote, adding that "he is destined to play a führer-role in future battles." Any National Socialist who picked up Elbertin's annual recognized Hitler instantly. His birth date was just as the astrologer had specified, and there was only one self-styled führer in Germany.

Four months later, Elbertin's prediction of "personal danger" and "uncautious action" was fulfilled when Hitler launched his putsch, an unsuccessful coup attempt in Munich. The police fired on the Nazis, killing some, and Hitler fell and dislocated his shoulder. Elbertin became famous, but the Nazi leader was not a believer. When shown Elbertin's prediction, Hitler snapped, "What on earth have women and the stars got to do with me?"

German astrologers advanced some striking and innovative theories during the 1920s. One such trailblazer was Herbert Freiherr von Kloeckler, who purged astrology of its medieval occult trappings and pioneered what was called psychological astrology, which sought to relate the stars and planets to the supposed psychological types then being studied in German universities. Another German, the successful novelist and playwright Oskar A. H. Schmitz, was an enthusiastic disciple of Swiss psychiatrist Carl G. Jung and probably spurred the analyst's interest in astrology.

Jung studied astrology, experimented with it, wrote about it, and at times used its principles in his practice. The famed psychiatrist felt that psychology's future lay in rebuilding what he described as lost connections between human beings and the cosmos. He thought some of the phenomena of astrology were the results of "synchronicity"—a mysterious force that Jung believed was behind such events as exceptional runs in gambling, predictive dreams, and other events that he termed meaningful coincidences. According to Jung, synchronicity was beyond mere chance but was not exactly a cause-and-effect relationship. To study this elusive principle statistically, he examined the horoscopes of 483 married couples to see if there were any correlations of the kind long claimed by astrologers.

Jung found a number of interesting correspondences, notably a highly significant tendency in married couples for the woman's moon to be in conjunction with the man's sun—that is, the position in the zodiac of the moon at the time of the wife's birth was close to the zodiacal position of the sun at the husband's birth. The psychiatrist did not count his experiment as a conclusive scientific study. But he felt that it demonstrated that astrology sometimes involved a synchronistic phenomenon.

The real importance of Jung's work, however, was that one of the most provocative thinkers of the century,

respected by the intellectual establishment, considered astrology sufficiently interesting and important to warrant so much attention. To this day, some institutions that train Jungian analysts offer courses in symbolic astrology as an aid to understanding the unconscious mind.

Although the Germans were looking at astrology in new ways, a Frenchman, Paul Choisnard, was the first to use statistics in an attempt to show that earthly affairs are indeed tied to the positions of heavenly bodies. A graduate of the famous École Polytechnique, Choisnard compared the horoscopes, cast for the moments of birth and death, of 200 people. Almost three times as often as chance would dictate, he reported in 1908, Mars at the time of death was in conjunction with the position of the sun at the moment of birth; the death Saturn was in conjunction with the birth sun twice as often as chance could account for.

Choisnard also charted the horoscopes of people with "superior natures"—presumably those who were outstanding for one reason or another—and claimed to find many more with Gemini, Libra, or Aquarius rising above the horizon at the time of birth than would happen by chance. In addition, he painstakingly examined collections of family horoscopes, searching for common astrological features in several members of the same family. Although Choisnard was satisfied that he had proved his various astrological theories statistically, his work does not now stand up to thorough scientific scrutiny.

Astrology in early twentieth-century America was more in the hands of charismatic personalities than of theorists like those who dominated the art in Europe. The most famous American astrologer of the time was Evangeline Adams, a supremely confident woman from Boston who learned the subject from books. At thirty-four, she arrived in New York City and created an immediate sensation. On her first day, she read the horoscope of the owner of her hotel and warned him that he was "under the worst possible combination of planets, bringing conditions terrifying in their unfriendliness."

The hotelier shrugged off the prediction as the work of

a charlatan, but that very day his wife and several relatives died in a fire that burned the hotel to the ground. His anguished report of Adams's warning made her an instant celebrity, and she eventually became America's best-known astrologer, a frequent consultant to the rich and famous.

Perhaps because of her huge success, Adams was arrested for fortunetelling in 1914. Instead of paying a fine, she decided to stand trial and argue her own defense. Armed with a pile of reference books, she told the court precisely how she analyzed horoscopes. To prove her point, she offered to make a reading from the birth date of someone she had never met and did not know.

The person chosen was the judge's son, and defenders of astrology have maintained ever since that the judge was so impressed by Adams's reading that he concluded, "The defendant raises astrology to the dignity of an exact science." However, the full court record shows that the often-cited quotation was taken out of context. The judge did not say that Adams *made* astrology an exact science; he said that she *claimed* it was an exact science. The actual reason he ruled in her favor was that she did not pretend to forecast the future, which was the charge against her, but simply explained to her clients what a horoscope was supposed to mean.

The trial made her more popular than ever. Her clients included Mary Pickford, the Prince of Wales, Enrico Caruso, and financier J. P. Morgan (for whom she was said to provide regular forecasts on politics and the stock market). In 1930, she began a radio series that pulled 4,000 letters a day from listeners eager for her advice. And after she died in 1932, her followers claimed that she had forecast her death by predicting that she would be unable to fulfill a lecture tour late that year.

British astrology in the first half of the century was spearheaded by Charles Carter, who pushed hard for a deeper understanding of astrology. In 1926, Carter started the magazine *Astrology,* and by 1948, he would become the first principal of the Faculty of Astrological Studies, sponsored by the London Theosophists. But Britain's signal contribution to the modern interest in astrology was to make horoscopes a feature in the popular press.

On August 21, 1930, Princess Margaret Rose, daughter of the duke and duchess of York and younger sister of the future Queen Elizabeth II, was born at Glamis Castle in Scotland. Since the news was already days old when the London *Sunday Express* for August 24 was being written, the editor decided to give the event a fresh angle by publishing a story on the princess's horoscope. The paper hired an astrologer named R. H. Naylor to "erect the chart," as astrologers put it. The half-page feature produced a torrent of admiring letters pleading for more horoscopes.

Six weeks later, in the first of what were to be regular columns for the *Sunday Express*, Naylor vaguely predicted that British aircraft were in "serious danger." Around noon that very day the BBC announced that the dirigible *R-101,* on its maiden voyage to Australia, had crashed and burned northwest of Paris. In its next issue the paper trumpeted the tragic verification of Naylor's remarkable prediction—and gave him a full page for his column. The popularity of the *Sunday Express*'s innovation caused astrology columns to sprout in publications throughout the Western world, especially in the British Empire and the United States.

During World War II, both the British and the Germans tried to use astrology to undermine enemy morale. One astrologer who played a pivotal role in this game, which was to become as twisted and involuted as any espionage thriller, was a Swiss named Karl Ernst Krafft, who came to the attention of the German authorities in spectacular fashion.

On the evening of November 8, 1939, the Bürgerbräu Beer Cellar in Munich was packed with a rowdy gang of beefy, middle-aged men. The featured speaker of the evening had left early and the room echoed with drunken laughter, stamping boots, and old military songs. Suddenly, a blinding flash of yellow light and an ear-splitting roar filled the air with dust and broken glass—then an eerie, pitch-dark silence broken only by the moans of the wounded.

A bomb had exploded just behind the speaker's plat-

MORE THAN A DOZEN LIVES LOST IN A FIRE WHICH DESTROYS THE WINDSOR HOTEL

RUIN IN BIG FIRE THAT RAZED THE WINDSOR HOTEL

ALL HEEDLESS OF THE CRY OF "FIRE"

Flames Raged While Futile Efforts Were Being Made to Convince Police and Employes That a Great Conflagration Was Threatening.

SCENES OF DEATH, SUFFERING AND RESCUES.

American astrologer Evangeline Adams (left) began her career in 1899 by predicting a disastrous fire at New York's stately Windsor Hotel. Her grim forecast, allegedly based on an astrological chart that she cast for the hotel's owner, brought her international fame. Adams, who claimed to be a descendant of President John Quincy Adams, was an enduring success. She had a large following among wealthy cosmopolites, but her down-to-earth style also appealed to skeptical, no-nonsense Yankees.

German astrologer and publisher Hugo Vollrath (right) rushed to join the Nazi party in 1933; for him, astrology justified the idea of Aryan supremacy. He had to abandon astrology in 1937 after the Nazis banned fortunetelling.

form. Seven were dead and sixty-three wounded. Within hours, German radio broadcast that an unsuccessful attempt had been made to assassinate Chancellor Adolf Hitler. The beer-cellar party celebrated the sixteenth anniversary of Hitler's 1923 Nazi attempt to overthrow the government. Fortunately, said the radio announcer who broke the news, the führer had left the festivities early and escaped unharmed.

In the tiny Black Forest village of Urberg, a short, dark-haired little gnome of a man heard the broadcast and broke into triumphant laughter. This was Karl Krafft, and he was overjoyed at the news. A pro-Nazi Swiss of German descent, Krafft was an astrologer who had immigrated to Germany in 1939 in hopes that his talents would be better recognized there than they had been in Switzerland. Krafft had published a monumental work entitled *A Treatise in Astro-biology.* Crammed with tables, it tried to prove the truth of astrology with statistics. For example, Krafft attempted to demonstrate that more musicians were born under certain signs and configurations than others.

Now, knowing that he had at hand a far more potent demonstration of his ability to read the stars, he hurried out to send a telegram to Deputy Führer Rudolf Hess, who was known to have an interest in astrology. In his wire, Krafft boasted that he had not only foreseen the attempt on Hitler's life but had sent his prediction to an official in Heinrich Himmler's secret intelligence service a week before the bomb exploded.

At the Reich Chancellery in Berlin, Krafft's telegram was almost as explosive as the bomb itself. A bureaucrat named Heinrich Fesel had recently put Krafft on the intelligence service payroll at 500 reichsmarks a month as a sort of consultant on astrology, politics, and the economy. A few days before the explosion in Munich, Fesel had indeed gotten a letter from his new employee predicting the "possibility of an attempt of assassination by the use of explosive material...." Krafft wrote that Hitler's life would be in danger between November 7 and 10. But Fesel knew that the practice of astrology had been under an official cloud in Germany since 1934 and that any astrological speculations

While casting horoscopes for neighbors, German astrologer Elsbeth Elbertin (above) supposedly concluded there would be a 1944 air raid on her neighborhood in Freiburg. Despite misgivings, she stayed in her home. The bombing raid came, and she died in it.

*Astrologer Karl Ernst Krafft's
accurate prediction of an attempt on
Adolf Hitler's life won him a job
as a Nazi propagandist. But Krafft (below)
later ran afoul of his bosses and
died en route to a concentration camp.*

about Hitler were strictly taboo. So instead of warning the führer, he had hastily stuffed the letter in a filing cabinet.

The morning after the explosion, Fesel's office door burst open. His boss strode in and curtly ordered the frightened Fesel to hand over Krafft's letter. It was taken to Hitler, who showed it to Joseph Goebbels, his propaganda minister, over lunch. The führer did not believe in astrology but apparently was impressed by the accuracy of Krafft's prediction. The Gestapo, too, was impressed—but not favorably. As Hitler lunched, four black-coated officers jumped into a staff car and sped out of their headquarters in Freiburg to arrest Krafft at his home deep in the Black Forest. After being bombarded for a full day with shouted accusations and questions, Krafft was taken to Berlin under heavy guard for interrogation by some of the Gestapo's more experienced persuaders.

Surprisingly, the little Swiss bore up well in Berlin. He finally convinced the Gestapo that he was not involved in the plot to kill Hitler. Then he went on to show his interrogators precisely how he had forecast the assassination attempt. With pencil, paper, and agile mind, Krafft demonstrated the exact astrological rules that had led him to his conclusion. It was such a bravura performance that Karl Krafft achieved his ambition: He was hired to practice astrology for the SS, the German Propaganda Ministry, and even the Foreign Office.

Officially, the Nazis did not believe in astrology; indeed, in the same month that they hired Krafft, they banned all privately published astrological almanacs and fortune-telling publications. But they knew that many people did believe and decided to use Krafft's astrological expertise as a psychological weapon. He was told to produce horoscopes and forecasts that would boost German morale while demoralizing the British, French, and Americans.

His first assignment was to produce a version of the rhymed prophecies of Nostradamus, the sixteenth-century French physician and astrologer. Translated and reprinted many times since first published in 1555, these verses are notoriously vague. Over the years, honest scholars have come up with radically different translations. Naturally, Krafft was instructed to search for quatrains to interpret in a way that seemed to forecast a Nazi victory. He did as he was told.

Krafft's version of the prophecies was circulated in Germany and abroad by the Propaganda Ministry. He also frequently cast the horoscopes of leading adversaries of the Reich, among them Winston Churchill and Franklin D. Roosevelt. The idea was to publish charts that made the future of such enemy leaders seem bleak. Krafft's work brought him into contact with many prominent Nazis. By the spring of 1940, the ambitious Swiss had become confident enough to reveal to sympathetic Nazis some of his unvarnished forecasts showing a pessimistic view of Germany's future after the winter of 1942-1943. Krafft advised any of the Nazis willing to listen that Germany should make peace before the end of 1942, while it was still winning the war.

Also in 1940, Krafft became the unwitting central figure in a complex game of astrological warfare between British and German agents. It all began with the Rumanian ambassador to London, a man named Virgil Tilea, who had once met Krafft in Switzerland. Tilea wrote to the astrologer asking for a forecast of coming events. Krafft showed the letter to Fesel, who remained his contact in Himmler's intelligence service, and Fesel immediately saw how Krafft's reply could be used as a weapon. A carefully slanted forecast of German victory was sent circuitously to Tilea in London.

As expected, the letter was passed on to the British, but not with the demoralizing effect that Krafft's masters intended. Instead, the letter had convinced the Rumanian that Krafft was on the Nazis' payroll, and perhaps close to Hitler. Tilea alerted British authorities and suggested that if the Germans were using an astrologer, perhaps the British could use one of their own to anticipate Hitler's moves. (The British and Tilea apparently gave credence to false rumors that Hitler believed in astrology.)

A British search for an astrological expert familiar with Karl Krafft's techniques turned up Hungarian-born Louis de Wohl, a huge walrus of a man and an accomplished self-promoter. "I had learned the technique of Karl Krafft, Hitler's favorite astrologer," said de Wohl afterward, "and I knew what his advice to Hitler would be long before he was even summoned by the Führer." All of this was a lie, but the British had no way of knowing it at the time. De Wohl was attached to the Department of Psychological Warfare, where he generated memos on what Karl Krafft was supposedly advising Hitler to do.

Of course, Krafft was not advising Hitler but instead concocting forecasts for propaganda uses, as were a number of other astrologers in German employ. London, too, began subsidizing astrologers in a number of foreign countries to publish horoscopes predicting British victory. And the British, like the Germans, enlisted Nostradamus in their secret war. While Karl Krafft turned out fudged translations for the Nazis, Louis de Wohl did the same for Britain. British planes dropped fake astrological forecasts over Germany while clever British forgeries of German astrological publications were distributed by underground channels.

Perhaps the most controversial—and highly secret—use of the astrological weapon in World War II was that involving the astonishing flight of Deputy Führer Rudolf Hess to Scotland in 1941. Ian Fleming, an officer in British naval intelligence who later became famous as the creator of fictional spy James Bond, apparently conceived the idea of luring Hess to England by playing on his interest in astrology. Unlike some other prominent Nazi leaders, Hess apparently believed fervently in the influence of the heavens. As the British analyzed what Hess was probably being told by his astrologers, they carefully circulated back to him false reports about high-ranking pro-German Britons, information ingeniously contrived to fit into the astrological advice that Hess was hearing.

Hess became convinced he could negotiate peace with the British. On May 10, 1941, a day that had an unusual conjunction of planets, he took off for Scotland to meet—he thought—with the duke of Hamilton. The duke was Lord Steward of the King's Household and commander of an RAF fighter squadron. When Hess parachuted onto Scottish soil, he was arrested for his trouble. The British had used astrology to achieve a spectacular coup, bagging Hitler's second in command. But they were unable to exploit their triumph because they feared it would draw attention to, and enable Berlin's propagandists to capitalize on, the very real pro-German sympathies of some upper-class Britons.

With Hess's bizarre adventure, Krafft's fortune took a decided turn for the worse. The Gestapo found papers indicating a connection between astrological advice and Hess's flight. Along with many other astrologers, Krafft was im-

India's Honored Astrologers

In India, perhaps as in no other culture, astrology is an integral part of daily existence. Almost every Indian visits an astrologer at least once in life—generally before a marriage—and more than 60 percent of the population consults an astrologer regularly.

Indian society is organized around a rigid class structure that makes it almost impossible to break out of the social caste of one's birth. Perhaps for this reason, Indians tend to be fatalistic. Many believe in a destiny that allows them few choices and minimal free will. Astrology is thus a relevant pursuit. It enables them to scan their futures with an eye toward mitigating probable misfortunes.

While astrologers are often shunned as charlatans in the West, in India they are considered members of a noble profession. Modern oracles such as Anand Shankar Vyas (right) of Ujjain are powerful figures who command large fees. Innumerable less-famous astrologers are available to people of modest means.

Whatever his stature, the astrologer's word is virtual gospel in India. Weddings have been called off because of astrological warnings. There have been cases where, on advice of astrologers, poor and primitive Indians have sacrificed children to ward off impending doom.

prisoned. After a year in solitary confinement, he was brought back to the Propaganda Ministry and evidently was promised his freedom if he followed orders. He produced a horoscope intended to prove that President Roosevelt and his wife, Eleanor, were puppets of Wall Street and "international Jewry." But after a few months, Krafft realized that the Gestapo was not going to release him no matter what he did, so he refused to fake any further horoscopes or forecasts. He was thrown into a small underground cell with fifty other men in Berlin's Lehrterstrasse Prison. He was shifted from jail to jail until he died of typhus January 8, 1945—on the train to Buchenwald.

Since World War II, the increasing public interest in astrology has inspired a number of scientists and others to devote time and effort attempting to disprove it. One of their arguments against astrology—or at least against astrology in half the world—confronts the proponents of astrological efficacy on their own terms. The thrust of this attack: Eastern and Western astrologers employ different, apparently contradictory systems to determine the heavenly positions of zodiacal signs at any given time.

The conflict stems from a phenomenon known as the precession of the equinoxes, the shift in the angle of the earth's axis that has caused a gradual change in alignment between the calendar and the whereabouts of constellations on which the zodiac is based *(page 11)*. For example,

Hungarian astrologer Louis de Wohl (above), who arrived in London as a refugee in 1935, was once described as a "tall, flabby elephant of a man" with a mesmerizing stare. De Wohl tried to convince British intelligence during World War II that Adolf Hitler was consulting an astrologer. The émigré even began reproducing the astrological advice the führer was supposedly receiving. The British were skeptical of de Wohl's forecasts, but they decided he might be useful as a propagandist. They had him edit faked astrological journals, such as the 1943 edition pictured at right. Some of the pamphlets, predicting Germany's defeat, were dropped behind enemy lines.

almost 2,000 years ago, in the time of Ptolemy, the sun was in the constellation Aries on the day of the spring equinox, March 21 by our current calendar. Most astrologers in the West, adhering to what is called the tropical zodiac, still apply the signs to the same periods of the year as Ptolemy did: Someone whose birthday falls on March 21 is said to be born under the sign of Aries, the Ram. But because of the equinoctial precession, the sun nowadays is actually in the constellation Pisces, the previous zodiacal sign, on that date. Eastern astrologers, who use what is known as the sidereal zodiac, based on the actual positions of the constellations, insist that Pisces—not Aries—is the true natal sign of persons who are born on March 21.

The difference is not insignificant, since Easterners and Westerners agree that people born under Aries tend to be energetic decision makers, while Pisceans are thought to be dreamily indecisive. The same conflict over zodiacal signs and the resulting contradictions of traits runs through the yearly calendar. Furthermore, Eastern astrologers do not take into account the three most recently discovered planets, Uranus, Neptune, and Pluto, whose influences are carefully plotted into astrological charts in the West.

Clearly, both systems of astrology cannot be correct, at least not in particulars. And if one is right, the other must be wrong. Some astrologers try to explain away this glaring inconsistency by saying the zodiacal signs are not as important as other factors, such as the positions of planets relative to one another. A small group of practitioners in America and England, however, has adopted the sidereal zodiac as the basis for their work.

Doubters of astrology, as well as a number of its proponents who yearn to see its validity confirmed by scientific examination, have subjected it to many tests over the years. Opponents of astrology say the results of the studies that have met the rigid standards required by science have been almost entirely—some would say completely—negative; that is, the tests offered little or no proof that astrology could do what its adherents claim. But believers in astrology interpret many of the same experiments differently, asserting they offer evidence that astrology does indeed work.

A case in point was a large study reported in 1978, involving no less than 2,324 people. Conducted by three London-based researchers, it was designed to test whether two major dimensions of personality—extroversion or introversion and emotionality or stability—actually coincided with the astrological expectation based on birth, or sun, signs. According to Western astrological tradition, the six odd-numbered signs, starting with Aries—that is, Aries, Gemini, Leo, Libra, Sagittarius, and Aquarius—are characterized by outgoing, or extroverted, traits. The even-numbered signs—Taurus, Cancer, Virgo, Scorpio, Capricorn, and Pisces—are thought to confer self-repressive, introverted qualities. Furthermore, the three water signs (Cancer, Scorpio, and Pisces) are considered indicative of volatile emotions, while the earth signs (Taurus, Virgo, and Capricorn) are associated with stability and practicality.

The subjects of the study answered questionnaires intended to reveal whether they were extroverted or introverted and emotional or stable. When the results were plotted, they showed that, at least by a small margin in each case, the averages of the self-evaluations tended to match what an astrologer would predict: The sun signs were associated with the expected traits.

An astrological journal pronounced these findings "possibly the most important development for astrology in this century." But critics, and the researchers themselves, perceived what they considered to be a flaw in the test— that some of the subjects were familiar enough with astrology to know what their sun signs indicated about their per-

Stars and Stocks

When the stock market crashed on October 19, 1987, many astrologers were not surprised. One stargazer pointed out that the planets had been in "expansive sectors for the last fifteen years or so, and they are now what you'd call in contractive areas." Another claimed a certain celestial arrangement of Saturn, Uranus, and Neptune led her to predict the debacle.

Skeptics insist that it did not take an intimate knowledge of the planets to conclude that the bull market would not last forever. In reply, astrologers say that the key to financial survival lay with pinpointing the time of the market's plunge. New York forecaster Mason Sexton, author of a newsletter whose predictions are based partly on astrology, began urging his customers on October 2 to sell. After his warnings proved well founded, his client list increased by almost 100 percent in less than a month.

Astrology is not new to the stock market. Financier J. P. Morgan reportedly frequented astrologer Evangeline Adams's studio above Carnegie Hall to consult her about planetary effects on stocks and bonds. Astrologers see the market as a natural forum for their talents: The stars, they say, are just as reliable a market predictor as any other. Sexton, who studied at the Harvard Business School, believes astrology supports his world view that nothing is random. He studies solar eclipses to chart market patterns.

Some astrologers predict the market by creating birth charts based on the date of a company's first trade, the date a stock goes public, or even the birth dates of a company's chief executives. Other advisers correlate individual stock prices with planetary cycles. Certain planetary movements are considered significant; for example, astrologers believe that a planet becoming retrograde—or appearing to move backward—can mean a downturn in the market.

Whatever their methods or special interests, most astrologers seek to impose order on a world that often seems chaotic. Perhaps it is not surprising that on ever-uncertain Wall Street, seekers of financial terra firma look upward to the immutable stars.

sonalities. Experiments have shown that if people know, or are told, that their astrological signs are associated with this or that characteristic, they tend to see those traits in themselves. Indeed, when the experimenters tried a similar test with schoolchildren, who could be presumed to know little or nothing about astrology, the results were strikingly different. There was no significant correlation between personality and what the sun signs predict. But because the results of some other trials appear to reinforce the original findings, many believers in astrology feel the first survey was valid.

An Indian bride and groom sit bound together by a symbolic cord at their wedding in 1955. That year, thousands of Indians rushed to marry before May 5—a date that, according to astrologers, began a thirteen-month period inauspicious for wedlock.

Some studies appear unequivocal. A 1984 survey by astronomers Roger B. Culver and Philip A. Ianna followed up more than 3,000 public predictions by astrologers over a five-year period, counting as inaccurate those that did not come true within the time limit set by the astrologer who made the forecast. The authors of the study granted exceedingly wide latitude for accuracy. A fulfilled prediction was counted as correct even if it was so obvious that it almost could not miss—foretelling continued trouble in the Middle East, say—or was extremely vague, such as predicting an unspecified disaster in a very large region, Africa, for instance. Even so, only 11 percent of the predictions—338 out of 3,011—were accurate.

Once in a while, however, a study produces findings suggesting there is something at work that cannot be explained away by chance or bias or experimental error—at least not to the satisfaction of some seemingly impartial observers. Interestingly, the most notable case comes from the work of a team that in other studies proved again and again that many of the assumptions of astrology are false—French psychologist Michel Gauquelin and his wife at the time, Françoise. One study by the Gauquelins that produced negative results involved the horoscopes of more than 600 French convicted murderers. The Gauquelins searched for some common factor in the murderers' horoscopes, and because Mars is astrologically associated with crime and violence, they paid particular attention to its position in the charts. But neither that planet nor any other discernible astrological factor had a statistical prominence that random chance could not explain.

Gauquelin also was intrigued by the statistical studies done decades earlier by Paul Choisnard and Karl Ernst Krafft. He decided to check the figures on which Krafft based his *Treatise on Astrobiology,* published in the late 1930s. With the help of a computer, Gauquelin proved that Krafft's results were invalid. One of Choisnard's most interesting studies had supposedly shown that, at the time of a typical person's death, Saturn or Mars was two to three times more likely to be in conjunction with the subject's sun sign than could be explained by chance. Choisnard's study had involved only 200 cases. When the Gauquelins tried the same survey on more than 7,400 cases, they found the two planets played no such role; Choisnard's findings apparently had been a quirk resulting from too small a sample.

The Gauquelin study that has attracted the most attention, however, had far different results. To test the notion that there is some relationship between the stars and certain occupations, the researchers collected birth data for 16,336 people who had distinguished themselves in various professions. The Gauquelins discovered that an unexpectedly large number were born when certain planets were in key sectors of their paths through the sky. For example, successful doctors and scientists tended to be born when Saturn was on the rise, or just over the midway point of its daily journey, as seen from Earth.

But the most famous of their findings from this study came to be known as the Mars effect—the striking connection between outstanding athletes and Mars. Some 22 percent of a sample of 1,553 sports champions were born when Mars was on or just above the horizon, or near its zenith. Chance alone would dictate that only 17 percent would have been born when Mars was in one of those two parts of the sky—which turned out to be the case for non-champion athletes. Equally intriguing, the Mars effect appeared to apply only to births timed by nature, not to artificially induced or Cesarean deliveries.

Skeptics—and supporters—abound. A Belgian research group, using data provided by the Gauquelins, appeared to confirm the effect—but then expressed some doubts about the results because of a statistical technicality. The devoutly skeptical Committee for the Scientific Investigation of Claims of the Paranormal (CSICOP) questioned the entire project, alleging that the claims of a Mars effect were "based on data gathered by the Gauquelins themselves, and none of the studies has been properly supervised. The Gauquelins have no way of proving that they did not cheat." Several CSICOP experimenters set out to test the findings by a similar survey, which, predictably enough, seemed to disprove the Gauquelins' conclusions. Critics, however, allege that the CSICOP experimenters misrepresented data to prove their thesis. Indeed, CSICOP later conceded that its

Indian priests in New Delhi burn offerings and chant sacred lines from Hindu texts. The ceremony was designed to avert the supposed malevolent influence from the conjunction of eight planets in the sign of Capricorn on February 4, 1962.

investigators had neglected to obtain "in advance a clear understanding with the Gauquelins on exactly what they were predicting and what directories of famous sports champions would be satisfactory according to their hypothesis."

In defense of the Gauquelins, two British psychologists, H. J. Eysenck and D. K. B. Nias, in 1982 weighed in with a book entitled *Astrology: Science or Superstition?* The authors, associated with the London University Institute of Psychiatry, reported that the Gauquelins' findings had been checked against a control group and the experiments had been successfully replicated. They concluded that the Gauquelins' research "compares favorably with the best that has been done in psychology, psychiatry, sociology or any of the social sciences." And in 1986, Professor Suitbert Ertel of West Germany's University of Göttingen reported on a follow-up survey to the Gauquelins' work, with an added dimension. Each of 4,331 sports champions was assigned to one of five categories of eminence, based on the frequency of citations. Ertel said he found that the Mars effect consistently increased as eminence increased: The greater the eminence of the champion, the more likely that Mars was in one of the key positions at the time of the individual's birth.

Some astrologers totally reject the idea that astrology should be tested by statistics or scientific studies of any kind, even those that might lend it credence. "Astrology is the language of individuality and uniqueness," declares Caroline Casey, a prominent American astrologer and a veteran of national television confrontations with would-be debunkers. "Statistics by their very nature are about non-individuality and non-uniqueness. So what if astrology doesn't stand up to scientific testing? What about music? What about poetry? What about religion? Do you want to put music and poetry to a double-blind test?"

When opponents attack astrology, they cite both the lack of scientific proof that it works and the absence of a credible theory as to how it could work, if it did. (Proponents have

The Uranian Influence

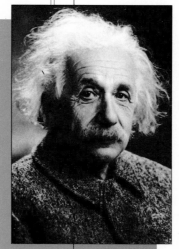

Uranus is something of a rogue planet to astrologers, the only one that appears to be misnamed. Its attributes do not fit the dour Greek sky god Uranus. Rather, astrologers say, it would be better named for Prometheus, the Titan who defied the Olympian gods to steal fire. Legend has it that Prometheus gave fire to mortals, launching the human journey toward civilization.

People whose charts feature Uranus in a prominent position are likely to be mavericks, like Prometheus. They are also apt to be brilliant, astrologers maintain, since Uranus signifies genius.

The Uranian influence is supposedly illustrated in the birth chart (below) of physicist Albert Einstein (above). At the moment of Einstein's birth in 1879, Uranus was in a very powerful position as the only planet other than the moon below the horizon line. Thus, insist astrologers, Einstein was gifted with genius and destined, like Prometheus, to change the world. Moreover, Uranus opposes Jupiter in his chart. Jupiter rules understanding and learning, so Einstein's breakthrough—his development of the theory of relativity—would necessarily challenge humanity's fundamental understanding of the universe.

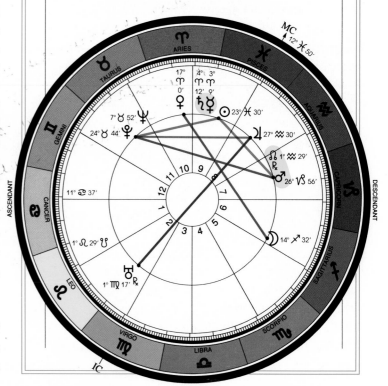

pointed out that this same attitude—"If you don't know how it works, it can't work"—caused most scientists to reject the theory of continental drift for nearly half a century before it was finally proved in the 1960s.) Certainly, astrologers do not present a unified front when it comes to discussions of how astrology works. In general, their explanations fall into one of two broad categories—causative or synchronistic—each of which consists of many variations.

Causative theories are those that postulate an actual cause-and-effect relationship between what happens in the sky and what happens in the course of people's lives on earth. The starting place for these explanations is generally that there are some widely recognized physical connections between the heavens and earth—the moon's gravity, for instance, which causes tides, or the sun's light, which affects the opening and closing of blossoms and the sleep periods of animals, including humans. And in recent decades, science has discovered many different kinds of energy from extraterrestrial sources and many new indications of life forms on earth responding, in ways not clearly understood, to stimuli from space. We know now that our world is constantly bombarded by the sun, stars, and remote, undefined sources deep in the far reaches of space not only with visible light, but with gamma rays and x-rays, ultraviolet and infrared rays, and radio waves of every conceivable length.

And even very faint signals have been shown to affect terrestrial behavior. The courses set by birds released inside a planetarium have convinced some researchers that migratory birds can navigate by the light of the stars, since they can be induced to take off in a different direction when the projected "stars" are shifted to a new position. Oysters once were thought to open and close their shells according to the movement of tides. But when the marine bivalves were transported to a sealed tank in a new geographical location, they adjusted their opening and closing rhythm to correspond to the movement of the moon in relation to their new home—even though they were in a tide-free environment. If birds and mollusks instinctively respond to faint or unseen messages from the heavens, why not human be-

ings? It is easy enough to see how the barrage of different kinds of radiation striking the earth presents a wealth of possibilities to anyone seeking explanations for astrology's alleged effects on life on earth.

Many people who believe in astrology do not think there is any such cause-and-effect mechanism at work at all. It is even possible that most Western astrologers do not believe that the movements of stars or planets or radiation from space control our lives on earth. Instead many people feel that the whole universe is synchronized so that certain celestial occurrences coincide with particular events below, as if earth and stars are different parts in a vast, wind-up watch, both moved simultaneously by a gigantic unseen mainspring. They feel the connections exist not only between people and heavenly bodies, but among particular materials, life forms, objects, energies, qualities, emotions—phenomena of every description. This is the so-called synchronistic explanation for astrology.

"Astrology is a language of correlation," says American astrologer Caroline Casey. "It says, for instance: There is an energy out there that we'll call Aries, which we also see in things that are bright red, and that describes things that start, and describes springtime and red berries and the spice cinnamon and stimulants. This language ties a lot of things together and says, here's how you can see this thing that we're talking about in different forms. There are herbs that are Aries. Springtime is the season. Red is the color. C-natural is the musical note. Astrology tracks the hidden relationship between things that are not obviously related on surface inspection. It's a language that says there is a harmony and correlation that runs through all of creation."

Dennis Elwell, a prominent British writer on astrological subjects, says astrology deals with "the seamless wholeness of the universe," whereas "the sceptics imagine that astrology must be about magic rays beaming through space." ("Sadly," he rues, "a few astrologers labour under the same delusion.") Britain's famous Charles Carter wrote in the 1930s that the astrologer's planets are not the actual,

The Dawning of the Age of Aquarius

In November of 1967, the American cast of the musical *Hair (left)* proclaimed the "dawning of the Age of Aquarius." The exuberant band of hippies sang of a time of universal understanding, peace, and happiness, and astrologers generally agree with that assessment of the future. The astrologers claim the new era will usher in undreamed-of levels of understanding and cooperation among people—and perhaps even a respite from war. A new spirituality will pervade humankind, the theory goes, and there will be a heightened respect for psychic and mystic phenomena.

Along with improved social and spiritual climates will come dramatic scientific advancements, say astrologers. The lively Aquarian Age is supposedly a period of innovation and creation. Space exploration, for example, epitomizes the age of the Water Bearer.

The Age of Aquarius supplants the Age of Pisces, which began about the time of Christ and is often spoken of in Christian terms: One astrologer describes that era as "an age of tears and sorrow, focused on the death of Christ." The differences between the Piscean and Aquarian ages could hardly be more pronounced—the former a time of conformity, largely static, passive, and somewhat self-indulgent, the latter a period of unconventionality and individual initiative, generous natured, active, and expansive.

While astrologers generally concur about the character of the two ages, they disagree about which one currently prevails. An astrological age, which lasts for about 2,160 years, is defined by the constellation in which the sun appears during the spring equinox *(pages 11-13)*. However, astrologers differ on where each of the zodiac's twelve constellations begins and ends. Thus while some astrologers insist that the sun slipped into the constellation Aquarius as early as 1904, others claim the new age will not dawn until well into the twenty-fourth century.

physical bodies circling the sun but "great categories of existence, animate and inanimate, operating upon all the planes of being." The physical planet, he said, is "the focusing point and the symbol of its category."

The ancients recognized these categories and associated them with their symbolic planets. Thousands of years ago, for instance, Saturn became linked to such apparently disparate things as gravity, the skeleton, lead, and growing old. "Strange bedfellows!" Elwell has written in a book called *Cosmic Loom*. "Such incongruous mixtures are a feature of astrology . . . it is worth pausing to ask why, if astrologers were making it all up, they did not do themselves the favor of settling for more plausible combinations."

is answer is that the stargazing sages of old were not making these connections up but had somehow divined relationships that science is confirming only now. Not until the space age, for example, did we learn that prolonged weightlessness—the absence of gravity—severely reduces the amount of calcium in the bones. And only recently has medicine discovered that the loss of bone minerals suffered by immobilized invalids can be counteracted by the patient's standing up for three hours each day, allowing gravity to strengthen the skeleton. It turns out, also, that lead taken into the body is stored in tissue, as well as the bones, and that lead concentration in the bones increases with age.

Scientists have not, of course, gone on to attribute these relationships to some influence of Saturn. Nor do astrologers contend that such a string of connections between otherwise unrelated items constitutes proof of astrology. But many of them view the discovery of these and similar relationships to be an indication of how modern science—in spite of the antithetical attitude of many scientists—is itself coming closer and closer to validating the old beliefs of astrology. They see particular promise in the work of physicists who are trying to come up with a new theory that would explain the interrelatedness of all things and forces.

During the twentieth century, the whole nature of physics has been dramatically transformed. The straightfor-

American expatriates gathered on August 16, 1987, at the Pyramids in Egypt to celebrate the Harmonic Convergence with singing and dancing. Believers urged everyone to stay outdoors for as long as possible to reap maximum psychic and spiritual benefits.

The Great Harmonic Convergence

On August 16, 1987, thousands of New Agers celebrated the Harmonic Convergence. All agreed it was an important event, though there was some question as to exactly what it signified.

The probable father of the Harmonic Convergence was art historian José Argüelles, who wrote that, according to ancient Mayan calendars, a collective outpouring of positive psychic energy on August 16 was humankind's last chance to save civilization. The date might be marked, he said, by Jesus' Second Coming and contact between earth and UFOs.

However, some suggested the real import of August 16 would be a rare alignment of the planets—a cosmic queue that would shower earth with beneficent psychic energy. There were predictions of various gods returning and of other portents and wonders.

Astronomers noted that no such planetary lineup was in the offing. Nevertheless, on the appointed day thousands turned out to add their positive energy to the heavenly spate. The result was a widespread and colorful party, although no momentous happenings were reported.

Holding a crystal aloft to catch dawn's first light, an enthusiast welcomes the Harmonic Convergence in the Black Hills of South Dakota. Crystals, said by some to amplify psychic powers, have been dubbed the "rabbit's foot of the '80s."

New Agers in Hawaii breathe incense and meditate before a Buddhist prayer gong. People of many cultures and religions took part in the Harmonic Convergence, undismayed by such critics as cartoonist Garry Trudeau, who labeled it the "moronic convergence."

American astrologer Dane Rudhyar, who died in 1985, was concerned that his readings might induce unhealthy fatalism in his clients. He used a birth chart not to predict the future, he stressed, but as a guide for realizing one's full potential.

ward, relatively easy-to-understand science outlined in the seventeenth century by Sir Isaac Newton has been greatly expanded by two comparatively abstruse revolutionary ideas: Einstein's general theory of relativity and the theory of quantum mechanics. Each of these complex notions provides a partial explanation for how the universe works, and together they add knowledge of astronomical and subatomic phenomena to Newtonian science.

Between the two of them, these theories cover almost all aspects of physical matter. But the scientific search is on for what British physicist Stephen Hawking calls "a complete unified theory that will describe everything in the universe," one consistent set of principles that would account for forces that set the courses of stars and planets and govern the behavior of the most minute subnuclear particles.

To believers in astrology, what the physicists seek is the very "seamless wholeness" that astrology has long ascribed to the universe. One physicist supposedly has pointed out that the quest for the theory of everything requires a kind of thinking that is halfway between physics and religion—"precisely this middle ground," says Elwell, that "we encounter in astrology." And Caroline Casey feels that the discovery of a unified order would be a clear vindication for astrology. "Once you get meaning in the pattern, so that the pattern of the planets and everything else actually means something instead of being random, then that is astrology. The astrological case is made. There is nothing for the skeptics to attack."

While others concern themselves with how astrology works, or whether it works at all, more and more people appear to be using it more and more often. A 1985 poll in France showed that nine out of ten people know their sun signs and about 70 percent of those sur-

The Heavens and Earth

The standard birth chart takes into account the time and place of birth in mapping cosmic influences. But enterprising San Francisco astrologer Jim Lewis has created an intricate variation he deems useful in this day of global travel. Astro*Carto*Graphy, as Lewis styles his system with a typographical flourish, uses a computer to chart the planets' relationship not just to one's birthplace but to a map of the entire earth. The aim, he says, is to determine which geographic locations will be significant in one's life—which places will bring out certain personality traits, for example, or serve as potential backdrops for disaster, or offer the best chance for business success or true love.

Lewis plots the location of all the planets and the sun and moon where they appear either directly above or directly below a location, or are visible on either horizon. Like the zodiacal houses in a birth chart, each of these positions has its own meaning. A planet on the eastern horizon, for instance, supposedly affects the way one presents oneself to others. In Astro*Carto*Graphy, the position's meaning is combined with the interpretation of the planet found there. Thus, according to Lewis, anyone born in a city where Jupiter appeared on the eastern horizon at the moment of his or her birth may exude self-confidence. On the other hand, someone born in a place where Neptune appeared on the western horizon might expect to develop marital problems.

*Astrologer Jim Lewis charted the position of the planets at the moment of John F. Kennedy's birth on May 29, 1917. This intriguing example of Astro*Carto*Graphy shows Pluto, the planet of death or transition, directly above Dallas, Texas. President Kennedy was assassinated in Dallas by Lee Harvey Oswald on November 22, 1963.*

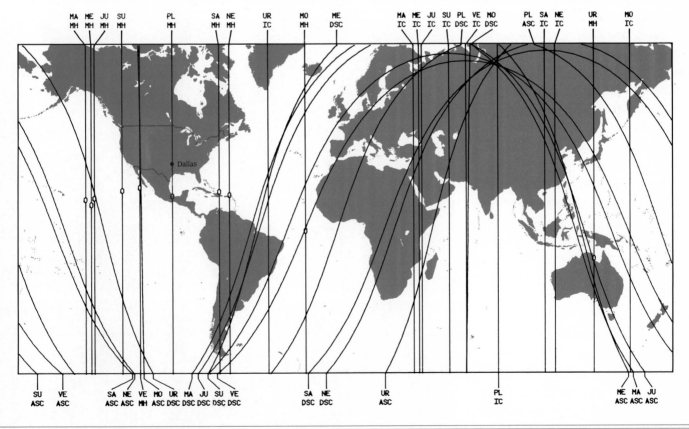

To the dismay of most astronomers, astrologers contend that there are parallels between their two pursuits. A case in point is NASA's Voyager 2 space probe, launched in 1977 and now gliding through the outer reaches of the Solar System. Voyager's route of exploration has taken it toward a rare alignment of Jupiter, Saturn, Uranus, and Neptune. Astrologers give mystical significance to the itinerary. They assert that Jupiter (left) and an aligned Saturn (below) signify expanding knowledge, reflecting the nature of Voyager's mission. Uranus (opposite) is a similarly apt metaphor, they say, since it is astrology's planet of discovery.

veyed consult their newspaper horoscopes at least occasionally. A similar poll in 1963 found that in those days only 58 percent of the French even knew their signs. Today, some mass-circulation American magazines carry astrology columns that have larger readerships than any other part of the publications.

To serious astrologers, however, the forecasts and advice in these columns, based only on sun signs, are merely entertainment. Most professional astrologers work individually with their clients and make readings on the basis of star-chart information that includes exact time and location of birth. Thus, the positions of all the pertinent celestial bodies can be taken into account.

In the Western world, the astrologer's work consists mainly of counseling, explaining what a client's chart means in terms of probable traits and preferences, discussing the client's problems, and helping to delineate solutions that are astrologically likely. During the early 1980s, one U.S. professor of psychology studied the work of astrologers and reported in the *American Journal of Psychotherapy* that their role was very much like that of psychotherapists. Clients got empathy, advice, and increased self-esteem—all

without the stigma sometimes attached to consulting a psychiatrist or psychologist. Another psychologist introduced some astrological elements into her own counseling sessions, discussing her clients' zodiacal signs and the traits that are traditionally associated with them. She discovered that the technique stimulated discussion and provided a focal point for clients to describe their personal qualities and problems. Such testimony evoked some approval even from CSICOP's journal, *The Skeptical Inquirer.* In a major piece on astrology, one of the magazine's writers declared: "Clearly, when used in this way, astrology can be valuable without needing to be true."

Astrological counseling may assume its most refined state in a form called humanistic astrology, introduced in the United States in the late 1960s by Dane Rudhyar, a Paris-born composer-poet-painter. In his own words, Rudhyar's astrology is "non-scientific, subjective, and purely symbolic." In contrast to those who see astrology as an art

or science, the humanistic astrologer regards it as a philosophy of life. The birth chart is viewed as a pattern of a person's potential, describing what the individual may, with effort, grow to become.

Although the current emphasis in Western astrology is on counseling, many astrologers do not ignore their original purpose as defined by their ancient antecedents—to foretell the future, to spy out the track of destiny before it is walked. This is the side of their art, after all, that still rivets the attention of most of us, believers and nonbelievers. Nancy Reagan, obviously, was no less interested in predictions concerning the fate of the nation's leader than was any Babylonian monarch consulting a ziggurat-climbing stargazer some 4,000 years earlier.

And according to writer Richard Deacon, an authority on secret security services, astrology has also played a part in planning a well-known modern military exploit. Deacon alleges that the daring and successful Israeli rescue of hostages from terrorists at the Entebbe, Uganda, airport in 1976 was preceded by consideration of its astrological prospects for success. Israeli officials have adamantly denied the whole story, but Deacon maintains that "close attention" was paid to a constantly monitored horoscope of Israel that had been kept up-to-date since the state was created in 1948.

Whether by cosmic accuracy or mere coincidence, fate occasionally fulfills an astrologer's prediction in a manner that can send a vaguely familiar shiver running up the spine of the public—and make even some nonbelievers momentarily feel the presence of unseen sages in long robes and conical hats, taking the measure of palpably powerful forces from the stars. One such instance occurred in 1987, when British astrologer Dennis Elwell became concerned about conditions indicated by a total eclipse of the sun that would occur on March 29.

"On 18 February," said Elwell, "I did something I had never done before in my 40 years' study of astrology—issue an uninvited warning." Elwell relates that he wrote identical letters to two major British shipping companies, Cunard

and P&O, to alert them "to the potential hazards locked into the March eclipse," which he said could endanger shipping for a year or more. The emphasis, he said, "is on the sudden and disruptive." He cautioned that their sailing schedules might be "upset for some unexpected reason" but warned that there was "a possibility of rather more dramatic eventualities, such as explosions." And his letter noted that the disastrous loss of the *Titanic* with 1,500 lives had coincided with similar planetary configurations and an eclipse seventy-five years earlier.

P&O declined Elwell's assistance, replying that the company's procedures were designed "to deal with the unexpected from whatever quarter." Nine days later, on March 6, 1987, the *Herald of Free Enterprise,* a big seagoing ferry belonging to a P&O subsidiary, capsized off Zeebrugge, Belgium, with the loss of 188 lives. Cunard, meanwhile, politely replied to Elwell that his letter had been passed to the Fleet Commodore. That officer was on board Cunard's *Queen Elizabeth II* a few months later when it made a much-publicized maiden voyage following a costly refit. The voyage, intended to usher in "a new age of truly gracious sailing," was a "debacle," according to the *Times* of London. "Ill-fated," the *Daily Telegraph* called it. Everything went wrong: The *QE II* listed, parts of the ship were unfinished, the crew was shorthanded, there were air-conditioning problems, cabins flooded. After a delayed arrival in New York, angry passengers received substantial refunds on their fares.

Elwell cites a long list of other mishaps at sea, major and minor, occurring in scattered locations around the world during the rest of the year. Of course, disasters at sea happen every year, total eclipse or no total eclipse. But even so, those who were aware of Elwell's warnings must have been given further pause in December of 1987, when the crowded ferry *Doña Paz* went down in the Philippines with more than 1,600 people on board—gaining the gloomy distinction of surpassing the death toll from the star-crossed ocean liner, the *Titanic,* when it sank in conjunction with that similar eclipse in 1912.

Views of the Coming Century

Astrologers now spend much of their time counseling clients about personal problems, but the aspect of astrology with the strongest grip on public imagination is still the foretelling of the future—especially the kind of sweeping predictions about the fate of the world that have made the sixteenth-century astrologer Nostradamus so fascinating to succeeding generations.

For this book, three astrologers were asked to chart what the heavens seem to hold in store for the twenty-first century. All three foresee the new century starting with upheaval—as, indeed, did Nostradamus, one of whose predictions seems to say that the world will be racked by war and havoc beginning in 1999. But as their predictions make clear, they are not as pessimistic as that prophet of old was, and all of them interpret the future in their own unique (and sometimes cryptic) styles, which may reflect their personal views of life as much as their readings of astral signposts.

Dennis Elwell is an English astrologer famed for two widely reported, seemingly fulfilled forecasts in 1987—one predicting sea disasters *(page 152),* the other a caution to underground travelers that was followed within days by the deaths of thirty-one people in a London subway fire.

With his record for gloomy accuracy, Elwell sees some disquieting confirmation for Nostradamus's melancholy forecast for 1999. According to many interpretations of his work, Nostradamus said that in the seventh month of that year ''the great King of Terror will come from the skies.'' The prediction foretells a tyrant originating in the Middle East who is destined to lay waste European civilization.

Elwell notes that in July of 1999—the seventh month—an eclipse of the moon will be caught up in a square ninety-degree aspect between Jupiter and Neptune. In that position, says Elwell, ''these planets signify an unstable overheating—like pumping up a balloon to the bursting point.''

Furthermore, a fortnight after the first eclipse of the moon, a second eclipse will occur, this time in a 180-degree opposition of Mars and Saturn. ''This is a ruthless combination, the iron fist,'' advises Elwell. ''Mars is the planet of aggression and hostility, and Saturn commonly manifests fear and coldness.'' The astrologer finds it no comfort that Mars will be in the constellation Scorpio, the traditional ''death sign of the zodiac''—nor that Saturn frequently indicates heavy loss.

But Elwell explains that relatively minor events can serve as what he terms blowholes, or safety valves, for pent-up cosmic forces. The Jupiter-Neptune configuration points to ocean travel, for instance. Thus, if Mars-Saturn indicates heavy loss, perhaps the threat is mainly to ships at sea, rather than to the whole world.

Whatever happens, Elwell goes on, neither Nostradamus nor modern astrologers ''see the turn of the century as visiting total disaster on the planet.'' On January 1, 2000, three major planets, Mars, Uranus, and Neptune, will be in Aquarius. ''This sign,'' says Elwell, ''has to do with social experiments. Working together, these three planets tell us that many of our existing and most revered social structures will be jettisoned as imperfect. There will be an increasing impatience to translate ideals into action.''

Elwell believes the Soviet Union will play an even larger role in world affairs than at present, but perhaps it will play a very different one, in the vanguard of a drive for universal brotherhood. ''The Russian soul may be sleeping,'' he says, ''waiting its time.'' He notes that Uranus, known for drastic upheaval, passed through Aquarius at the time of the 1917 Russian Revolution—and that Uranus enters Aquarius again in 1996, there to remain for seven years. Those years may see another Russian revolution, suggests Elwell, or at least significant change in the USSR.

The mainspring for change in the new century will be a dazzling renaissance of science. But the rebirth will be more in human than technological terms—''not so much the cleverness of gadgetry as a fresh perception of universal principles.''

Indeed, the twenty-first century may well be that ''Age of Aquarius'' celebrated by popular folklore, an era of enlightenment and fraternal spirit. According to Elwell, other celestial combinations seem to bear out the idea: In the century's horoscope, Pluto, the planet of breakthroughs, will be in conjunction with the recently discovered planetoid Chiron, named after the mighty centaur who conducted a school for heroes. Both will be in Sagittarius, sign of widening horizons, which suggests to Elwell the "training up" of men and women to astounding heights of achievement. There may even be the means at hand to produce a breed of supermen and superwomen.

In all of this, Elwell says, society will no longer accept less than the best in its leaders. Democracy, with its many political compromises, may give way to a sort of benign elitism. Humanity will at last face up to the finite nature of natural resources and acknowledge that there are limits to the ecological burden the earth can bear.

Instead of unbridled economic growth, concludes Elwell, "an era of relative contraction seems to be favored, along with a simpler and more authentic lifestyle." People will be the earth's greatest resource and they will be entitled to chief consideration; the emphasis on the perpetuation of mere institutions becomes irrelevant in comparison. "In the twenty-first century, any institution or system that fails to support human goals will be peremptorily dispatched."

Jim Lewis of San Francisco has been a practicing astrologer since the late 1960s and specializes in the effects of geographical location on astrological influences *(page 149)*. He, too, believes that the coming century will be a time of intense crisis and change, although he focuses primarily on America.

Lewis divides the century into six

periods of varying lengths, based on the positions of the outer planets in the horoscope of the United States. The outer planets are thought to control large-scale, long-term developments. The first period, from the year 2000 to 2012, will be shaped by Pluto in Sagittarius, the sign of cultural institutions, and by Uranus in Aquarius and Pisces, signs of idealism and humanitarianism. Lewis holds that this period will see "the metamorphosis of social institutions," brought about by ever-accelerating technology.

The electronic revolution will produce "informational subgroups linked by common interests through computers—and these are to be the dominant organizational form for this century, just as national and corporate groups held sway in the twentieth." In this new "human monoculture," electronic data will be universally available. "Every being on the planet is to be linked electronically." Thus, "as all cultures become accessible, each begins to lose its uniqueness and individuals, too, lose their sense of identity."

It will be a time of philosophical anarchy, Lewis foresees, "with collective group beliefs achieving a brief dominance, one after the other." American democracy is likely to change radically since the will of the people will be instantly measurable.

He thinks scientists will find that "people, cells, organs and societies all respond predictably to external electronic stimulation, setting the stage for *the* scientific revolution of the twenty-first century—the harnessing of electronic wave energy, which will culminate midcentury with 'rays' that heal, educate or genetically program."

The years between 2012 and 2030 will see Pluto in Capricorn, a condition

affecting governmental structures, and Uranus in Aries and Taurus, signs of individualism and the ecosystem. This will be a time of consolidation and rethinking. With its economic and military primacy on the wane, the U.S., says Lewis, "is thrown back on itself to develop internal values and identity." These may be the years when China and Canada, the former for its supremely well organized population, the latter for its vast resources, arrive at center stage. People will demand an end to pollution. And, predicts Lewis, "a world race, more yellow and brown than white, becomes inevitable."

The next fifteen years will be marked by Pluto in Aquarius, Neptune in Aries and Taurus, and Uranus in Gemini, Cancer, and Leo. To Lewis, these positions foretell a sudden polarization of ideas and a resurgence of an "us and them psychology." Who the "us" and "them" will be is difficult to forecast, but he thinks that because of resource distribution, disputes seem more likely along north-south lines than between East and West.

Meanwhile, says Lewis, science will have achieved the means by which "moods, feelings and complex nonverbal ideas can be communicated among individuals and groups through the broadcast of electromagnetic frequencies." Now, for the first time, there can be communication between all the species of the earth. "But the big news," suggests Lewis, "may be that similar emanations are picked up from extraterrestrial sources."

The middle years, from 2045 to 2063, could be the most disruptive. Among the most important planetary influences will be Uranus passing through Virgo, Libra, and Scorpio, pointing to increasing polarization. Lewis says anarchy and dissolution are likely, as counterforces stressing individualism and ethnic pride challenge "the new, homogenized, worldwide monoculture." Struggles between the haves and the have-nots add to the disarray.

The stars foretell a return to peace and relative quiet in the years 2063 to 2078. The U.S., Lewis says, will fall into a sort of "somnolent, self-congratulatory idealism and isolationism, not unlike the early 1900s . . . an idealized and xenophobic perfection."

Worldwide, he continues, "a racial narcissism takes hold, powered by the fact that the last 'natural' humans with genes unmodified by conscious intention are being born." The rise of genetic manipulation will largely result from the need to reduce mutations caused by environmental toxins. Science may finally find that genetically engineered microorganisms can be developed to control the poisons.

In the last quarter of the century, as Neptune moves into creative and artistic Leo, "genetic engineering may well become almost an art form," predicts Lewis, "with the 'improved' human being itself the ultimate artistic expression." Lewis forecasts a flowering of art, a sort of "hedonistic Renaissance." Yet the century ends on a depressing note. "In the absence of a sense of self that comes from the family and ethnic identity," says Lewis, "individuals have only their own evolution to look forward to."

Caroline W. Casey, of Washington, D.C., holds a degree in semiotics (symbol systems) from Brown University and enjoys a wide astrological practice on radio, television, and the lecture circuit as well as through her writings and personal counseling.

Casey sees the period ahead as a time of massive upheaval yet great opportunity. The planet Neptune, she says, represents "the Intelligence of Vision, how a culture turns imagination into reality." With Neptune in Capricorn, the years leading up to 1998 will witness the dissolution of what she calls the greedy and self-indulgent economic structure of old. Most of the polluting industries, particularly "the chemical and nuclear power trusts," will be driven into bankruptcy. A new global power structure will "implement the solution-oriented Visions of the Neptune-in-Aquarius period," which lasts from 1998 until 2011.

Casey believes that during this time advances in physics will reveal the universe to be "an organic, unfolding and continually evolving Intelligence." She says the dispute between ancient metaphysics and modern physics will end; the two will join in what Casey calls Reverent Science—a science that will "release the earth's first human seeds out into the galaxy."

Viewing the planet Pluto as "the Intelligence of death, rebirth and renewal," Casey predicts that its passage through Capricorn from 2008 to 2024 will signal the increasing irrelevance and final death of the nation-state. "Clans—modern tribes by choice—develop without any spatial boundaries," she prophesies. "And global families develop through creative affinity. Music and arts become the agents of world change and contribute to the creation of true participatory global democracy."

By 2020, Casey states, cultural leadership will fall to two main groups. Uranus represents radical change and innovation. The planet will be in Taurus, the realm of the traditional

and biological. Therefore, one group will be what Casey terms "the Radical Traditionalists, whose function will be the Taurean task of restoring the earth to its pristine state." They will be the guardians and stewards of the gene pool. The second group, according to Casey, "will be the Visionary Technocrats, who will undertake the colonization of space, beginning with the moon, Mars and the asteroids."

Commencing in 2025, with Neptune in Aries, a great out-migration from the home planet will occur. "This," advises Casey, "will reduce the population stress on earth, allowing the Radical Traditionalists to get on with restoration and healing." The world will see the "age of marvelous solutions": more energy with less waste, greater understanding of electromagnetic fields around both the earth and the human body, the healing of the ozone layer, the elimination of crude surgery, the regeneration of human limbs. "A whole new cycle of humanity begins," says Casey.

By 2038, with Neptune in Taurus, "the earth should be well on its way to a full healing. A rich gene pool is now assured." There is more human communication with other species, particularly whales and dolphins.

The outer-space colonies are thriving, and in 2067, with Pluto in Aries, says Casey, "we have the beginning of star travel, and the infinite opening universe in which to play." At this time, too, continues the astrologer, "there is initial physical contact with extraterrestrials in a large-scale societal way." Thus, concludes Casey, "life continues to serve the Great Order, with increasing love and efficiency, with accelerated evolution in consciousness."

ACKNOWLEDGMENTS

The editors wish to express their appreciation to the following individuals and institutions:

Robert Amadou, Paris; Dr. Hans Bender, Institut für Grenzgebiete der Psychologie und Psychohygiene, Freiburg, West Germany; Nicholas Clarke-Lowes, Society for Psychical Research, London; Elena Corradini, Galleria Estense, Modena, Italy; Giancarlo Costa, Milan, Italy; Antoinette Decaudin, Documentaliste, Département des Antiquités Orientales, Musée du Louvre, Paris; Dr. LeRoy Doggett, U.S. Naval Observatory, Washington, D.C.; Dr. Baldur von Ebertin, Bad Wildbad, West Germany; Dennis Elwell, Stourbridge, West Midlands, England; Germana Ernst, Università di Firenze, Florence, Italy; Hilary Evans, London; Prof. Claudio Gallazzi, Università di Milano, Milan, Italy; Gabrielle Kohler Gallei, Archiv für Kunst und Geschichte, West Berlin; Michel Gauquelin, Paris; Leif Geiges, Staufen, West Germany; Charles Harvey, Frome, Somerset, England; Kitty Higgins, Washington, D.C.; Manfred Kage, Lauterstein, West Germany; James B. Kaler, Department of Astronomy, University of Illinois, Urbana; Heidi Klein, Bildarchiv Preussischer Kulturbesitz, West Berlin; Dr. Theodor Landscheidt, Lilienthal, West Germany; Jim Lewis, Astrocartography™, San Francisco; Brenda Marsh, Weybridge, Surrey, England; Mary Ellen Miller, New Haven, Conn.; Giuseppe Monaco, Rome, Italy; Doris Montagne, Fondation Saint Thomas, Strasbourg, France; Danielle Muzerelle, Conservateur, Bibliothèque de l'Arsenal, Paris; Eleanor O'Keeffe, London; Derek Parker and Julia Parker, London; Royal Library, Copenhagen, Denmark; Leyla Rudhyar, San Francisco, Calif.; G. C. Shekhar, Madras, India; Dr. Rolf Streichardt, Institut für Grenzgebiete der Psychologie und Psychohygiene, Freiburg, West Germany; Masako Watanabe, New York, N.Y.; Matthew Zalichin, Takoma Park, Md.

PICTURE CREDITS

The sources for the illustrations in this book are shown below. Credits from left to right are separated by semicolons; credits from top to bottom are separated by dashes.

Cover: Art by Bryan Leister. 1, 3, and initial alphabet art by John Drummond. 8, 9: Robert Harding Associates, London, from *Early Man and the Cosmos*, by Evan Hadingham. 10: Courtesy of the Trustees of the British Museum, London. 11-13: Art by Yvonne Gensurowsky/SRW Inc. 14, 15: Art by Tina Taylor. 16: Daniel Bouquignaud, Agence TOP. 18, 19: Gerald Ponting/Janet & Colin Bord, Wales. 20: © T. Middleton/The Telegraph Colour Library, London. 21: Vincenzo Negro, Modena, courtesy Galleria Estense, Modena. 22: Luisa Ricciarini, Milan, courtesy Museo Archeologico Nazionale. 24: Musées Royaux D'Art et D'Histoire, Bruxelles. 25: Courtesy George Lovi—art by Walter Hilmers, Jr. from HJ Commercial Art. 26: Courtesy of the Trustees of the British Library, London. 27: Antikenmuseum Staatlich Museen Preussischer Kulturbesitz, West Berlin, Foto Jürgen Liepe. 28, 29: Beijing Cultural Relics Publishing House. 30: Kodansha Publishing Co. Ltd., Tokyo, courtesy Egyptian Museum of Cairo. 31: Kodansha Publishing Co. Ltd., Tokyo, courtesy Egyptian Museum of Cairo—courtesy of the Trustees of the British Museum, London; Giraudon, Paris. 32, 33: *Sky and Telescope*—G. Dagli Orti, Paris. 35: Nikos Kontos—inset art by Allen Davis from *Uranometria* by Johannes Bayer, courtesy the University of Illinois Library. 38: Scala, Florence, courtesy Musei Vaticani, Rome. 39: Scala, Florence, courtesy Tempio Malatestiano, Rimini. 40: Nikos Kontos. 41: Scala, Florence, courtesy Museo Archeologico Nazionale, Florence. 42: National Gallery of Art, Washington, D.C., Andrew W. Mellon Collection. 43: Scala, Florence, courtesy Musei Vaticani, Rome. 44: Scala, Florence, courtesy Tempio Malatestiano, Rimini. 45: Emmett Bright, courtesy Musei Vaticani, Rome. 46: Courtesy of the Board of Trustees of the Victoria and Albert Museum, London. 47: Scala, Florence, courtesy Galleria Borghese, Rome. 49: Royal Astronomical Society, London. 50, 51: Courtesy of the Trustees of the British Library, London. 53: Artephot/Promophot, Paris. 54: Courtesy Edinburgh University Library. 55: Courtesy Chester Beatty Library, Dublin. 56: Phillip Pocock, courtesy the Spencer Collection, the New York Public Library, Astor, Lenox and Tilden Foundations. 57: Bibliothèque Nationale, Paris. 58: Det kongelige Bibliotek, Copenhagen. 60, 61: John B. Carlson; Hillel Burger, 1972, courtesy Peabody Museum, Harvard University—Marc Riboud, Magnum, Paris. 62: Bibliothèque Nationale, Paris. 63: Giancarlo Costa, Milan, courtesy Bibliotech Amabrosiana, Milan. 65: Giraudon/Art Resource. 66: Courtesy the Huntington Library, San Marino, California—courtesy The Master and Fellows of Peterhouse, Cambridge. 67: Scala, Florence, courtesy Duomo, Florence. 68, 69: Giovanni Roncaglia, courtesy Biblioteca Estense, Modena. 70: Courtesy of the Trustees of the British Library, London. 71: Andre Held/Artephot-Ziolo, Paris. 72: Giraudon, Paris. 73: Jean-Loup Charmet, Paris. 74: Scala, Florence, courtesy Galleria Borghese, Rome—Donato Pineider, Florence, courtesy Biblioteca Medicea Laurenziana, Florence—Donato Pineider, Florence, courtesy Museo Nazionale del Bargello. 75: BBC Hulton Picture Library, London. 76: National Portrait Gallery, London. 77: From *Astrology: The Celestial Mirror* by Warren Kenton, Avon publishers, London, 1974. 78: Giraudon, Paris. 79: Jean-Loup Charmet, Paris. 80: Scala, Florence. 81: Courtesy the Librarian of the Glasgow University Library, Glasgow. 82, 83: Bibliothèque Nationale, Paris. 84: Bodleian Library, Oxford. 85, 86: Bibliothèque Nationale, Paris. 87: Courtesy of the Trustees of the British Library, London. 88: Bodleian Library, Oxford. 89, 90: Bibliothèque Nationale, Paris. 91: Bibliothèque Royale Albert 1er, Brussels. 94: Explorer Archives, Paris. 95: Giraudon, Paris—Explorer Archives, Paris. 96: Explorer Archives, Paris. 97: Mary Evans Picture Library, London—detail from the portrait in the Royal Observatory, Edinburgh. 98: Courtesy Fondation St. Thomas, Strasbourg. 99: Jean-Loup Charmet, Paris. 100, 101: Courtesy Istituto e Museo di Storia della Scienza, Florence—Scala, Florence, courtesy Galleria degli Uffizi, Florence; Scala, Florence. 102: Courtesy of the Trustees of the British Museum, London. 103: Courtesy of the Trustees of the British Library, London. 105: The Ashmolean Museum, Oxford. 106: Courtesy of the Trustees of the British Library, London. 107: Bodleian Library, Oxford. 108: Images Colour Library, London/Charles Walker Occult Collection. 109: Ann Ronan Picture Library, Taunton Somerset. 110, 111: © Robert Holmes. 114, 115: Courtesy of the Trustees of the British Library, London. 116: From *The Art of Synthesis (How to Judge a Nativity, Part 2)* by Alan Leo, 1909/courtesy the Theosophical Society, London. 117: Field Museum of Natural History (transparency #16231C), Chicago—Western History Collections, University of Oklahoma Library; National Anthropological Archives, Smithsonian Institution. 118: Scala, Florence, courtesy Museo Correr, Venice. 119-125: Art by John Drummond. 126: Mary Evans Picture Library, London/Sigmund Freud Copyrights/courtesy of W. E. Freud. 127: Art by John Drummond. 133: New York Historical Society, New York City—Nicholas Muray, courtesy Time Inc. Picture Collection. 134: Ellic Howe, London—from *The Cosmic Influence* by Francis King, Doubleday and Company, Inc., Garden City, N.J., 1976. 135: Foto Leif für Grenzgebiete der Psychologie und Psychohygiene, Freiburg. 137: Roland and Sabrina Michaud/Rapho, Paris. 138: Keystone Collection, London—courtesy Imperial War Museum, London. 140, 141: T. S. Satyan, Life Magazine © Time Inc. 142: Courtesy Library of Congress—art by John Drummond. 144: Martha Swope. 146, 147: Elkoussy/Sygma; Bruce Wagman/Gamma Liaison—Gamma Liaison. 148: Betty Freeman. 149: Courtesy Astro*Carto*Graphy. 150, 151: NASA/JPL. 153-155: Background courtesy Science Photo Library, London.

BIBLIOGRAPHY

Adams, Evangeline, *The Bowl of Heaven*. New York: Dodd, Mead, 1926.

Addey, John M., *Harmonics in Astrology*. Chadwell Heath, Essex, England: L. N. Fowler, 1976.

"Anti-Astrology Packet." *Skeptical Inquirer,* summer 1983.

Armstrong, J., "An Italian Astrologer at the Court of Henry VII." In *Italian Renaissance Studies,* ed. by Ernest F. Jacob. London: Faber and Faber, 1960.

Arroyo, Stephen, *The Practice and Profession of Astrology*. Reno, Nev.: CRCS, 1984.

"Astrology Disclaimer." *Skeptical Inquirer,* summer 1986.

Baigent, Michael, Nicholas Campion, and Charles Harvey, *Mundane Astrology*. Wellingborough, Northamptonshire, England: Aquarian Press, 1984.

Bastedo, Ralph W., "An Empirical Test of Popular Astrology." *Skeptical Inquirer,* fall 1978.

Best, Simon, ed., *Correlation* (Hants, Great Britain), December 1986.

Boczkowska, Anna, *Hieronim Bosch: Astrologiczna Symbolika Jego Dziel.* Wroclaw, Poland: Wydawnictwo Polskiej Akademii Nauk, 1977.

Bok, Bart J., "R. B. Culver and Philip A. Ianna, *The Gemini Syndrome*" (book review). *Skeptical Inquirer,* winter 1980-1981.

Bok, Bart J., and Lawrence E. Jerome, *Objections to Astrology*. Buffalo: Prometheus Books, 1975.

Boorstin, Daniel J., *The Discoverers*. New York: Random House, 1983.

Brau, Jean-Louis, ed., *Larousse Encyclopedia of Astrology*. New York: McGraw-Hill, 1980.

Camden, Charles C., *Astrology in Shakespeare's Day.* Bruges, Belgium: Saint Catherine Press, 1930.

Campion, Nicholas:
An Introduction to the History of Astrology. London: Institute for the Study of Cycles in World Affairs, 1982.
The Practical Astrologer. New York: Harry N. Abrams, 1987.

Capp, Bernard, *English Almanacs 1500-1800: Astrology and the Popular Press.* Ithaca, N.Y.: Cornell University Press, 1979.

Cavendish, Richard, ed.:
Man, Myth & Magic. Vol. 3. Freeport, N.Y.: Marshall Cavendish, 1983.
Mythology: An Illustrated Encyclopedia. London: Orbis, 1980.

Cornell, James, *The First Stargazers: An Introduction to the Origins of Astronomy.* New York: Charles Scribner's Sons, 1981.

Cosmology + 1: Readings from Scientific American. San Francisco: W. H. Freeman, 1977.

Cramer, Frederick H., *Astrology in Roman Law and Politics.* Philadelphia: American Philosophical Society, 1954.

Cronin, Vincent, *The View from Planet Earth.* New York: William Morrow, 1981.

Culver, R. B., and Philip A. Ianna, *The Gemini Syndrome: A Scientific Evaluation of Astrology.* Buffalo: Prometheus Books, 1984.

David, Rosalie, *Cult of the Sun: Myth and Magic in Ancient Egypt.* London: J. M. Dent & Sons, 1980.

Deacon, Richard:
The Book of Fate: Its Origins and Uses. London: Frederick Muller, 1976.
A History of the British Secret Service. New York: Taplinger, 1969.
The Israeli Secret Service. London: Hamish Hamilton, 1977.
John Dee. London: Frederick Muller, 1968.

Dean, Geoffrey:
"Does Astrology Need to Be True? Part 1: A Look at the Real Thing." *Skeptical Inquirer,* winter 1986-1987.
"Does Astrology Need to Be True? Part 2: The Answer Is No." *Skeptical Inquirer,* spring 1987.
"Guardian Astrology Study: A Critique and Reanalysis." *Skeptical Inquirer,* summer 1985.

Dean, Geoffrey, comp., *Recent Advances in Natal Astrology: A Critical Review, 1900-1976.* Bromley, Kent, England: Astrological Association, 1977.

Ehresman, Nancy, and Stephen Albaugh, *The Saturn Return.* Tempe, Ariz.: American Federation of Astrologers, 1984.

Elwell, Dennis, *Cosmic Loom: The New Science of Astrology.* London: Unwin Hyman, 1987.

Ertel, Suitbert:
"Further Grading of Eminence: Planetary Correlations with Musicians, Painters, Writers." *Correlation* (Hants, Great Britain), June 1987.
"Grading the Eminence, or: Raising the Hurdle for the Athletes' Mars Effect." Unpublished manuscript, October 1987.

Eysenck, H. J., and D. K. B. Nias, *Astrology: Science or Superstition?* New York: St. Martin's Press, 1982.

Firenze e la Toscana dei Medici nell'Europa del Cinquecento—Astrologia, magia e alchimia (exhibition catalog). Florence, Italy: Edizioni Medicee, 1980.

French, Peter J., *John Dee: The World of an Elizabethan Magus.* London: Routledge and Kegan Paul, 1972.

Friedrich, Otto, "New Age Harmonies." *Time,* December 7, 1987.

Friedman, Jack, "Hum If You Love the Mayans." *People Weekly,* August 31, 1981.

Gallant, Roy A., *Astrology: Sense or Nonsense?* Garden City, N.Y.: Doubleday, 1974.

Garcia, Beatrice E., "An Appraisal: From Stats to Stars, Wall Street Searches for Guidance." *Wall Street Journal,* February 22, 1988.

Gardner, Martin, *In the Name of Science.* New York: G. P. Putnam's Sons, 1952.

Garin, Eugenio, *Astrology in the Renaissance.* London: Routledge and Kegan Paul, 1983.

Gauquelin, Michel:
Astrology and Science. Transl. by James Hughes. London: Peter Davies, 1969.
The Cosmic Clocks: From Astrology to a Modern Science. London: Peter Owen, 1969.
Dreams and Illusions of Astrology. Buffalo: Prometheus Books, 1979.
"K. E. Krafft, *Traite d'Astrobiologie,* and Edmund Van Deusen, *Astrogenetics*" (book review). *Skeptical Inquirer,* spring/summer 1978.
The Scientific Basis of Astrology. Transl. by James Hughes. New York: Stein and Day, 1969.
"Second Eysenck Research Seminar, Freiburg-im-Brisgau, West Germany, April 13-14, 1987." *Correlation* (Hants, Great Britain), June 1987.
The Truth about Astrology. Transl. by Sarah Matthews. Oxford, England: Basil Blackwell, 1983.
"Zodiac and Personality: An Empirical Study." *Skeptical Inquirer,* spring 1982.

Gauquelin, Michel, et al., "Discussion of the 'Mars Effect' Studies." *Skeptical Inquirer,* summer 1980.

Glass, Justine, *They Foresaw the Future: The Story of Fulfilled Prophecy.* New York: G. P. Putnam's Sons, 1969.

Gleadow, Rupert, *The Origin of the Zodiac.* New York: Atheneum, 1969.

Good, I. J., Paul A. Reeves, and Geoffrey Dean, "Statistics on Dean's Astrology Article." *Skeptical Inquirer,* summer 1987.

Graubard, Mark, *Astrology and Alchemy.* New York: Philosophical Library, 1953.

Graves, Robert:
The Greek Myths. Vols. 1 and 2. Harmondsworth, Middlesex, England: Penguin Books, 1955.
The White Goddess. London: Faber and Faber, 1961.

Gray, John, *Near Eastern Mythology.* London: Hamlyn, 1969.

Greek Ministry of Culture and Sciences, *The Search for Alexander* (exhibition catalog). Boston: Little, Brown, 1980.

Gribbin, John R., and Stephen H. Plagemann, *The Jupiter Effect.* New York: Walker, 1974.

Hadingham, Evan, *Early Man and the Cosmos.* London: William Heinemann, 1983.

Hall, Manly Palmer, *The Story of Astrology.* Philadelphia: David McKay, 1943.

Hawking, Stephen W., *A Brief History of Time: From the Big Bang to Black Holes.* Toronto: Bantam Books, 1988.

Hill, Joylyn, *The Discovery of the Outer Planets.* Tempe, Ariz.: American Federation of Astrologers, 1985.

Howe, Ellic:
Astrology: A Recent History Including the Untold Story of Its Role in World War II. New York: Walker, 1967.
Astrology and the Third Reich. Wellingborough, Northamptonshire, England: Aquarian Press, 1984.
The Black Game: British Subversive Operations against the Germans during the Second World War. London: Michael Joseph, 1982.

Nostradamus and the Nazis. London: Arborfield, 1965.
Urania's Children: The Strange World of the Astrologers. London: William Kimber, 1967.

Ianna, Philip A., and Chaim J. Margolin, "Planetary Positions, Radio Propagation, and the Work of J. H. Nelson." *Skeptical Inquirer,* fall 1981.

Ianna, Philip A., and Charles R. Tolbert, "A Retest of Astrologer John McCall." *Skeptical Inquirer,* winter 1984-1985.

"It's in the Stars, Mr. President." *Discover,* January 1985.

Jackson, Eve, *Jupiter: An Astrologer's Guide.* Wellingborough, Northamptonshire, England: Aquarian Press, 1986.

Jerome, Lawrence E., *Astrology Disproved.* Buffalo: Prometheus Books, 1977.

Jung, C. G., *Synchronicity: An Acausal Connecting Principle.* Transl. by R. F. C. Hull. Princeton, N.J.: Princeton University Press, 1960.

Kelly, Ivan W., and R. W. Krutzen, "Humanistic Astrology: A Critique." *Skeptical Inquirer,* fall 1983.

Kelly, Ivan W., and Don H. Saklofske, "Alternative Explanations in Science: The Extroversion-Introversion Astrological Effect." *Skeptical Inquirer,* summer 1981.

Kenton, Warren, *Astrology: The Celestial Mirror.* New York: Avon Books, 1974.

King, Bruce (Zolar, pseud.), *The History of Astrology.* New York: Arco, 1972.

King, Francis, *The Cosmic Influence.* Garden City, N.Y.: Doubleday, 1976.

Kleinfield, N. R., "Seeing Dollar Signs in Searching the Stars." *New York Times,* May 15, 1988.

Koestler, Arthur, *Walkers: A History of Man's Changing Vision of the Universe.* New York: Macmillan, 1959.

Komaroff, Katherine, *Sky Gods.* New York: Universe Books, 1974.

Kowalski, Jeff Karl, *The House of the Governor.* Norman: University of Oklahoma Press, 1987.

Krupp, E. C., *Echoes of the Ancient Skies.* New York: Harper & Row, 1983.

Kurtz, Paul, "H. J. Eysenck and D. K. B. Nias, *Astrology: Science or Superstition*" (book review). *Skeptical Inquirer,* spring 1983.

Kurtz, Paul, and Andrew Fraknoi, "Tests of Astrology Do Not Support Its Claims." *Skeptical Inquirer,* spring 1985.

Kurtz, Paul, and Lee Nisbet, "Are Astronomers and Astrophysicists Qualified to Criticize Astrology?" *Zetetic,* fall/winter 1976.

Kurtz, Paul, Marvin Zelen, and George Abell:
"Response to the Gauquelins." *Skeptical Inquirer,* winter 1979-1980.
"Results of the U.S. Test of the 'Mars Effect' Are Negative." *Skeptical Inquirer,* winter 1979-1980.

Lamy, Lucie, *Egyptian Mysteries.* Transl. by Deborah Lawlor. New York: Crossroad, 1981.

Lewis, Jim, *Astro*Carto*Graphy.* San Francisco: Astro*Carto*Graphy, 1976.

Lindsay, Jack, *Origins of Astrology.* New York: Barnes & Noble, 1971.

Luck, Georg, comp. and transl., *Arcana Mundi: Magic and the Occult in the Greek and Roman Worlds.* Baltimore: Johns Hopkins University Press, 1985.

Lum, Peter, *The Stars in Our Heaven: Myths and Fables.* New York: Pantheon, 1948.

McCann, Lee, *Nostradamus.* New York: Farrar, Straus & Giroux, 1982.

McGervey, John D., "A Statistical Test of Sun-Sign Astrology." *Zetetic,* spring/summer 1977.

McIntosh, Christopher, *The Astrologers and Their Creed:*

An Historical Outline. New York: Frederick A. Praeger, 1969.

Maclagan, David, *Creation Myths: Man's Introduction to the World.* London: Thames and Hudson, 1977.

Mailly Nesle, Solange de, *Astrology: History, Symbols and Signs.* New York: Inner Traditions International, 1983.

Mann, A. T., *The Round Art: The Astrology of Time and Space.* Ed. by Donald Lehmkuhl and Mary Flanagan. Limpsfield, Surrey, England: Dragon's World, 1979.

"The Mars Effect." *Psychology Today,* July 1982.

Martin, Malachi, *The Decline and Fall of the Roman Church.* New York: G. P. Putnam's Sons, 1981.

Mechler, Gary, "Response to the *National Enquirer* Astrology Study." *Skeptical Inquirer,* winter 1980-1981.

Meyer, Michael R., *A Handbook for the Humanistic Astrologer.* Garden City, N.Y.: Anchor Books, 1974.

Miller, Mary Ellen, *The Murals of Bonampak.* Princeton, N.J.: Princeton University Press, 1986.

Moore, Patrick, *Suns, Myths and Men.* New York: W. W. Norton, 1968.

Morrow, Lance, "The Five-and-Dime Charms of Astrology." *Time,* May 16, 1988.

Mountbatten, Viscount Louis, *Mountbatten: Eighty Years in Pictures.* New York: Viking Press, 1979.

Murase, Miyeko, *Tales of Japan* (exhibition catalog). New York: Oxford University Press, 1986.

Naylor, P. I. H., *Astrology: An Historical Examination.* London: Robert Maxwell, 1967.

Needham, Joseph, *Mathematics and the Sciences of the Heavens and the Earth.* Vol. 3 of *Science and Civilisation in China.* Cambridge: Cambridge University Press, 1959.

Neugebauer, O., and H. B. Van Hoesen, *Greek Horoscopes.* Philadelphia: American Philosophical Society, 1959.

Oates, Joan, *Babylon.* London: Thames and Hudson, 1979.

"The Origin of the Zodiac." *Sky & Telescope,* March 1984.

"Overloaded." *New Yorker,* February 9, 1987.

Paltrinieri, Mario, and Elena Rader, with Dr. Rosanna Zerilli, *The Book of Practical Astrology.* New York: Macmillan, 1981.

Parker, Derek, *Familiar to All.* London: Jonathan Cape, 1975.

Parker, Derek, and Julia Parker:
The Compleat Astrologer. London: Mitchell Beazley, 1971.
A History of Astrology. London: André Deutsch, 1983.

The Planets: Readings from Scientific American. New York: W. H. Freeman, 1983.

Rawlins, Dennis:
"Report on the U.S. Test of the Gauquelins' 'Mars Effect.'" *Skeptical Inquirer,* winter 1979-1980.
"What *They* Aren't Telling You: Suppressed Secrets of the Psychic World, Astrological Universe, and Jeane Dixon." *Zetetic,* fall/winter 1977.

Ridpath, Ian, *Universe Guide to Stars and Planets.* New York: Universe Books, 1984.

Robbins, F. E., ed. and transl., *Ptolemy: Tetrabiblos.* Cambridge, Mass.: Harvard University Press, 1971.

Rowan, Roy, "The Stars Rule Siam." *Life,* November 21, 1949.

Russell, Eric, *Astrology and Prediction.* Secaucus, N.J.: Citadel Press, 1972.

Sagan, Carl, *Cosmos.* New York: Random House, 1980.

Sagan, Carl, and Ann Druyan, *Comet.* New York: Random House, 1985.

Smilgis, Martha, "A New Age Dawning." *Time,* August 31, 1987.

"A Stampede into Marriage in India." *Life,* May 23, 1955.

Stephenson, F. Richard, "Historical Eclipses." *Scientific American,* October 1982.

Sullivan, Walter, "New Era Dawns—or Just a New Day." *New York Times,* August 11, 1987.

Tarnas, Richard T., "Uranus and Prometheus." *Spring: An Annual of Archetypal Psychology* (Dallas), 1983.

Tester, S. J., *A History of Western Astrology.* Woodbridge, Suffolk, England: Boydell, 1987.

Thomas, Hugh, *A History of the World.* New York: Harper & Row, 1979.

Thomas, Keith, *Religion and the Decline of Magic.* New York: Charles Scribner's Sons, 1971.

Thompson, C. J. S., *The Mystery and Romance of Astrology.* New York: Causeway Books, 1973.

Thorndike, Lynn, *A History of Magic and Experimental Science.* Vols. 4-6. New York: Columbia University Press, 1934.

"Venus: Not Simple or Familiar, but Interesting." *Science,* January 1980.

Westrum, Ron, "Scientists as Experts: Observations on 'Objections to Astrology.'" *Zetetic,* fall/winter 1976.

"Where There's Hope." *Time,* March 29, 1963.

Wulff, Wilhelm, *Zodiac and Swastika: How Astrology Guided Hitler's Germany.* New York: Coward, McCann & Geoghegan, 1973.

Xi, Ze-zong, "The Cometary Atlas in the Silk Book of the Han Tomb at Mawangdui." *Chinese Astronomy and Astrophysics* (Great Britain), March 1984.

Yourcenar, Marguerite, *Memoirs of Hadrian.* Transl. by Grace Frick. New York: Farrar, Straus & Giroux, 1954.

Zinner, Ernst, *The Stars above Us.* Transl. by W. H. Johnston. New York: Charles Scribner's Sons, 1957.

INDEX

Time-Life Books Inc.
is a wholly owned subsidiary of
TIME INCORPORATED

FOUNDER: Henry R. Luce 1898-1967

Editor-in-Chief: Jason McManus
Chairman and Chief Executive Officer: J. Richard Munro
President and Chief Operating Officer: N. J. Nicholas, Jr.
Editorial Director: Ray Cave
Executive Vice President, Books: Kelso F. Sutton
Vice President, Books: George Artandi

TIME-LIFE BOOKS INC.

EDITOR: George Constable
Executive Editor: Ellen Phillips
Director of Design: Louis Klein
Director of Editorial Resources: Phyllis K. Wise
Editorial Board: Russell B. Adams, Jr., Dale M. Brown,
Roberta Conlan, Thomas H. Flaherty, Lee Hassig, Donia
Ann Steele, Rosalind Stubenberg
Director of Photography and Research:
John Conrad Weiser
Assistant Director of Editorial Resources: Elise Ritter Gibson

PRESIDENT: Christopher T. Linen
Chief Operating Officer: John M. Fahey, Jr.
Senior Vice Presidents: Robert M. DeSena, James L. Mercer,
Paul R. Stewart
Vice Presidents: Stephen L. Bair, Ralph J. Cuomo, Neal
Goff, Stephen L. Goldstein, Juanita T. James, Hallett
Johnson III, Carol Kaplan, Susan J. Maruyama, Robert H.
Smith, Joseph J. Ward
Director of Production Services: Robert J. Passantino

Editorial Operations
Copy Chief: Diane Ullius
Production: Celia Beattie
Library: Louise D. Forstall

MYSTERIES OF THE UNKNOWN

SERIES DIRECTOR: Russell B. Adams, Jr.
Series Administrator: Myrna Traylor-Herndon
Designer: Herbert H. Quarmby

Editorial Staff for *Cosmic Connections*
Associate Editors: Sara Schneidman (pictures); Janet Cave,
Jim Hicks (text)
Writer: Laura Foreman
Assistant Designer: Lorraine D. Rivard
Copy Coordinators: Marfé Ferguson Delano, Mary Beth
Oelkers-Keegan
Picture Coordinators: Richard A. Karno, Adrienne L.
Szafran
Researchers: Susan Stuck (principal, pictures), Christian D.
Kinney, Sharon Obermiller, Elizabeth Ward
Editorial Assistant: Donna Fountain

Special Contributors: Christine Hinze (London, picture
research); Patricia A. Paterno (pictures); Beth DeFrancis,
Denise Dersin, David Mitchell, Evelyn S. Prettyman
(research); Sarah Brash, Champ Clark, George Daniels,
Marilynne R. Rudick, Sandra Salmans, Charles C. Smith,
John Tompkins, Bryce Walker (text); John Drummond
(design); Karen Siatras (copyediting); Hazel Blumberg-
McKee (index)

Correspondents: Elisabeth Kraemer-Singh (Bonn), Vanessa
Kramer (London), Maria Vincenza Aloisi (Paris), Ann
Natanson (Rome)
Valuable assistance was also provided by Mirka Gondicas
(Athens); Barry Iverson, Nihal Tamraz (Cairo); Laurie
Levin (Copenhagen); Arti Ahluwalia, Deepak Puri (New
Delhi); Judy Aspinall (London); Elizabeth Brown, Christina
Lieberman (New York).

The Consultants:
Marcello Truzzi, the general consultant for the series, is a
professor of sociology at Eastern Michigan University. He
is also director of the Center for Scientific Anomalies
Research (CSAR) and editor of its journal, the *Zetetic
Scholar.* Dr. Truzzi, who considers himself a "constructive
skeptic" with regard to claims of the paranormal, works
through the CSAR to produce dialogues between critics
and proponents of unusual scientific claims.

John B. Carlson worked in extragalactic and radio
astronomy before developing a new interdisciplinary
specialty, the study of astronomy in ancient cultures.
Carlson concentrates on the astronomy of pre-Columbian
America and is the founder and director of the Center for
Archaeoastronomy in College Park, Maryland.

Caroline W. Casey of Washington, D.C., is a professional
astrologer and lecturer on astrological subjects. A graduate of Brown University, where she studied semiotics
(symbol systems), she has written many articles and has
frequently discussed astrology on television and radio.

Patrick Curry, who holds degrees from the University of
California, the London School of Economics, and
University College, London, is an authority on the history
of astrology. His writing on the subject includes two
books, *Astrology, Science and Society* and *Prophecy and
Power: Astrology in Early Modern England.* Curry lives
in London.

Other Publications:

THE TIME-LIFE GARDENER'S GUIDE
TIME FRAME
FIX IT YOURSELF
FITNESS, HEALTH & NUTRITION
SUCCESSFUL PARENTING
HEALTHY HOME COOKING
UNDERSTANDING COMPUTERS
LIBRARY OF NATIONS
THE ENCHANTED WORLD
THE KODAK LIBRARY OF CREATIVE PHOTOGRAPHY
GREAT MEALS IN MINUTES
THE CIVIL WAR
PLANET EARTH
COLLECTOR'S LIBRARY OF THE CIVIL WAR
THE EPIC OF FLIGHT
THE GOOD COOK
WORLD WAR II
HOME REPAIR AND IMPROVEMENT
THE OLD WEST

*For information on and a full description of any of the
Time-Life Books series listed above, please call 1-800-621-
7026 or write:*
  Reader Information
  Time-Life Customer Service
  P.O. Box C-32068
  Richmond, Virginia 23261-2068

This volume is one of a series that examines the history
and nature of seemingly paranormal phenomena. Other
books in the series include:

Mystic Places	*Phantom Encounters*
Psychic Powers	*Visions and Prophecies*
The UFO Phenomenon	*Mysterious Creatures*
Psychic Voyages	*Mind Over Matter*

Library of Congress Cataloging in Publication Data
Cosmic connections / by the editors of Time-Life Books.
  p. cm.—(Mysteries of the unknown)
Bibliography: p.
Includes index.
ISBN 0-8094-6340-7. ISBN 0-8094-6341-5 (lib. bdg.)
1. Astrology—History. 2. Astrology.
I. Time-Life Books. II. Series.
BF1671.C67 1988
133.5'09—dc19   88-20118 CIP

© 1988 Time-Life Books Inc. All rights reserved.
No part of this book may be reproduced in any form or by
any electronic or mechanical means, including informa-
tion storage and retrieval devices or systems, without
prior written permission from the publisher, except that
brief passages may be quoted for reviews.
First printing. Printed in U.S.A.
Published simultaneously in Canada.
School and library distribution by Silver Burdett Company,
Morristown, New Jersey 07960.

TIME-LIFE is a trademark of Time Incorporated U.S.A.

Time-Life Books Inc. offers a wide range of fine record-
ings, including a *Rock 'n' Roll Era* series. For subscription
information, call 1-800-621-7026 or write Time-Life
Music, P.O. Box C-32068, Richmond, Virginia 23261-2068.